NEW
BRITAIN

Tony Blair is the leader of the Labour Party. He has
been shadow spokesman for Employment and shadow
Home Secretary and has represented Sedgefield as an
MP since 1983. He is married to Cherie and they
have three children, Euan, Nicholas and Kathryn.

NEW BRITAIN

My Vision of a Young Country

Tony Blair

WestviewPress

A Division of HarperCollinsPublishers

First published in Great Britain in 1996 by
Fourth Estate Limited
6 Salem Road
London, W2 4BU

Copyright © 1996 by The Office of Tony Blair

Cover photograph © 1996 Richard Avedon. All rights reserved.

Copyright © 1997 by Westview Press, A Division of
HarperCollins Publishers, Inc.

Published in 1997 in the United States of America by
Westview Press, 5500 Central Avenue,
Boulder, Colorado 80301-2877

A CIP catalog record for this book is available from the
Library of Congress.

ISBN 0-8133-3338-5

The paper used in this publication meets the requirements of the
American National Standard for Permanence of Paper for Printed
Library Materials Z39.48-1984.

10 9 8 7 6 5 4 3 2 1

Contents

My Kind of Britain   ix

INTRODUCTION: OUT OF THE WILDERNESS

1   *The Challenge for Labour*   3
2   *The Radical Coalition*   4
3   *New Labour, New Life for Britain*   22

PART I: NEW LABOUR

4   *Accepting the Challenge*   29
5   *New Labour, New Britain*   35
6   *New Clause IV*   51
7   *Why I am a Christian*   57
8   *The Young Country*   62

PART II: OUR ECONOMIC FUTURE

9   *The British Experiment*
     – an Analysis and an Alternative   75
10   *New Industrial World*   98
11   *New Labour, New Economy*   107
12   *The Global Economy*   118

13   *New Labour and the Unions*   130

PART III: EQUALITY AND OPPORTUNITY

14   *Social Justice*   141

15   *Hearing from Women*   151

16   *Realising Our True Potential*   159

17   *A New Vision for Comprehensive Schools*   173

18   *The One-Nation NHS*   177

19   *The Age of Consent*   186

20   *Housing*   190

PART IV: SECURITY AND RESPONSIBILITY IN A WORLD OF CHANGE

21   *Security in a World of Change:*
       The New Politics of the Left   203

22   *New Community, New Individualism*   215

23   *Our Common Environment*   223

24   *The Rights We Enjoy, the Duties We Owe*   236

25   *Crime and Family Breakdown*   244

26   *Valuing Families*   249

27   *Dear Kathryn . . .*   251

28   *The Stanley Matthews Culture*   254

Contents

PART V: THE UNITED KINGDOM AND THE NEW WORLD ORDER

29	*New Nation-state*	259
30	*Devolution*	269
31	*The Northern Ireland Peace Process*	276
32	*Five Questions for John Major on Europe*	278
33	*Britain in Europe*	280

PART VI: STAKEHOLDER BRITAIN

34	*The Stakeholder Economy*	291
35	*The Stakeholder Society*	297
36	*Stakeholder Politics*	310

| *Index* | 323 |

My Kind of Britain

This is a book about Britain: its past, its future and above all its people. It is motivated by a simple idea – that we have the potential to create a much better future for ourselves and our children but will only do so if we work together with new purpose, new direction and new leadership.

I was brought up to form my views on the basis of what I saw around me, what I read, what I learnt from friends and colleagues – in other words to study reality rather than theory. Today, as I travel around Britain, I see many people with great strengths. We have some of the world's best scientists and engineers, businesspeople and teachers, artists and sportsmen and -women. We have fine traditions of tolerance, openness, sticking up for the underdog. And British governments have often been at the forefront of changes that have then been followed elsewhere. We are ready to take bold steps when they are justified.

But all across Britain today I also see enormous untapped potential. Sometimes there are simple things that bring it home. Children in classes too big for them to learn properly; young people in their twenties who have never had a job; trains vandalised, city centres clogged up, the countryside spoiled; elderly people unable to enjoy their retirement because they live in fear; political institutions so remote that they no longer seem to serve the people but to serve only themselves.

There is a deeper sense too in which our potential remains just that. People want to be proud of Britain, but they have lost confidence. They want us to be strong, but they sense we are losing an old identity without finding or developing a new one. They know in their hearts we cannot do this by looking back. They know that the riskier but ultimately more satisfying search for a new future is necessary; but they want to be convinced that we can keep the best of the past as we move forward.

My ambitions for Britain are defined by this gap between potential and performance. We are a country with a great past but too often we seem to live in it rather than learn from it. Changing that mind-set, so that we are masters of change rather than victims of it, is what I mean when I talk about making Britain a 'young country'. It is a country convinced that its best times can lie ahead, fired with ambition but improved by idealism, compassion and justice.

People used to say that the Conservatives were 'cruel but efficient'. Labour, they said, was caring but incompetent. That was foolish, for many reasons. The Conservatives have shown themselves to be monumentally incompetent. More important, we cannot afford the costs of mass unemployment and poverty. We cannot escape the crime that comes from despair. Britain cannot be strong and confident when the majority of its people are insecure and fearful. We live as one nation, and must act as one too.

Social justice, the extension to all of a stake in a fair society, is the partner of economic efficiency and not its enemy. We do not have to choose between a less divided society and a more productive economy. We can and must seek both. To do so, we need to work in radically new ways. We live in a world of dramatic change and the old ideologies that have dominated the last century do not provide the answers. They just do not connect with a new world of global competition, abrupt technological advance, a revolution in the role of women, new environmental danger and widespread demands for a more empowering and open form of politics.

But there is a big idea left in politics. It goes under a variety of names – stakeholding, one nation, inclusion, community – but it is quite simple. It is that no society can ever prosper economically or socially unless all its people prosper, unless we use the talents and energies of all the people rather than just the few, unless we live up to the ambition to create a society where the community works for the good of every individual, and every individual works for the good of the community.

In the 1980s, the Conservatives effectively presented themselves as the party of the majority in Britain. They claimed to offer hard-working families the chance to get on, the power to control their lives. They talked about popular capitalism and promised an economic miracle in which income and wealth would trickle down from people at the top and benefit the rest of us. Today, that claim seems absurd. Millions of people fulfilled their side of the bargain – they bought houses, set up businesses, changed jobs, bought personal pensions. Yet the government did not honour its pledge. Taxes have been raised 23 times, mortgage repossessions are running at 1000 a week, pensions regulation has been shown to be inadequate. Instead of helping the majority, government has been hurting them. The result is a growing number of people at the bottom without work and often without hope, joined by a discontented, anxious class in the middle, insecure about the future.

There are two responses. One is easy: it is to fall into an old British trap – contenting ourselves with the thought that things could be worse, rather than asking and demanding that they be made better. But we are not condemned to a future of fractured communities, inadequate public services, environmental decay. Such things are only inevitable if we believe them to be. In fact, they aren't. I do believe that government can challenge the country to work together, because I know that when people are enabled to give of their best, they do. Government can give a lead, set priorities, work in partnership with private and voluntary sectors, stand up for the majority and not just the few.

It is to provide this sort of government that the Labour Party has undergone fundamental change. We have a new constitution, more members than for a generation, a modern relationship with the trade unions, and our MPs selected by one member one vote. We have developed a new policy agenda for the challenges facing Britain: never before has an opposition political party developed policy in as much detail and in as many areas as today's Labour Party.

Now we seek the honour of leading change in Britain. This book is a testament to the hard learning and hard thinking done throughout the Labour Party to put us in that position. It provides an important complement to the daily diet of political news. The pressure in politics today is to make simple and polarised what is in fact more complex and nuanced. A book can take a soundbite and show its context, its provenance and its depth. Where other media are reactive, the articles here are intended to be proactive in setting an agenda for the future. Two points come through again and again.

First, Labour has returned to its values and is now seeking the clearest and most effective ways of putting them into practice. This is a historic shift, liberating us from the terrible tyranny of confusing means and ends. Second, no one reading this book can say either that Labour has no policies, nor that they do not represent a decisive alternative to the failed politics advocated by the Conservatives. The election will present a clear choice – between more of the same under the Tories, and a new direction with Labour.

The four cornerstones of the new Britain we seek to build provide the main themes throughout this book. They are the building blocks of a more secure and successful Britain. First, we want to improve the standards of living of all Britain's families through an economic strategy based on investment in people, infrastructure and industrial research and development. Government should not be running business. Nor should it abandon its key strategic responsibilities. To compete in the global economy every country needs a partnership of public and private sectors to harness the power of the market to the public interest.

Second, we need to build a new social order in Britain, a genuine modern civic society for our own time, based on merit, commitment and inclusion. The spirit of solidarity on which the Labour Party was founded has a very modern meaning – the creation of a true community of citizens involving all the people and based on rights and responsibilities together. Divided Britain is weak. Struggling alone we are ineffective. Social and economic inclusion – the insistence that it is the responsibility of government to extend to every citizen a stake in society – is a radical and necessary goal.

Third, we seek to decentralise and make accountable the institutions of political power in Britain. The organisation of government has not traditionally been an area of great political debate. But secrecy, centralisation, patronage are of benefit to those who are already powerful. That is why the Conservatives defend the current regime. Opening up politics to put the people in charge has been the task of left-of-centre parities throughout the ages, and it will be Labour's mission in government too.

Finally, the condition of Britain at home is intimately connected to our influence abroad. Insecure in our homes and streets and workplaces, we lack leadership and confidence in our foreign policy. We should say loud and clear that Britain has a lot to offer, especially in partnership with other countries. Britain is an important European country; we should be leading reform in Europe, not tailing along behind.

This book is intended to help show not just why these things are important, but how they can be achieved. The ideas here do not offer a quick fix. They show how we can make a start, but also set out a programme of change to last well beyond one Parliament. They are a challenge to our country, as well as a remedy for its problems.

For a generation, the Conservatives have argued that the way to make people cope with insecurity is to make them more insecure. They believed that fear was the best spur to initiative and action. But in fact it has bred caution and apathy. Confidence, not insecurity, is the real foundation of progress – confidence that merit and hard work will be rewarded, that family finances are secure, that education and health services are available to the highest standards when we need them, that our political intitutions are governed by public good not private interest.

These are the building blocks of the young country I want to lead – confident in itself, and confident in its future.

Out of
the Wilderness

To change our country, we must show that we have the
courage to change ourselves.

Guardian, 9 June 1993

1 The Challenge for Labour

At four successive general elections, the British people have refused to grant the Labour Party their trust. They have sent us back to the exile of opposition.

Most important, they have tried to tell us something. They have not told us to retreat or to retire: they have told us to rethink and to review, and to come back with a new prospectus for a new government. For our generation and our time, Labour must exist not only to defend the gains of the past but to forge a new future for itself and our country. Our job is to honour the past but not to live in it. I have never believed that Labour's essential principles and values were its problem. On the contrary, they still retain their validity and their support among the public. But the public have longed for us to give modern expression to those values, to distinguish clearly between the principles themselves and the application of them. That is the difference between honouring the past and living in it.

With Neil Kinnock's election as leader we began a long march of renewal. That project was taken forward by John Smith. We owe it to them both, and above all to the people who most need a Labour government, to finish the journey from protest to power.

To win the trust of the British people, we must do more than just defeat the Conservatives on grounds of competence, integrity and fitness to govern. We must change the tide of ideas. Our challenge is to show that in our policies, in our commitment and in our optimism we are ready to meet the country's call for change and its hopes for national renewal. Britain stands at a crossroads, and Labour stands ready. Our challenge is to forge a new and radical politics for a new and changing world.

From 'Change and National Renewal', Leadership Election Statement 1994

2 The Radical Coalition

In 1945 the people of Britain elected a Labour government which rebuilt this nation. We now step up our attempts to rebuild the bond of trust with the people so that we may take on the task of building a new Britain. So this is a good moment to look back to 1945 and to look forward to the future.

Then, as now, we faced enormous changes in the global economy and in society. Then, as now, Labour spoke for the national interest and offered hope for the future; the Tories spoke for sectional interest and represented the past. Then, as now, Britain needed rebuilding and the voters turned to Labour to take on that task; because, then as now, the people knew that market dogma and crude individualism could not solve the nation's problems. I want here to honour the 1945 generation, to learn the lessons of their victory and their achievements, and to set out how the enduring values of 1945 can be applied to the very different world today.

Labour Past, Present and Future

I have no hesitation whatsoever in describing the 1945 Labour government as the greatest peacetime government this century. It was led by statesmen of enduring stature: Attlee, Morrison, Bevin, Bevan. Its achievements were immense: demobilisation and full employment, the welfare state, the NHS, as well as significant contributions to international relations. And it was so secure in the affections of the British people that it lost no by-elections, gained votes on its re-election in 1950, and gained votes again in 1951, when it won more votes but fewer seats than the Tories. The record of that government makes me proud to call myself a democratic socialist. Its confidence, exuberance and commitment to the jobs that needed to be done are an inspiration to all in the labour movement. 26 July 1945: 393 Labour seats, 209 gains, overall majority 146.

But it is important to understand where that government's strength came from, what it really represented as well as what it did not. The reality is that its agenda grew out of the coalition government of the war; that it cut decisively with not against the grain of political thinking; and that its prospectus at the election was strongest in the new direction it offered, not in the minutiae of policy detail.

The real radical strength of the 1945 government was the utter clarity and determination with which its purposes were defined and carried through. Its objectives – jobs for all, decent housing, proper health and education services – were magnificent. It was a government massively driven by a sense of national purpose and renewal, extraordinarily unified in its aims, and entirely unashamed of building a broad consensus to achieve them. It was truly a government that changed the agenda for a generation.

But the government did not emerge out of the blue. Wartime experience was critical to the election result. The genius of Labour leaders was to capture the national mood and, at the same time, to lead that national mood. But in terms of its programme, too, the 1945 government built on what had gone before. Earlier progressive social and economic reform laid the legislative and intellectual foundations. The debates of the 1930s helped shape the outlook of a generation of leaders. And wartime experience in government gave them the skills to implement their programme. They were elected ready to govern, and they did.

With the possible exception of 1964, Labour has hitherto been unable to recreate the strong political consensus of 1945. The truth that we must take seriously is that 1945 was the exception and not the rule. Labour in 1945 overcame but did not resolve fundamental issues of ideology and organisation facing the Labour Party. In wartime, these became obscured. But later they reasserted themselves. In the late 1970s and early 1980s they were almost fatal. Essentially both ideology and organisation became out of date. What Neil Kinnock, John Smith and I have sought to do is to cure these weaknesses and so transform the left-of-centre in British politics.

By reason of the need to distinguish itself from the Liberal reformers, the 1918 Labour constitution identified itself with one particular strand of socialist thinking, namely state

5

ownership. This meant that the party's ideology came to be governed by too narrow a view of democratic socialism. Over time, Clause IV took on the status of a totem. Our agenda was misrepresented. And as statist socialism lost credibility, so did we lose support. Further, the gap between our stated aims and policies in government fed the constant charge of betrayal – the view that our problem was that the leadership was too timid to tread the real path to true socialism. This did immense harm to the party. And it was compounded by our organisational weakness.

The party grew out of the trade unions' legitimate desire to defend their interests and their members in Parliament. As a result, Labour's organisation has traditionally been dominated by its large affiliated membership and a strictly activist-based structure of democracy. Of course, a party of ordinary working people should by definition have at its heart the interests of the majority. But producer interests have over the century become increasingly varied and diffuse. And in any event they need to be balanced by the needs of consumers. In terms of democratic organisation, as mass activism died and people stopped turning up in large numbers to union or party meetings, so the party machine became a shell, prey to factionalism and sectarianism. It looked democratic but it wasn't. The key democratic link – which should be that between the party and the real people it seeks to represent – disappeared. Members of a 1970s general committee might say they represented the membership; union executive members might say they represented their members; but the truth was that often they didn't.

So the ideology was out of date; and yet the structures of the party had no means of bringing that home. In the end, of course, the country brought it home, by rejecting – repeatedly – the prospect of a Labour government. The task today is to reconstruct our ideology around the strength of our values and the way they are expressed. And then to create an organisation to match and reflect the ideology.

We are well on our way. The first task came to fruition in the rewriting of Clause IV, in which, far from escaping our traditions, we recaptured them. The second is proceeding too.

The ultimate objective is a new political consensus of the left-of-centre, based around the key values of democratic socialism and European social democracy, firm in its principles but capable of responding to changing times, so that those values may be put into practice and secure broad support to govern for long periods of time. To reach that consensus we must value the contribution of Lloyd

We must value the contribution of Lloyd George, Beveridge and Keynes and not just Attlee, Bevan or Crosland

George, Beveridge and Keynes and not just Attlee, Bevan or Crosland. We should start to explore our own history with fresh understanding and an absence of preconceptions.

The 1995 Conservative leadership contest saw a Conservative Party afraid to ask and answer hard questions about itself, its character and its direction. The debate began, but was so painful, it had to be abandoned. We should not flinch, and we need not do so, because we are so much stronger, so much more liberated by our voyage of rediscovery. Part of that rediscovery is to welcome the radical left-of-centre tradition outside of our own party, as well as celebrating the achievements of that tradition within it. The strength of the latter was its attack upon the abuses of economic power, its commitment to social justice and its ability to mobilise the country

---

If you look back at why people came into the Labour Party in the early part of this century, they came in because the Labour Party represented to them the party of change. They didn't say the existing political structures and systems were fine for them. In fact what they said was, 'Look the Liberal Party can't represent us. We need our own political party. We need a party that stands for the values that we stand for.' And so they formed the Labour Party. And they would be astonished to find that seventy, eighty, ninety years on people were concerned about change as if it were something to be frightened of. This is the party of change.

From a party members' forum meeting in London, 19 April 1995

---

for change. The strength of the former has been in its sensitivity to the abuse of political as well as economic power and its independent free thinking which has this century helped to promote our economic objectives. The task of the left-of-centre today is to put these two strengths together, led by Labour and providing the same broad consensus for change that a previous generation did in 1945.

I am not interested in governing for a single term, coming to power on a wave of euphoria, a magnificent edifice of expectations, which dazzles for a while before collapse. I want to rebuild this party from its foundations, making sure every stone is put in its rightful place, every design crafted not just for effect but to a useful purpose.

Looking Back

There is of course dual significance in the year 1945: the end of the Second World War, and Labour's first absolute parliamentary majority. The two events are intimately connected, because Labour's crushing victory was testimony to the fact that it embodied the hopes of war-torn Britain better than the Tories. Labour's vision chimed with the vision for which the British people had been fighting. Labour became the voice of the nation, in a sense never recognised as true before and rarely accepted as true since.

The 1945 election and the government which followed are therefore a source of immense pride for the Labour Party. By 1945 the people of Britain wanted national renewal: change from the depression years of the 1930s; change from the war years of the early 1940s. And they trusted Labour, whose leaders played a central part in the wartime coalition, to deliver that renewal. Labour promised to build a future for all the people. As Barbara Castle has described it, 'We were washed into Westminster on a wave of popularity, acceptability, hope and faith that we would have a new society.'

It was not a raft of detailed policies that took that government to power, but the clear sense of purpose and direction. There was, of course, Beveridge, and the Labour plans for social security developed during the war. And the coalition government had passed the 1944 Education Act. But in the

8

1930s the debate on economic policy and the role of planning, though long, was rather confused. Other things were done on the hoof – for example, Aneurin Bevan and the structure of the health service. What the 1945 government did have, however, was a very strong sense of direction based on core Labour values – fairness, freedom from want, social equality.

In 1945 Labour was the patriotic party, as it is today. It embodied national purpose and personal advancement – nowhere more so than in its slogan, 'Now Let us Win the Peace'. The Second World War was a people's war. On the battlefield, men of all classes fought together. On the home front, the evacuation of the cities brought people together in a way not seen before or since. To follow the people's war, Labour pledged to build a people's peace. It spoke for the people's vision of what Britain ought to be – a generous, brave, forward-looking bastion of decency and social justice. National unity and patriotic purpose were brought together to build a better society.

What is more, Labour did not just promise change, it delivered it, combining idealism and practicality in equal measure. The achievements were immense by any standard:

★ Labour engineered the transition from wartime to peace-time economy without a reversion to mass unemployment or the re-emergence of depressed areas.

★ Labour implemented the Beveridge Report, abolishing the hated means-test, raising old age pensions from ten shillings to twenty-six shillings a week, setting up a universal system of national insurance to cover sickness, unemployment and retirement, and supporting children and families with a welfare system that was at the time the envy of the world.

★ Labour set up the National Health Service, three years after its election. For the first time, the fear of illness was removed from the great mass of people. Defying the great Tory lie that equality meant levelling down, the government showed that socialism is about the abolition of second-class status: not attacking excellence, but making it available to all.

★ Overseas, Labour also made its contribution. Attlee's determination to grant independence to India signalled a readi-
ness to reconsider the role of empire, and Ernest Bevin's
contribution was central to the Marshall Plan, to NATO
and to the UN, which finally gave proper expression to the
bonds of interdependence and mutuality that exist between
peoples. Nor should we forget the role the party played in
helping socialist and progressive forces all round the world:
Denis Healey was not International Secretary for nothing.

By 1950, Sam Watson, the Durham miners' leader, claimed
at party conference, 'Poverty has been abolished. Hunger is
unknown. The sick are tended. The old folks are cherished,
our children are growing up in a land of opportunity.' The
Tories were constantly on the defensive. They tried to bury the
Beveridge Report. They said full employment was impossible.
They voted against the second and third readings of the NHS
Bill. But the public mood turned against them. Labour did
not just embody a new consensus: it helped to create it and
sustain it.

In retrospect, of course, we can see that there were some
mistakes and omissions. Peter Hennessy, a sympathetic biogra-
pher of that government, highlights three: first, a failure to
recognise fully the realities of the new world order, manifested
in the attitude of the government towards Europe; second, a
reluctance to modernise the institutions of government itself
– what Kenneth Morgan calls the Labour government's 'stern
centralism'; and, third, a tendency to look back to the problems
of the 1930s not forward to the challenges of the 1950s.

Unsympathetic biographers – Corelli Barnett leading among
them – argue that, by trying to build a New Jerusalem, Labour
and Britain chose social comfort over economic gain. But the
reality is different. The 1945 government did pursue the goal of
social justice. But it also laid enormous emphasis on economic
modernisation. What is more, by pursuing social and economic
goals *together*, it laid the basis for the most rapid period of
economic growth in Britain's history. And, because it got
employment up and poverty down, the government was good
value. Little wonder a nine-year-old Neil Kinnock watched

his grandfather weep as the news came through that Labour had lost the 1951 election.

The Lessons of 1945

The truth is that the government had intellectual vitality, moral courage and organisational effectiveness. It was a government that was willing to draw on the resources of the whole progressive tradition. The ideas of Keynes and Beveridge were the cornerstone of reform. Attlee proclaimed that 'the aim of socialism is to give greater freedom to the individual'. And the political philosopher T. H. Marshall avowedly linked the socialist project with its political ancestry. He divided the history of three hundred years of political reform into three phases:

★ the struggles for civil citizenship – liberty of the person; freedom of speech, thought and faith; and the right to justice – in the eighteenth century;

★ the campaigns for political citizenship – above all the right to vote – in the nineteenth century; and

★ the enactment of social citizenship – above all, minimum standards of economic welfare and social security – in the twentieth century.

I am a socialist not through reading a textbook that has caught my intellectual fancy, nor through unthinking tradition, but because I believe that, at its best, socialism corresponds most closely to an existence that is both rational and moral. It stands for cooperation, not confrontation; for fellowship, not fear. It stands for equality, not because it wants people to be the same but because only through equality in our economic circumstances can our individuality develop properly. British democracy rests ultimately on the shared perception by all the people that they participate in the benefits of the common weal.

From Tony Blair's maiden speech in the House of Commons,
6 July 1983

Democratic socialism in Britain was indeed the political heir of the radical Liberal tradition: distinctive for its own roots, priorities, principles and practices, but with recognisable affinities when put next to its progressive Liberal cousin.

What is more, the 1945 Labour Party backed up intellect with organisation. The party had 500,000 members in 1945. By 1951 it had over a million. It appealed and gained support throughout the country. And Labour won in 1945 because it reached beyond its traditional base, especially in the South.

The electoral map of 1945 is remarkably similar to that of the 1994 European elections. We won six of seven seats in Norfolk, seven of nine in Essex, four of five in Northamptonshire and two in Somerset. Labour single-mindedly set out to reach beyond the traditional industrial areas — and no one more so than Herbert Morrison, who gave up safe Hackney and fought marginal Lewisham East. He won by 15,000 votes.

We should therefore feel pride as we celebrate those achievements today. But we should also feel humility. Our moment of greatest success remained just that — a moment. Since 1945, Labour in government has achieved a great deal, often in very difficult circumstances. But, looking back over the years since that great postwar government, it is clear that the coalition forged in 1945 has not been maintained: since 1951, we have been out of power for more than three-quarters of the time.

To create the conditions in which Labour is once again capable of leading a governing consensus — in which it is truly the 'people's party' — we have to learn the lessons of 1945

The 1964 Labour government expanded higher education and created the Open University, reformed social legislation, kept unemployment down, spent more on education than defence, and carried forward the attack on class barriers and prejudice started in 1945. In the 1970s, Labour dealt with the consequences of the world financial crisis of 1973, without the benefit of North Sea Oil. It consolidated progress in the field of pensions with the introduction of SERPs, and in women's rights with the passage of the Sex

12

Discrimination Act. It passed the pioneering Race Relations Act, which still sets a standard across Europe for legislative action against racial discrimination.

But despite the high hopes, especially of Harold Wilson's first government, Labour did not succeed in establishing itself as a natural party of government. To create the conditions in which Labour is once again capable of leading a governing consensus – in which it is truly the 'people's party' – we have to learn the lessons of 1945. For me these are:

★ the need for a clear sense of national purpose;

★ the need to win the battle of ideas;

★ the need to mobilise all people of progressive mind around a party always outward-looking, seeking new supporters and members.

The Progressive Dilemma

Since 1945, some elections have been lost for reasons of bad luck, bad timing or bad policies, but the historical record demands something more than an election-by-election analysis of contingent factors that have contributed to election results. We need a more systematic analysis of Labour's history. As early as 1952, the younger Peter Shore was asking the right question: 'How is it that so large a proportion of the electorate, many of whom are neither wealthy or privileged, have been recruited for a cause which is not their own?'

That question is as relevant today as it was then. I believe it goes to the heart of what has been termed the 'progressive dilemma', defined by David Marquand as follows:

> The Labour Party has faced essentially the same problem since the 1920s: how to transcend Labourism without betraying the labour interest; how to bridge the gap between the old Labour fortresses and the potentially anti-Conservative, but non-Labour hinterland; how to construct a broad-based and enduring social coalition capable, not just of giving it a temporary majority in the House of Commons, but of sustaining a reforming government thereafter.

One part of the explanation is obvious: our very success in 1945 forced the Conservative Party to adapt and change, to embrace the key components of the welfare state and the mixed economy. The 1945 government built a durable post-war settlement that forced the Tories to move on to our ground. The historian Peter Clarke puts it as follows: by the 1950s, 'much of the 1945 agenda was no longer radical and contentious; it had become part of the political furniture which both parties were now competing to rearrange rather than replace'. Even during Mrs Thatcher's counter-revolution in the 1980s, the Conservatives pulled back from a full-frontal assault on the enduring legacies of the 1945 settlement.

However, the record of Conservative adaptation is only part of the story. The 'progressive dilemma' is rooted in the history of social and economic reform in Britain. Up to 1914, that history was defined by the Liberal Party's efforts to adapt to working-class demands. This involved the gradual replacement of the classical liberal ideology, based on non-intervention and 'negative freedom', with a credo of social reform and state action to emancipate individuals from the vagaries and oppressions of personal circumstance. Following the growing assertiveness of trade unions from the 1860s and after the foundation of the Labour Representation Committee in February 1900, working people were able to put new demands on the Liberal Party. These were the forces that were eventually to swamp the Liberals, but for a time they found political manifestation inside that party in the rise of New Liberalism. Radical liberals saw that the electorate was growing and changing, and realised that liberalism could survive only if it responded to the new demands.

The intellectual bridgehead was established by Leonard Hobhouse and others. They saw the nineteenth-century conception of liberty as too thin for the purposes of social and economic reform, so they enlarged it. They realised that theoretical liberty was of little use if people did not have the ability to exercise it. So they argued for collective action – including state action – to achieve positive freedom, even if it infringed traditional *laissez-faire* liberal orthodoxy. And they recognised that socially created wealth could legitimately be used for social

14

purposes, even if this required change in the existing order of property rights. They did not call themselves socialists, though Hobhouse coined the term 'liberal socialism', but they shared the short-term goals of those in the Labour Party – itself then not yet an avowedly socialist party.

This became clear after the crushing defeat of the Balfour administration in 1905. The Liberal-led majority of 1906 to 1914 spanned a wide divergence of political views. On the left, Labour MPs gave it their support. On the right, relics of Gladstonian liberalism, still espousing the agenda of nineteenth-century liberal *laissez-faire*, were kept on board. But the intellectual energy came from the New Liberals. It was their ideas that drove the 1910 government, which legislated for reform of the House of Lords, improved working conditions, an embryonic welfare system and progressive taxation.

The New Liberals were people who were both liberals with a small 'l' and social democrats, also in lower case, living on the cusp of a new political age – transitional figures, spanning the period from one dominant ethic to another. All sought far-reaching social reform. However, the Liberal coalition disintegrated after the 1916 split, and by 1918 the Tories had captured Lloyd George and wiped out Asquith's Liberals. It was therefore the Labour Party which began to take the lead. But the ideas of the pre-war reformers lived on: sometimes in the Labour Party, sometimes in the Liberal Party, sometimes beyond party. J. A. Hobson was probably the most famous Liberal convert to what was then literally 'new Labour'. But Labour never fully absorbed the whole tradition: we had our own agenda.

Labour's ideological compass was set in 1918, when it adopted its first statement of objects. At the behest of Sidney Webb, the party established 'clear red water' between itself and the Liberals, in the form of Clause IV of the party constitution. Seventy years on, Clause IV and especially Part 4 have assumed a particular meaning, but at the time Sidney Webb saw the 'socialist clause' as a fudge. He would have been astonished to learn that Clause IV was still in existence three-quarters of a century later. He would have been amused that his clause had assumed totemic status on the left of the party. And he would have been appalled that the party's whole economic and social debate was subsumed for so long under the question of ownership.

The organisational structures of the party are also important. Quite naturally, as a party born out of the trade unions and formed largely to represent people at work, the trade unions had a major say in party structures. As the class contours of society changed, however, this has meant that the party has struggled against a perception that it had too narrow a base in its membership, finance and decision-making.

New Labour, New Britain

The phrase 'New Labour, New Britain' which the party is using today is therefore intended to be more than a slogan. It describes where we are in British politics today. It embodies a concept of national renewal led by a renewed Labour Party. It has three elements: ideology, organisation and programme.

The ideological refoundation of the party took place through the revision of Clause IV. The party clearly said that we are in politics to pursue certain values, not to implement an economic dogma. Since the collapse of communism, the ethical basis of socialism is the only one that has stood the test of time. This socialism is based on a moral assertion that individuals are interdependent, that they owe duties to one another as well as to themselves, that the good society backs up the efforts of the individuals within it, and that common humanity demands that everyone be given a platform on which to stand. It has an objective basis too, rooted in the belief that only by recognising their interdependence will individuals flourish, because the good of each does depend on the good of all. This concept of socialism requires a form of politics in which we share responsibility both to fight poverty, prejudice and unemployment, and to create the conditions in which we can truly build one nation – tolerant, fair, enterprising, inclusive. That, fundamentally, was Attlee's kind of socialism, and it is also mine.

Once socialism is defined in this way – as social-ism – we can be liberated from our history and not chained by it. We

16

can avoid the confusion of means and ends inherent in the 1918 definition of socialist purpose. Most important, by re-establishing our identity on our terms, we can regain the intellectual confidence to take on and win the battle of ideas, because, as I have said again and again since becoming leader, the choice is not between principle and power. That was the foolishness of the early 1980s.

But to be a people's party we must also look at the kind of party we are. The party was born out of the desire of working people to gain a voice in the government of the country. That is why Labour was founded as the Labour Representation Committee. But the bedrock of the party in the hopes and aspirations of trade unionists was quickly broadened to include people who joined out of belief in Labour's aims and values.

In organisational terms the consequence of the origins of the party was the block vote, which sustained the leadership of the party until the 1960s and 1970s, when the structure of the accountability and organisation broke down. The party lost contact with the electorate, and in the name of internal party democracy gave away its ultimate source of accountability – the people at large. That is why the change to One Member One Vote and the changes in the organisation of party conference are so important.

The nature of the party – who is in it, how their interests are articulated, how the decisions are made, the boundaries of what is possible and desirable, even how we behave towards each other – help define the politics and the policies of the party. That is why I attach such importance to mass membership. In 1945 we were truly representative of the country at large: we had candidates from all classes, all professions, all regions. George Orwell spoke of the 'skilled workers, technical experts, airmen, scientists, architects and journalists, the people who feel at home in the radio and ferro-concrete age' who would lead Labour's drive for change after the war. Today, I want Labour to be a party which has in its membership the self-employed and the unemployed, small businesspeople and their customers, managers and workers, home-owners and council tenants, skilled engineers as well as skilled doctors and teachers.

In addition to having more members, plans are in hand to give them greater say in conference decisions. We shouldn't forget that it was the unions themselves who proposed gradually reducing the block vote. We want to repeat the success of the Clause IV consultation exercise, except this time on policy issues. We want the Policy Forum to establish itself as a platform for more open and constructive discussion than is possible on the floor of conference.

On the basis of values and organisation we can develop our programme. Socialists have to be both moralists and empiricists. Values *are* fundamental. But if socialism is not to be merely an abstract moralism it has to be made real in the world as it is and not as we would like it to be. As Tony Wright put it in his book *Socialisms*, 'If a socialism without a moral doctrine is impossible, then a socialism without an empirical theory can become a mere fantasy.'

Our values do not change. Our commitment to a different vision of society stands intact. But the ways of achieving that vision must change. The programme we are in the process of constructing entirely reflects our values. Its objectives would be instantly recognisable to our founders:

★ to equip our country for massive economic and technological change;

★ to provide jobs and security for all in this new world;

★ to ensure that there are available to all strong public services that depend on the needs and not the wealth of those who use them;

★ to attack poverty by reform of the welfare state and the labour market;

★ to rebuild a sense of civic pride and responsibility out of the chaos of lawlessness and social breakdown around us; and

★ to define Britain's place in the world, not in isolation but as a leader among a community of nations.

What have changed are the means of achieving these objectives. Those should and will cross the old boundaries between Left and Right, progressive and conservative. They did in 1945. What marks us out are the objectives and the sense of unity and national purpose by which we are driven.

On the economy, we move beyond the old battles between public and private sector. Instead we promote a modern industrial partnership between government and industry and at the workplace to achieve sustainable growth and high employment.

On welfare, the Labour objective is not to keep people on benefit, but to grant the financial independence that comes from employment. The world has changed since Beveridge – unemployment is often long-term; the family is changing as women go out to work; and many pensioners live long enough to need care and not just income. We need a new settlement on welfare for a new age, where opportunity and responsibility go together.

On education, we seek excellence for all and not just a few, because Britain's problem has never been the education of an élite. Schools should be free to run their own affairs. Local education authorities should be judged by whether they raise standards. And parents should have more say in the education of their children.

On crime, hardly mentioned in the 1945 campaign – though who can doubt that the securities and solidarities of the postwar settlement contributed to the tranquillity of the postwar decades? – we must recognise that it is traditional Labour voters who are most vulnerable to the terror of gangs and burglars and muggers. We all know some of the sources of antisocial behaviour: social decay, unemployment, lack of opportunity. But we know too that alienation is no excuse for crime, which is why Labour in government will be committed to attack crime itself and its causes.

On health, Labour's objective is a public health system that promotes good health and an NHS rebuilt as a people's service, free of market dogma, but also free of the old and new bureaucratic constraints, serving all the people, with doctors, nurses and administrators working as part of a unified system. That means GPs and health authorities teaming up to plan care, hospitals with operational freedom, and resources directed to meet need.

On the constitution, we face a massive task that the 1945 government did not address: to modernise our institutions of government to make them fit for the twenty-first century. There is no place for hereditary voting peers in the House of Lords. There should be no assumption of government secrecy, which is why a Freedom of Information Act is essential. And there should be no scope for the abuse of people's rights, which is why we are committed to a Bill of Rights.

And on Europe, our objective must surely be international cooperation for mutual benefit. That benefit should come in the form of better economic performance, environmental improvement, and secure defence. Labour will work for these goals, driven by the knowledge that the peoples of Europe prosper when they work together.

The Long Haul

I hope I have said enough to make it clear that I am in this for the long haul. We were set up as a majority party in Britain, and the time has come to fulfil that destiny in government.

It is not enough to win an election, or even to push through important changes after winning, or even to force other parties to adapt to the political parameters that you establish. The 1945 government did all these things: its great glory was that, unlike other progressive or left-of-centre governments this century, it did establish an enduring social and economic settlement. But the 1945 government did not presage a further period of Labour rule.

Our task now is nothing less than national renewal, rebuilding our country as a strong and active civil society backing up the efforts of the individuals within it. That requires economic renewal, social renewal, and political renewal. But, in setting out on our project, we should gain confidence from the government of 1945. Confidence in our values. Confidence in our insights. Confidence in our ability not just to promise change but to deliver it. For that and many other reasons, I am delighted to honour the generation of

20

1945. They have set an example which it is a privilege to follow.

From a speech at a Fabian Society commemoration of the fiftieth anniversary of the 1945 general election, 5 July 1995

3 New Labour, New Life for Britain

We are months from a general election. Months from a historic choice which will decide the country's direction as we enter a new millennium. That choice is simple: Conservative or Labour. Same old Tories versus New Labour.

New Labour, New Life for Britain will form the basis of the manifesto on which we will fight that election when it comes. It is not a policy compendium. It is not the last word. But it lays New Labour's foundations for the new Britain we seek to build. It is about people, about their lives, about the dreams shattered by the Tories, about people's hopes and fears.

The principles underlying this document would be very familiar to Labour leaders and Labour activists in the past. It is a rediscovery of the essence of Labour: a party that speaks up for the weak as well as the strong; a party that knows that the individual thrives best within a strong community; a party that believes in standards and a basic moral code. The Labour Party has given this country some of its greatest achievements but in the seventies and eighties we simply lost touch with those basic beliefs. We lost touch with the people. The only people to gain were the Conservatives.

So, yes, there has been a revolution inside the Labour Party. We have rejected the worst of our past, and rediscovered the best. And in rediscovering the best of our past, we have made ourselves fit to face the future, and fit to govern in the future. There is a big idea here. It is about creating a society that is genuinely One Nation in which we seek to realise the potential of all our people.

New Labour, New Life for Britain puts the Labour Party back where it belongs, as the party of the people. That is the divide in British politics. A Tory Party that runs Britain in the short-term interests of an élite at the top. A New Labour Party that will govern Britain for you, the people of Britain, all the people. Your ambitions are our ambitions. You should be able to send your child to a state school that's as good as any private school, to be treated at a hospital that is as good, if not better than what you can buy privately. Your streets should be safe no matter what part of the town or country you live in. You should have not just a job but a career with prospects and decent pay.

Consistent with the high-quality services we need, you should be able to keep as much of the money you have earned to spend as you like. You want a Britain that holds its head high in the world, and a Britain of which other countries take notice. You want a government capable of giving strong leadership, direction and purpose. My pledge to you is that nothing will stand in the way of our setting about achieving those aims by the best method possible; no special or privileged interests, no outdated thinking, no government bureaucracy. In every single area of policy we now set out both a vision and clear, direct and practical proposals.

For industry and jobs, there's no switching the clock back, but measures to modernise and equip our business and people for the new global markets. Practical proposals for improving

---

We must build a programme for government which embodies our beliefs and principles in strong communities and responsible citizens, in equality of opportunity and social justice. We will win the next election by applying these timeless values of the Labour Party anew for a changed world.

That is why I am so passionate in the belief that we need a mass-membership party, reaching into every community, to be the driving force for achieving government. We need to continue pilot membership schemes to attract new people and, in particular, young people to the party. But we must do more than attract new members. We need to change the whole culture of the party so that the Labour Party becomes a source of fun and enjoyment as well as the focal point for campaigns and organisation.

From Labour Party News, *September/October 1994*

---

skills, harnessing new technology, helping small businesses, upgrading road and rail, developing British science and innovation, opening up markets abroad, and for fairness at work. In schools: keeping the comprehensive principle but modernising it to take account of different abilities. Practical proposals to revolutionise primary school standards and teaching; getting a fair balance in university funding between public subsidy and student contributions. In health: getting money out of NHS bureaucracy and getting it to front-line services that help the patients. Practical proposals to improve preventive health care. In crime: tough on crime, tough on the causes of crime. Practical proposals to tackle young offenders, drug abuse, reform criminal justice, help the police but also give the chance of decent work or education to all our youngsters. In Europe: leadership not isolation, winning not losing. Practical proposals for EU reform. A taxation and expenditure system where we are spending less on welfare and more on investment for the future; aware, when we can cut tax, that it is the hard-working majority's turn to see the benefit, not simply those at the top.

In every area, policy is New Labour. New Labour against the same tired old Tories. We have changed for good. The document contains many policy commitments which a first term Labour government would seek to fulfil.

We have concentrated, as an example of what can be done, on five early pledges. They meet the direct needs of the people. They are about the choices governments face on behalf of the people. They will give new life to Britain. I make this pledge to you, the people of the country we seek to serve:

★ We will cut class sizes to 30 or under for 5-, 6- and 7-year-olds by using money saved from the assisted places scheme;

★ We will bring in fast track punishment for persistent young offenders by halving the time from arrest to sentencing;

★ We will cut NHS waiting lists by treating an extra 100,000 patients as a first step by releasing £100m saved from NHS red tape;

★ We will get 250,000 under-25-year-olds off benefit and

into work by using money from a windfall levy on the privatised utilities;

★ We will set tough rules for government spending and borrowing; ensure low inflation; strengthen the economy so that interest rates are as low as possible.

Smaller classes. Tough on crime. Shorter waiting lists. More jobs for our young people. An economy run efficiently for the many not the few: that is my pledge to the people. Those are the people's concerns. They are my concerns too. They are Labour's concerns.

People said that New Labour would never happen. It has. As our enemies have been forced to concede, it is real: a new constitution, a doubled membership, a new programme, a turning point in British politics. New Britain will happen too.

From a speech at Millbank Tower, London, 4 July 1996

PART I

New Labour

Parties that do not change die, and this party is a living
movement not a historical monument.

From a speech to the Labour Party conference, Blackpool, 4 October 1994

4 Accepting the Challenge

I came into Parliament in 1983.

Those were dark days: they required great courage and determination from our new leader then. We got those qualities in full measure.

It was a great achievement to make Labour electable once more, and we will never forget the contribution to us and our country's history by Neil Kinnock. Now it is *our* values and ideas that are the battleground of politics in the 1990s.

The Tories have failed. But I will wage war in our party against complacency wherever it exists. The Tories have lost the nation's trust. But that does not mean we inherit it automatically. We have to work for it. We have to earn it. Above all, we must show not just that they have failed, but how we can succeed.

I will tell you what our task is. It is not just a programme for government. It is a mission of national renewal: a mission of hope, change and opportunity.

It is a mission to lift the spirit of the nation, drawing its people together, to rebuild the bonds of common purpose that are at the heart of any country fit to be called one nation:

★ a country where we say, We are part of a community of people – we do owe a duty to more than ourselves;

★ a country where we help those who cannot help themselves;

★ a country where if it's not good enough for my children it's not good enough for theirs;

★ a country where there is no corner – not in its length and breadth – where we shield our eyes in shame and look away because we dare not contemplate what we see;

★ a country with pride in itself because it has pride in its people;

★ a country that knows it is not just a group of individuals and families struggling on their own, but a society, strong and united and confident, and where we harness the power of that society to advance the individuals within it – the power of all for the good of each.

That is what socialism means to me.

I will tell you how it works. It works not through some dry academic theory or student Marxism. It works when every person who wants to can get up in the morning with a job to look forward to, and prospects upon which to raise a family. When our children go to school in classrooms with teachers, books on desks, and a roof on the school building, and when they can come home and go outside and play without fear. When our nurses are nursing, not filling out forms; when our doctors are caring for patients, not billing them; and when government is spending on improving health care in the NHS, not on management, accountants and bureaucrats.

It is time to talk a new language of social justice – of what is just and unjust, fair and unfair, right and wrong. Let me tell you what that means, and what we will do.

It is wrong that we spend billions of pounds keeping able-bodied people idle, and right that we spend it putting them to work to earn a living wage – as a Labour government will do.

It is wrong that we spend more to keep families in miserable bed-and-breakfast accommodation than we do to build homes for them to live in, and right that we allow local authorities to use capital receipts locked up by Tory dogma to give them a home – and Labour will do that.

It is wrong that we have people appointed to run local services because of Tory patronage, that people in the House of Lords make the laws of this country simply because of their birth, and right that those who wield power do so based on democracy and merit – and Labour will insist that this is so.

It is wrong that we live in a society where our elderly are terrified in their own homes, women can't walk in the streets at night, and children can get drugs even in the school play-ground, and right that we are tough on crime and tough on

the causes of crime – and Labour will act to make our communities safe for people to live in.

And it is wrong that we should tell old-age pensioners that
they will have to choose between paying VAT on fuel or
freezing in their home, while the executives of privatised utility
companies pay themselves six-figure sums for three-day weeks
– something no civilised society should tolerate, and a Labour
government will not tolerate it.

There is a place for anger, for passion, when we look at
our country today. But ours is a passion allied to reason.
Because a society that is unjust, a society that rewards privilege
not hard work, a society that ignores its industry and under-
values its skills, a society in which only one in fifty crimes is
punished and the majority are unrecorded, a society that is
divided, unequal, set against itself – such a society is not only
unjust but inefficient; not just unfair but unfit for any decent
person to raise a family and live in. And the need for society
to act for the individuals in it is greater now than ever.

Look around the world today: its chief characteristic is
change. The force of change outside our country is driving
the need for change within it.

The task of national renewal is to provide opportunity and
security in this world of change. That can be done only if we
act together as a society, to equip our people and our industry
for change, allowing them to prosper through change.

This means taking our historic principle of solidarity, of
community, but applying it anew and afresh to the world
today. It can't be done by a return to the past or by staying
with the failed policies of the present. We need neither the
politics of the old Left nor new Right but a new left-of-centre
agenda for the future – one that breaks new ground, that does
not put one set of dogmas in place of another, that offers
the genuine hope of a new politics to take us into a new
millennium.

Socialism is not some fixed economic theory defined for
one time but a set of values and principles definable for all
time. This is how we should apply those principles:

★ On the economy, we should replace the choice between

31

the crude free market and the command economy with a new partnership between government and industry, workers and managers – not to abolish the market, but to make it dynamic and work in the public interest, so that it provides opportunities for all.

★ On education, we should provide choice and demand standards from the teachers and schools, but run our education system so that all children get that choice and those standards, not just the privileged few.

★ On welfare, we do not want people living in dependency on state hand-outs, but should create a modern welfare system that has a nation at work not on benefit.

★ On Europe, we should be committed Europeans, restoring influence and dignity to our country after the shambles of the past few years and then using that influence to cut waste, bring democratic reform and end the scandal of a food policy that costs British and European families twenty pounds a week.

★ On the constitution, we reject the desire of governments to centralise and we will not run the quango state of the Tories with different managers – we will get rid of it, and return power to local people over local services.

I know this may not suit everyone's purposes, but as important as anything else is changing the membership of the Labour Party. That is absolutely vital. I mean, let's just be quite brutal about this, the reason why the block vote held sway for so many years was because people felt you had small groups of activists in the Labour Party and the block vote if you like was the brake on their enthusiasms. Now what is actually happening is a process of change whereby we are going to have One Member One Vote coming into many, many of the decisions of the Labour Party.

From Walden, *London Weekend Television, 26 September 1993*

These are the principles and foundations of policy on which we will build socialism in action today – rooted in our values, in our traditions; learning from our history, but never chained to it; with both the certainty of conviction in our principles and the confidence that only real conviction breeds, to let those principles work anew, in different ways for a different age.

It is the confident who can change and the doubters who hesitate. A changed Labour Party, with the vision and confidence to lead Britain in a changing world – that is our pledge to the people of this country. But the challenge of the Labour Party is not just to govern but to inspire; not just to show how politics matter to us, but what politics can do for them.

I say this to the people of this country – and most of all to our young people – join us in this crusade for change. Of course the world can't be put to rights overnight. Of course we must avoid foolish illusions and false promises. But among all of the hard choices and uneasy compromises that politics forces upon us there is a spirit of progress with which we must keep faith.

There is much to be done, but much has been done. It was done by individuals of will and principle, working together for change. These were the people who saw exploitation and injustice at work and began the trade-union movement; who saw, at the beginning of this century, a land of ignorance and squalor, founded our party, and brought us mass education and housing; who created the NHS in the teeth of Tory hatred and opposition; who formed the United Nations and the European Community out of the rubble of world war.

Recently I sat and talked with a man who only a few years back had been a refugee, fleeing from his country because he had campaigned for freedom and democracy. Today he has the right to vote and he is Vice-President of a new South Africa. Is that not progress?

And how did it come about? Not by chance or accident, but because he and millions before and after him have been prepared to risk all for what they believed. They refused to accept that the world as it is is the world as it is meant to be. They have changed it through courage and compassion and intelligence, but most of all through hope – the small, broken moments of hope that for ever are worth an eternity of dull despair. That is the tradition in which we stand.

'A chance to serve, that is all we ask' – John Smith, London, 11 May 1994. Let it be his epitaph, and let it be our inspiration.

I am ready to serve. We are ready to serve. And together we can make this a turning-point – we can change the course of our history, and build a new and confident land of opportunity in a new and changing world.

From a speech accepting leadership of the Labour Party, London,
21 July 1994

5 *New Labour, New Britain*

Here is my vision for our party and our country: what we are; where we stand; how we will govern.

Labour: The Party of the Majority
Across the nation, across class, across political boundaries, the Labour Party is once again able to represent all the British people. We are the mainstream voice in politics today.

To parents wanting their children to be taught in classrooms that are not crumbling, to students with qualifications but no university place, let us say: The Tories have failed you. We are on your side. Your ambitions are our ambitions.

To men and women who get up in the morning and find the kitchen door smashed in again, the video gone again; to the pensioners who fear to go out of their homes, let us say: The Tories have abused your trust. We are on your side. Your concerns are our concerns.

To the small businesses, pushed to the wall by greedy banks, to employers burdened by government failure, to employees living in fear of the P45, to the thousands of others insecure in their jobs in every part of this county, let us say: The Tories have forgotten you, again. Your anxieties are our anxieties.

To middle- and lower-income Britain, suffering the biggest tax rises in peacetime history to pay the bills of economic failure, let us say: The Tories have betrayed you, again. Labour is on your side. Your aspirations are our aspirations.

We are back as the party of the majority in British politics, back to speak up for Britain, back as the people's party.

Rebuilding Community
Look at Britain fifteen years after Mrs Thatcher first stood on the steps of Downing Street.

Where there was discord, is there harmony? Where there was error, is there truth? Where there was doubt, is there faith? Where there was despair, is there hope?

Harmony? When crime has more than doubled?

Truth? When they won an election on lies about us and lies about what they would do?

Faith? When politics is debased by their betrayal?

Hope? When 3 million people are jobless, almost 6 million are on income support, and one in three children grow up in poverty?

They have brought us injustice and division, but these have not been the price of economic efficiency. Because tax is also up – £800 a year extra for the average family. Spending is up, and growth over the last fifteen years is down.

Look at what they wasted on the way. Billions of pounds gifted by nature – the God-given blessing of North Sea oil. Billions we could have invested in our future. Billions they squandered. One hundred and eighteen billion pounds – £5,000 for every family in this country – gone, wasted, vanished.

And to hide the truth of the nation's problems they have sold our nation's capital assets, built up over many years, and have used the proceeds not to invest but to cover current spending. Seventy billion pounds gone for ever.

It's time to take these Tories apart for what they have done to our country. Not because they lack compassion – though they do – but because they are the most feckless, irresponsible group of incompetents ever let loose on the government of Britain.

And why are they incompetent? Not just because of the individuals. It is not this or that minister that is to blame: it is an entire set of political values that is wrong. The Tories fail because they fail to understand that a nation, like a community, must work together in order for individuals within it to succeed. It is such a simple failing, and yet it is fundamental.

Go and look at a company that is succeeding. It will treat its workforce not as servants but as partners. They will be motivated and trained and given a common purpose. Of course sweatshop conditions in the short term can make do. But in the end they fail. The quality and commitment aren't there.

It's the same with a country. It can be run on privilege and greed for a time; but in the end it fails.

This is not theory. We have living proof of it. At the end of fifteen years, we are taxing and spending more – not to invest in future success but to pay for past failure.

I don't mind paying taxes for education and health and the police. What I mind is paying them for unemployment, crime and social squalor.

After fifteen years we spend more of our national income on unemployment and poverty and less on education. If the share of national wealth invested in housing was the same as in 1979, we would spend £11 billion more; next year we will spend £11 billion on housing benefit.

Now they want to cut the benefit. Instead of cutting benefit, why not cut the homeless queue, cut unemployment, and build houses? And if it needs an initial capital investment, release the money tied up in local-authority bank accounts and put it to work to start the house-building programme.

The Tories' economics is based on a view of the market that is crude, out of date and inefficient. And their view of society is one of indifference – to shrug their shoulders and walk away. They think we choose between self-interest and the interests of society or the country as a whole. In reality, self-interest demands that we work together to achieve what we cannot do on our own.

We can learn from the family. The Tories have posed as the party of the family for too long. They are no more the party of the family than they are the party of law and order. They have done more to undermine stable family life in this country than any other government in memory.

The Tories' view of the family is the same as their view of the individual: you are on your own. But the essence of family life is that you are not on your own – you are in it together. Families work best when their members help and sustain each other. The same is true of communities, and of nations.

Community is not some piece of nostalgia. It means what we share. It means working together. It is about how we treat each other.

So we teach our children to take pride in their school, their town, their country. We teach them self-respect – and we teach them respect for others too. We teach them self-support and self-improvement – and we teach them mutual support and mutual improvement too.

The Tories despise such principles. Their view is simple: Let's just watch as the hospitals spring up, as the schools rise in green and pleasant playing-fields. Let's just sit tight on this planet of miracles, where the free market builds business, trains employees, controls inflation, preserves demand, ensures everlasting growth. Let's congratulate ourselves that, thanks to our inspiring inaction, the elderly live in comfort and the young play in safety.

All around, people on this planet sing hymns of gratitude to the invisible hand of the market, as it brings equality and prosperity to all, as 'cascades of wealth' tumble down from generation to generation. Welcome to Planet Portillo. It is the theatre of the politically absurd.

Market forces cannot educate us or equip us for this world of rapid technological and economic change. We must do it together.

We cannot buy our way to a safe society. We must work for it together.

We cannot purchase an option on whether we grow old. We must plan for it together.

We can't protect the ordinary against the abuse of power by leaving them to it. We must protect each other.

That is our insight. A belief in society, working together, solidarity, cooperation, partnership – these are our words.

This is my socialism – and we should stop apologising for using the word.

It is not the socialism of Marx or state control. It is rooted in a straightforward view of society: in the understanding that

---

The solutions of neither the old Left nor the new Right will do. We need a radical centre in modern politics ... And today's Labour Party – New Labour – is a party of the centre as well as the centre-left.

From a speech to the British American Chamber of Commerce, New York, 11 April 1996

---

the individual does best in a strong and decent community of people, with principles and standards and common aims and values. It is social-ism. We are the party of the individual because we are the party of community.

Our task is to apply those values to the modern world. It will change the traditional dividing lines between Right and Left. And it calls for a new politics – without dogma, and without swapping our prejudices for theirs.

Today's politics is about the search for security in a changing world. We must build the strong and active society that can provide it. That is our project for Britain.

It will be founded on four pillars: opportunity; responsibility; fairness; trust.

Labour Offers Opportunity

A society of opportunity must be built around a strong and stable economy in which all of us have a stake.

It is time to state clearly, in the words of the pioneering White Paper of 1944, that it is the duty of government to maintain a high and stable level of employment. It is a responsibility we share as a society. That commitment – the goal of full employment – I reaffirm here. Achieving it will take time. The means of doing it will change. But it must be done if this is to become a society of which everyone feels a part.

Above all, we must conquer the weaknesses of our economy

A mistake that several left-of-centre parties have suffered from is to try and divide society up into a set of different interest groups, give them each a policy, put it together, amalgamate it, and then – hey presto – you've got a majority for government. And life just doesn't work like that, because most people don't look at themselves in that way. I think particularly in relation to the economy you require a unifying economic theme, which I think is based around the notion of community action to provide and enhance individual opportunity, and that is something that will be applied to all groups in society.

From The Revisionist Tendency, *BBC Radio 4, 18 March 1993*

---

that hold our country back. This won't be done by state control, and it won't be done by market dogma. It can only be done by a dynamic market economy based on partnership between government and industry, between employer and employee, and between public and private sector.

Take investment in infrastructure. Only in Tory Britain could the government have tried to build the Channel Tunnel without public investment. Government must take the lead. We would get public and private finance working together in transport, in housing, in capital projects, in health and in education.

In technology, there is an information revolution under way. Fifty per cent of employees in Britain now work in information processing, 70 per cent of wealth will in the next century be created in information industries, and 80 per cent of all the information stored anywhere in the world is in English. These are massive markets, we have a massive competitive advantage, and yet we see massive Tory failure.

We should be investing in the new electronic superhighways – satellite and telecommunications technology that is the nerve-centre of a new information economy, doing for the next century what roads and railways have done for this one. The government failed to see this revolution coming, and because of that failure a new market is operating under old rules which work against our companies, large and small. We will set the framework which encourages the new investment, so we coordinate a new national effort so that British companies are at the head of the competition, not falling behind.

We have to invest for the long term. In the Tory years, dividends have risen by 12 per cent per year in manufacturing, profits by 6 per cent, and investment by only 2 per cent. That is short-term private interest crowding out long-term public good. Labour is examining how we can encourage long-term investment agreements between finance and industry to develop the stable source of investment funds that every company needs.

We have to invest in economic regeneration. There are areas of the country laid waste by the shedding of old industry. The market won't rebuild them on its own. A partnership economy will – and where imaginative Labour authorities have worked with business it is. But we want more of it. That is why we have proposed one-stop-shop development agencies for our regions, to help create the wealth they need.

Most of all, we need to train and educate our people. Education will be the passion of my government. I know how important the education of my children is to me. I will not tolerate children going to run-down schools, with bad discipline, low standards, mediocre expectation or poor teachers, and nor should anyone else. If schools are bad they should be made to be good, and if teachers can't teach properly they shouldn't be teaching at all. And if the Conservative government can't see why education matters then sack the government and get one that does.

If schools are bad they should be made to be good, and if teachers can't teach properly they shouldn't be teaching at all

Nowadays, if you want to earn you have to learn, throughout life. The University for Industry – the Nineties equivalent of the Open University – will use satellite, cable and the new information highways to give every home and workplace access to information, to skills and to teaching, to achieve our objective of permanent educational opportunity for all. Switching on your computer for opportunities should be as natural as switching on your TV to watch a football match.

Education is just one of the public services we provide together to improve the quality of opportunity for each of us. It cannot be left to the market. Nor can our health service, or our armed forces, or our police. Nor should the railways or the Post Office. These are public services: they should be run for the public, and they should stay in public ownership for the people of this country. And if the Tories say there is no money to fund better public services, then let us tell them the cuts they could make.

They could save £700 million on the costs and fees and City charges of railway privatisation. That £700 million could have been used to build a high-speed link from London to Manchester and Liverpool, and to upgrade lines between there and Hull and Middlesbrough, and there would still be enough left over to improve commuter services on Network South East.

While waiting-lists are past 1 million, when patients are lying unattended on hospital trolleys, when dentistry has virtually gone out of the NHS, they could save on the £1.6 billion extra they are spending on the NHS changes and spend it on patient care.

Or the £30 million to turn police authorities into quangos – let that money go on putting police on the beat.

And while students scrimp to get through college, a university vice-chancellor gets a 98 per cent vote of no confidence from the staff and is rewarded with a £500,000 pay-off. We could have bought half a million exercise books with that. It's their system, their dogma, their shambles. But it's our children.

Labour's way is to fund the front line of the public services. I want hospital resources released from the administrative chaos of opting out, so that nurses can nurse again. I want schools released from form-filling and red tape, so that teachers can teach again. And I want our uniformed services freed from paper-pushing, so that we can put police officers on the beat again.

Responsibility
For the Tories, the language of responsibility is what those at the top preach to the rest, while neglecting it themselves. But the Left has undervalued the notion of responsibility and duty, and it is time we understood how central it is to ourselves.

Parents should have responsibility for their children – fathers too. Companies should have responsibility to their employees and their community, ministers to the truth, citizens to each other.

Responsibility is at the heart of our message about crime. The Labour Party is now the party of law and order in Britain today – and quite right too.

We can all get angry because crime hurts – and it hurts most the people who are least able to fight back. But it is not enough to get angry, to stamp your feet and shout from the Tory conference platform. That is the soft option.

42

We need a new approach – one that is tough on crime and tough on the causes of crime.

Tough on crime – with measures to tackle juvenile offending; to crack down on illegal firearms; to punish properly crimes of violence, including racial violence; to give victims the right to be consulted before charges are dropped or changed.

Tough on the causes of crime – with a comprehensive crime-prevention programme; an anti-drugs initiative; long-term measures to break the culture of drugs, family instability, high unemploy-

Responsibility is a value shared. If it doesn't apply to everyone it ends up applying to no one

ment and urban squalor in which some of the worst criminals are brought up.

Responsibility means a recognition that there is no divorce from the outside world. Social responsibility is for all. The unemployed youngster has no right to steal your radio – but let's get just as serious about catching the people in the City with an eye on your pension. This is where the Tories fall down.

Responsibilty is a value shared. If it doesn't apply to everyone it ends up applying to no one. It applies to those who defraud the state of benefits. It applies to those who evade their taxes. And it also applies to those water, gas and electricity-company bosses, running monopoly services at our expense, awarding themselves massive salaries, share options, perks and pay-offs – they have responsibility too.

It applies in the health service. Remember how the reforms were sold in the name of better, quicker patient care? We'd all be able to get the doctor we want, at the time we want, in the hospital we want. Who have those reforms benefited? Not the patient but the pen-pusher, getting the carpet he wants, the wallpaper he wants, and the nice big company car he wants. And can we get his wife on the board too?

A society without responsibility is the enemy of the society built on merit and hard work. It creates an economy in which enterprise is just another word for the quick buck.

The Thatcherites used to boast they were anti-establishment. But the trouble with them is that they never wanted to bust the establishment, just buy their way into it. And the new establishment is not a meritocracy but a power élite of money-shifters, middle men and speculators – people whose self-interest will always come before the national or the public interest. So it is hardly surprising that fifteen years of sleaze in high places has given birth to the yob culture. Tory philosophy is the most effective yob-creation scheme ever devised.

We have one further proposal to make here. There are nearly 1 million young people in this country who have no work, or training or education. This is not just a waste of talent but breeds resentment, crime and drug-abuse. The Social Justice Commission has called for a new civilian service – a voluntary national task force of young people given constructive tasks to do. I support that, and I think young people do as well. Working on environmental projects or caring for the elderly – something useful to the community and personally fulfilling – will instil a sense of responsibility, self-discipline and self-respect – a sense of achievement and value.

Labour Stands for Fairness
Responsibility and opportunity require fairness, justice, the right to be treated equally as a citizen. That means a strong stand against discrimination on grounds of race, sex, creed or sexuality.

But justice is about much more than fighting discrimination. It is about our lives at work, the laws we live under, and the tax we pay.

If you ever want to know whose side the Tories are on, look at the tax system. Millionaires with the right accountant pay nothing, while pensioners pay VAT on fuel. Offshore trusts get tax relief, while home-owners pay VAT on insurance premiums. Middle-income taxpayers get stung, while perks and privileges at the top roll on unstopped. And, because the government changed the rules, 2 million more people now pay the top rate of tax.

We will create a tax system that is fair: where the abuses end, the perks stop, and where ordinary families are not squeezed to pay for the privileged. Tax should be related to ability to pay.

It sticks in my gullet when I see Tory MPs – some of whom earn more for a half day's consultancy work than some of my constituents earn in a month – denounce our plans for a minimum wage. And it is also wrong that the taxpayer ends up paying more than a billion pounds on benefits to subsidise poverty pay. A minimum wage exists in every European country – and in America too – for the simple reason that it makes social and economic sense. Of course the minimum wage should be set sensibly – and it will be. But there will be no retreat from its basic principle, because it is right.

And we will sign the Social Chapter because it is right for our country. And we will give people at work the right to join a trade union and, where they want it, to have that union recognised. And let one small but significant act be a signal of our commitment to people at work – that is, the restoration to the workers of Cheltenham GCHQ of their trade-union rights.

The Tories always complain that the welfare state costs too much. The answer is not just increasing benefits, adequate though those benefits should be. The people on benefits need and deserve better – not more benefits, but help in getting off benefits. Welfare should be about opportunity and security in a changing world. It is about helping people to move on and move up.

Because the world has changed, the welfare state has to change with it. And we are the only people who can be trusted to change it, because we are the people who believe in it.

We moved around a lot when I was young, before we finally settled in Durham. I never felt myself very anchored in a particular setting or class. One of the things really wrong with Britain is that there are still hangovers from the class system that are great brakes on our ability to be a proper mobile, modern society. Sometimes it has taken the form in the Labour Party of inverted snobbery.

From the Observer, *2 October 1994*

The Tories will cut benefits and make poverty worse. We will put welfare to work.

A nation at work, not on benefit – that is our pledge.

Trust
But there is one big obstacle in the way of all our plans for change. It is the greatest legacy of the Tory years – disillusion with politics itself. And if we want to remove it we must show that our politics is not theirs. Not just that our vision for Britain is different, but also our means of achieving it. A new politics – a politics of courage, honesty and trust.

It means being open. It means telling it as it is, not opposing everything every other party does for the sake of it. If the government is getting it right, as over Northern Ireland, we give credit. We welcome without reservation new hope beginning there. We pay tribute to our own government, the Irish government, Unionist and Nationalist opinion in the North for their efforts in the peace process. And let us pay a special word of tribute to John Hume, leader of our sister party, for his unceasing commitment to that cause.

It means speaking the same language to each other as we know we need to speak to the country.

People look to politicians for leadership, and leadership is about having the courage to say no as well as yes. Even this week I have heard people saying a Labour government must repeal all the Tory trade-union laws. Now there is not a single person in this country who believes that to be realistic, or that we will do it. No one believes strike ballots should be abandoned. So why do we say it? We shouldn't, and I won't.

I am absolutely committed to the goal of full employment. We will develop the plans to achieve it. But let's not pretend that we can deliver it overnight. Let's not seek to fool the unemployed into thinking we will walk into power on Thursday and they will walk into a job on Friday. Let us be honest, straight, realistic.

Those most in need of hope deserve the truth. Hope is not born of false promises; disillusion is. They are tired of dogma. They are tired of politicians pretending to have a monopoly

46

on the answers. They are tired of glib promises broken as readily in office as they were made on the soapbox. When we make a promise, we must be sure we can keep it. That is page 1, line 1 of a new contract between government and citizen.

But we should do more. We have to change the rules of government, and we will.

We are putting forward the biggest programme of change to democracy ever proposed by a political party:

★ Every citizen to be protected by fundamental rights that cannot be taken away by the state or their fellow citizens, enshrined in a Bill of Rights.

★ Government will be brought closer to the people. We will legislate for a strong Scottish Parliament, an Assembly for Wales, in the first year of a Labour government. And the Tory quangos will be brought back under proper democratic control.

★ We will enact a Freedom of Information Act to attack secrecy wherever it exists, in public or private sector.

★ We will reform the House of Commons to make its working practices and its powers to investigate more effective, and to achieve through our party the increase in the number of women MPs that we have talked about for so long.

★ We will make history by ending the ancient and indefensible practice of hereditary peers voting on the law of the land.

★ We will tighten the rules of financing of political parties. And, since trade unions are balloted on their political contribution, it is only fair that in this free country shareholders are balloted on theirs.

Labour Offers Leadership

The people of this country are not looking to us for a revolution. They want us to make a start.

I want you with me in that task – I want you with me head and heart – because this can only be done together. Leaders lead, but in the end the people govern.

Some of you will think we are too modest in our aims, too cautious. Some of you support me because you think I can win. But it is not enough. We are not going to win despite our beliefs. We will only win because of them. I want to win not because the Tories are despised but because we are understood, supported, trusted.

We should win and we can win. This is no choice between being principled and unelectable or electable and unprincipled. We have tortured ourselves with this foolishness for too long. We should win because of what we believe.

The task of renewing our nation is not one for the faint-hearted or the world-weary or cynical. It is not a task for those afraid of hard choices, for those with complacent views, or for those seeking a comfortable life.

At the next election, the voters will have had this Tory government for seventeen or eighteen years. They may hate them, but they know them. I want them now to know us – our identity; our character as a party. And change is an important part of that.

If the world changes and we don't, then we become of no use to the world. Our principles cease being principles and just ossify into dogma. Parties that do not change die, and this party is a living movement not a historical monument.

The Tories didn't win four elections. We lost them. And we lost them because we lost touch with the people. In 1995 we got back in touch. In 1996 we will show that it is Labour, not the Tories, that understands the modern world and the issues of concern to the people.

It is Labour that can deliver prosperity through a dynamic economy. It is Labour that can rebuild Britain as one nation. It is Labour that can tackle crime, improve schools and hospitals, provide a transport system that works.

From the Sun, *1 January 1996*

We have changed not to forget our principles but to fulfil them; not to lose our identity but to keep our relevance.

Let us have the confidence once again that we can debate new ideas, new thinking, without forever fearing the taunt of betrayal. Let us say what we mean and mean what we say – not just what we are against but what we are for. We should stop saying what we don't mean and start saying what we do mean, what we stand by, what we stand for.

It is time we had a clear, up-to-date statement of the objects and objectives of our party. John Prescott and I will propose such a statement to the NEC. Let it then be open to debate. I want the whole party involved. I know the whole party will welcome that debate. And if it is accepted, then let it become the objects of our party for the next election and take its place in our constitution for the next century.

This is a modern party living in an age of change. It requires a modern constitution that says what we are in terms the public cannot misunderstand and the Tories cannot misrepresent. We are proud of our beliefs, so let's state them – and in terms that people will identify with in every workplace, every home, every family, every community in our country. And let this party's determination to change be the symbol of the trust they can place in us to change the country.

The British people are a great people. We have proud democratic traditions. We are a nation of tolerance, innovation and creativity. We have an innate sense of fair play. We have a great history and culture. And when great challenges face us – as they have twice this century – we rise to them. But if we have a fault it is that, unless roused, we tend to let things be. We say 'Things could be worse' rather than 'Things should

---

I want to make one thing very, very clear indeed. New Labour is not some public-relations exercise. It's not a marketing gimmick. It is a new and different changed Labour Party. It is changed in opposition and it will remain changed in government, and nobody should be in any doubt about that at all.

From Breakfast with Frost, *BBC Television, 14 January 1996*

---

be better.' And the Tories encourage this fault. They thrive on our complacency.

I say it is time we were roused.

Let us be blunt. Our system of government has become outdated. Our economy has been weakened. Our people have been under-educated. Our welfare state and public services have been run down. And our society has been made more divided than at any time for 100 years. But our politics need not be like this. Our country need not be like this.

Conclusion

Ours is a project of national renewal, renewing our commitment as a nation, as a community of people, in order to prepare and provide for ourselves in the new world we face.

I want to build a nation with pride in itself – a thriving community, rich in economic prosperity, secure in social justice, confident in political change; a land in which our children can bring up their children with a future to look forward to.

That is our hope: not just to promise change – but to achieve it.

Our party – New Labour. Our mission – New Britain. New Labour: New Britain.

From a speech to the Labour Party conference, Blackpool, 4 October 1994

6 *New Clause IV*

The debate about Clause IV has been the widest consultation exercise ever undertaken by a British political party. Our party can look back on it with pride.

Tens of thousands took part, almost half the party participated in the membership ballots, and all but three constituencies that balloted showed overwhelming support for change.

I asked for you to be with me head and heart, and I believe you are. Those ballots were the answer to the Tory charge that Labour's head is separate from Labour's body. This is a leader in step with his party – and this is a party in step with the people.

Our project is to redefine radical left-of-centre politics for the new millennium. It is to create a new political agenda for the country. It will break new ground and it should. Change and modernisation does not stop at four o'clock this afternoon.

The new Clause IV puts our values of community, of social justice, democracy, equality, partnership, at the forefront. It advocates both strong public services and a thriving private sector and a partnership between the two for change. It commits us for the first time to ending prejudice and discrimination, to safeguarding the environment, to promoting international solidarity. These key values, which are bringing people into the Labour Party in ever greater numbers today, give us the genuine framework of political ideology on which our policies can be based. And they mean one very important thing: that there's no longer any disjunction, any division, between what we say to the public and what we profess to ourselves as a party. It is politics that is clear and simple and straight, and that is the type of politics that people need.

From a party meeting in London, 19 April 1995

51

It goes on. In the development of the party. In the development of policy.

The strongest impression of the consultation meetings on Clause IV was not the disagreement but the consensus. No one disputed the need for some public ownership. That is why we fought the privatisation of the Post Office. That is why we will fight to keep our railways as a proper public service, publicly owned and accountable to the people. But no one seriously argued against the need for a thriving private sector. The new Clause IV expresses what we really believe.

'A dynamic economy.' Markets and enterprise are a necessary part of any developed economy. But markets alone are not enough.

Examine the challenges we face:

★ ending Tory boom and bust;

★ tackling structural levels of unemployment;

★ regenerating run-down inner cities and regions;

★ long-term investment in industry and infrastructure;

★ a modern transport and energy policy;

★ helping the self-employed and small businesses;

★ harnessing technology and science; and

★ above all, education and skills.

What modernisation to me is about is not about dumping principle. It's the opposite. It's retrieving what the Labour Party is really about.

From a party members' forum meeting in London, 19 April 1995

What you don't often hear from people opposed to the change is actually a defence of Clause IV itself. That's because when you look at it and try and marry it up to what the Labour Party stands for today it's very difficult to do.

From a party members' forum meeting in London, 19 April 1995

None of this can be done by intoning the words 'market forces' like druids around the ancient stones of worship. It has to be done in partnership, together, as a society of people working with a common purpose.

And we need the strength of partnership and cooperation at the workplace too. There is no future for Britain as a low-wage, low-skill, low-tech economy. That is the Tory way, and it will fail. Successful companies know it. Decent minimum standards at work achieve commitment to the enterprise. That is why part-time workers should not be treated as second-class. It is why we will sign the European Social Chapter. And it is why, introduced sensibly and flexibly, we will have a statutory minimum wage.

'Strong public services.' Let me tell you this: I will renationalise the National Health Service, to make it once more a service run for the whole nation, and we will make education the great liberator.

The goal is nursery education for all; raising school standards; broadening A-levels; bringing vocational and academic learning closer together; ensuring no one is shut out of higher education through poverty; reforming our outdated methods of skills and training to put education throughout life within the reach of all.

What have the Tories done? First classroom chaos under Patten; now complacency under Shephard. We need neither. What we need is David Blunkett's crusade for change and achievement. David may have taken some flak, but I believe he has shown courage. But then that is typical of someone once told that he had three options in life – he could be a lathe operator, a piano tuner or a braille typist. He won't be any of those things. He will be a Cabinet minister in a Labour government.

'The opportunity for all to work and prosper.' Of course, given the huge change in the labour market, the goal of full employment must be pursued today in a different way. But you cannot build a strong, unified society unless all its people have a stake in it. A Labour government that did not strive for a high and stable level of employment would not be a government worthy of the name Labour.

'A just society': a government which empowers the poor – unlike this government, which enriches the privileged and allows a small Tory élite to use the public utilities to line their pockets.

'Justice at work' – and that includes the right to be a member of a trade union and to be represented by it.

'Equality of opportunity' that delivers people from the tyranny of prejudice, discrimination and the abuse of power.

'A healthy environment': for the first time a commitment in the party constitution by this generation to the next to cherish and enhance the environment for the future.

'An open democracy.' I say it is time to end the quango state and put power back where it belongs – in the hands of the people. This means devolving power in Scotland and Wales, rebuilding local democracy, reforming Parliament, and a Freedom of Information Act for government.

Let no one say radical politics is dead. In fact the new statement is much more radical than the original – because we intend to put it into practice. I can be the first leader in our history to stand up and say, 'I will implement Clause IV, Part 4 of our constitution.'

It is radical, but it is also relevant, sensible and modern – definitively new; definitively Labour.

For far too long the Conservatives have defined what it is to be a democratic socialist. It is time we defined our socialism for ourselves.

We can win new friends without losing old values. At one of the official consultation meetings a woman stood up and said, 'Tony, I have to be honest – I'm suspicious. I mean, I know *Tories* who are voting for you.' Well, long may it continue.

I did not come into the Labour Party to join a pressure group. I didn't become leader of this party to lead a protest movement. Power without principle is barren. But principle without power is futile. This is a party of government, and I will lead it as a party of government.

We are reclaiming this ground in British politics because it is rightfully ours. It is the Tories who are the intruders. It is Labour that provides the real thing. We are reoccupying ground that we should never have vacated.

For sixteen years we have been out of power, but for far longer we had lost our way. Not just the Labour Party, but the left-of-centre the world over.

★ We confused means with ends, allowing one economic prescription to eclipse the aims it was supposed to serve.

★ We permitted the party's structure and organisation to fall into disrepair, prey to the politics of the vanguard, not the people.

★ The idea of social action became dominated by the notion of a central state.

★ And the party that came into being to change the world became frightened of changing itself.

We paid the penalty. We have learned the lesson. Today, we set our thinking free. Our organisation is growing. Our political culture is opening up. There is a strength in our party now. There is a vigour in our policy-making.

The new Clause IV is much more than a symbol of change for the Labour Party: it is a symbol of hope for the country. It is time to move Britain on beyond the old battles of the twentieth century. The days of the all-embracing theories of politics – religious in nature, whose adoption would solve all human problems – are over. This is a wiser, chastened, if still dangerous world.

The twenty-first century won't be a battle between public and private sectors. It will be a search for the defining principles of a modern civic society in a world of constant economic change. But don't let this more practical world rob us of vision, or sour our souls. The noble causes remain:

★ to ally progress and science with justice and equality;

★ to push further the boundaries of human potential;

★ to end war between nations and wage war instead on poverty and ignorance;

★ to bring prosperity to the one-fifth of the world who hunger.

These are and have been our causes since time immemorial.

Our aim is a country that is proud to call itself one nation

This is a generation in need of inspiration, because its new challenges and the pace of change dwarf our imaginations. Look around. A new, global economic market; a microchip the size of a fingernail that can store a library of knowledge; a labour market our grandparents wouldn't recognise; and how many of us know elderly people who have saved their whole lives for a nest-egg for old age, only to see their savings, even their home, swallowed up in the costs of nursing care? The old attitudes, the old ways, the old politics won't do any more.

What do the Conservatives offer? Nothing. They are the old politics, the old ways. They are all about selling off, breaking up, the short term, the narrow, the selfish.

This country needs new energy, ideas and vision – a government free of dogma, not hidebound by ideology but driven by ideas.

Our aim is a country that is proud to call itself one nation. One nation where, by the strength of our common endeavour, we achieve more than we achieve alone; where we recognise we are not just isolated figures struggling to compete against each other, but human beings, members of a community and a society, who owe obligations to one another as well as to ourselves and who depend on each other to succeed.

That is the spirit of solidarity. That is the socialism I believe in.

From a speech to a special conference of the Labour Party, 29 April 1995

7 *Why I am a Christian*

First a politician's health warning: I can't stand politicians who wear God on their sleeves; I do not pretend to be any better or less selfish than anyone else; I do not believe that Christians should only vote Labour; and I do not discuss my religious beliefs unless asked, and, when I do, I discuss them personally. Of course, they influence my politics, but I do not wish to force them on anyone else.

As a private individual, I find prayer a source of solace and I read the Gospels. They are compelling texts, and a most extraordinary expression of sensitive human values. I also read the Old Testament, which is in some ways more detailed and vivid than the New Testament.

Easter, a time of rebirth and renewal, has a special significance for me and, in a sense, my politics. My vision of society reflects a faith in the human spirit and its capacity to renew itself. But Easter is not only a celebration of the Resurrection: it is also a time to recall the events that led to Christ's crucifixion and what they mean.

There are three parts of the Easter message – best described in St Matthew. First there is Pontius Pilate, taking his decision as Jesus stood before him. One of the things that lends power to the Gospels is that the characters are so real. Pilate is fascinating because he is so obviously human and imperfect, torn between principle and political reality. Were the Gospels simply a didactic tale, his choice would be remembered as an easy one. But it is not described in this way.

The intriguing thing about Pilate is the degree to which he tried to do the good thing rather than the bad. He commands our moral attention not because he was a bad man but because he was so nearly a good man. One can imagine him agonising, seeing that Jesus had done nothing wrong, and wishing to release him. Just as easily, however, one can envisage Pilate's advisers telling him of the risks, warning him not to cause a

It is possible to view Pilate as the archetypal politician, caught on the horns of an age-old political dilemma

riot or inflame Jewish opinion. It is a timeless parable of political life.

It is possible to view Pilate as the archetypal politician, caught on the horns of an age-old political dilemma. We know he did wrong, yet his is the struggle between what is right and what is expedient that has occurred throughout history. Should we do what appears principled or what is politically expedient? Do you apply a utilitarian test or what is morally absolute?

The two images of Easter. Peter, the rock of Christ, who falls from grace, and in weakness denies him; Judas betraying Christ and in remorse hanging himself. Neither man simply good or bad, yet in Peter's case, an ordinary man who went on, by faith, to achieve the extraordinary.

Lastly, there is Christ himself in the Garden of Gethsemane: the knowledge of suffering to come and the very human agony − 'let this cup pass from me'; putting duty first − 'not my will, but thine, be done'.

Duty leads to renewal. John Smith, whose faith was central to what he was and stood for, always spoke of service and duty as the defining elements of his politics. He epitomised the decency of the Scottish Presbyterian tradition.

I am often asked how my religious convictions have played a role in the emergence of my political thinking. First, my view of Christian values led me to oppose what I perceived to be the narrow view of self-interest that Conservatism − particularly its modern, more right-wing form − represents. But Tories, I think, have too selfish a definition of self-interest. They fail to look beyond, to the community and individual's relationship with the community. That is the essential reason why I am on the Left rather than the Right. The key point is that Christianity is more than a one-to-one relationship between the individual and God, important as that is. The relationship also has to be with the outside world.

Second, Christianity helped to inspire my rejection of Marxism. Whatever subtleties can be placed upon it, Marxism was essentially determinist. It was an attempt to make politics scientific, which it isn't. Politics is about people, and they are, of course, influenced by the conditions around them. But human nature is complex. There is free will, individual responsibility. We can choose and decide. The problem with Marxist ideology was that, in the end, it suppressed the individual by starting with society. But it is from a sense of individual duty that we connect the greater good and the interests of the community – a principle the Church celebrates in the sacrament of communion.

The Left got into trouble when its basic values became divorced from this ethical socialism, in which Christian socialism is included. Marxism obscured the importance of personal responsibility, concentrating only upon the social determinants that contribute to individual behaviour. For the left-of-centre, the great rediscovery has been the early social-democratic view that better social conditions enhance personal responsibility; they are not a substitute for it.

> It is from a sense of individual duty that we connect the greater good and the interests of the community

I recognise that people can by their own volition exert themselves to become better, more decent, people. Human beings have free will: the choice to act well or badly. What distinguishes me from Conservatives is that I believe people are more likely to act well and improve themselves in a society where opportunities are offered to them to do so; which strives to be cohesive and treats people as of equal worth. This, I think, is the crucial difference between my own position and the Marxist and Tory extremes.

Many writers have influenced my interest in religion and philosophy – Kierkegaard, Jung and Kant among them. One of the best things I have read on the subject of Christian duty was an essay by the Scottish philosopher John Macmurray, a socialist thinker whose writings I was introduced to as a student at Oxford.

Describing his experience in the First World War and how it changed his life, Macmurray said that his comrades had divided into two categories in response to the horror of the conflict. The first group reacted as Epicureans. The second group, in contrast, was gripped by a profound belief that their lives had to have a purpose – a moral purpose that encompassed the notion of duty. One could liken this to Kant's categorical imperative. What Macmurray meant is that there is a human impulse within, which can be fulfilled only through duty. For a politician this idea has important consequences. It means that you see the need for change around you and you accept your duty to do something. Christian belief means you cannot detach yourself from the world around you.

Some years ago Margaret Thatcher caused controversy in a speech by quoting St Paul's letter to the Thessalonians: 'If a man will not work, he shall not eat.' This injunction by Paul should never be used to justify the withdrawal of support from the helpless. We must always be willing to assist the vulnerable and disadvantaged. But what I think Paul meant was this: that everyone had a duty to get on and work for the common good. To participate in the benefits, they had to give as well as take. He was referring to the work of the early Church, but his message remains relevant. Unless each of us accepts personal responsibility, the community in which we live suffers as a result.

'Sin' as a word conjures up images of strait-laced piety and frowning disapproval. It seems old-fashioned today. Yet the concept is simple and important. In theological terms, it is

---

I've never believed that the problems of the Labour Party are simply political. They are also if you like almost cultural, they're organisational and they're cultural. This mass membership – extending the membership of the party – that's not a glorified recruitment drive to me, it's about transforming the way the Labour Party works and it operates and it thinks . . . What we are finding as a result of going out and making a priority of campaigning and recruiting members is that we are changing the whole culture of the party and the way it works. Different issues are coming up. Crime and law and order is a much bigger issue for Labour Party members now as a result of a larger membership.

From Walden, *London Weekend Television, 26 September 1993*

---

alienation from God. In everyday terms, it is the acknowledgement of right and wrong. It is the rejection of a purely libertarian ethos. This is an area that will become of increasing
importance in politics. I don't mean 'sin' in the sense of personal morality, but there is a desire in the modern world to
retrieve and re-establish a sense of values, of common norms
of conduct. They have to be relevant to today's world, not
leaps back to the past. But there is an increasing rejection,
interestingly among young people, of an amoral society. Not
that people want to be preached at over their lifestyles or
controlled; but rather they recognise that unless boundaries
are set and agreed, and judgements of good and bad are made,
society cannot function well or fairly.

Christianity is full of mercy and compassion. Jesus said, 'He
that is without sin among you, let him first cast a stone.' He
was not saying that sin does not exist – far from it. He was
saying that those who pass moral judgement must first examine
their own moral position.

I am an ecumenical Christian. I find many of the angry
debates between Catholic and Protestant completely baffling.
I have a deep respect for other faiths, and relish the religious
pluralism of this country.

There is the restless searching after truth in the Gospels.
Jesus challenged, he changed, he asked why: Sabbath was made
for man, not man for the Sabbath. Yet what is shown in both
Old and New Testaments – though perhaps more marked in
the Old – is an honesty with which human nature is confronted. Christianity is optimistic about the human condition,
but not naïve. It can identify what is good, but knows the
capacity to do evil. I believe that the endless striving to do
the one and avoid the other is the purpose of human existence.
Through that comes progress.

From the Sunday Telegraph, *7 April 1996*

8 *The Young Country*

I know that for some New Labour has been painful. There is no greater pain to be endured in politics than the birth of a new idea. But I believe in it, and I want to tell you why.

Socialism to me was never about nationalisation or the power of the state; not just about economics or politics even. It is a moral purpose to life; a set of values; a belief in society, in cooperation, in achieving together what we are unable to achieve alone. It is how I try to live my life.

The simple truths: I am worth no more than anyone else. I am my brother's keeper. I will not walk by on the other side. We aren't simply people set in isolation from each other, face to face with eternity, but members of the same family, the same community, the same human race. This is my socialism. And the irony of our long years in opposition is that those values are shared by the vast majority of the British people.

I joined the Labour Party because it represented those values. But I felt something else: that, however great and timeless our values, our party's politics, its structure and even its ideology no longer reflected those values in a way that brought them alive for the people. We were separated from the very people we said we represented. We called them 'our people' while forgetting who they were.

Nineteen eighty-three was, for me, a watershed. Since then we have transformed our party – our constitution rewritten; our relations with the trade unions changed; our party organisation improved; political education on an unprecedented scale; new policy; breaking new ground.

But I didn't come into politics to change the Labour Party. I came into politics to change the country. And I honestly believe that if we had not changed, if we had not returned our party to its values, freed from the weight of outdated ideology, we could not change the country. We could not win, and even if we did we would not have governed in the

62

way Britain needs. For I do not want a one-term Labour government that dazzles for a moment then ends in disillusion. I want a Labour government that governs for a generation and changes Britain for good.

It has been hard, I know. Hard for me sometimes – 1994 Bambi; 1995 Stalin. From Disneyland to dictatorship in twelve short months. I am not sure which one I prefer. OK, I prefer Bambi. Honestly.

There have been good moments. In 1995, for the first time since I became leader, my children were impressed by something I did. Did you really meet Kevin Keegan, Dad? Did you really do twenty-seven consecutive headers?

I love my party. I just hate it being in opposition

I have spent years being angry, passionate and indignant – about young people huddled in doorways, families made wretched by unemployment, the poor unable to make ends meet. I am fed up with anger. I tell you, they don't need our anger – they need action. And they will get it not through the rage of opposition but through a Labour Party that has had the courage to take hard choices, get into government, and do something for them.

And let me tell you, the hard choices get harder in government:

★ when we refuse to take risks with inflation because this country cannot be rebuilt on boom and bust, even to boost short-term employment;

★ when we want more children at university but know that, though the Student Loan Scheme will be replaced, we face hard choices about what its replacement will be;

★ on public-sector pay, when a Labour government, like any other, will have to say no as well as yes – even to people in this hall.

Hard choices are what good government is about.

I love my party. I just hate it being in opposition. I love my country. And I hate what the Tories have done to it. Every promise ever made they have broken: taxes, unemployment, crime, NHS, education – theirs is a record of incompetence

63

and dishonesty on an epic scale. And now they plead with the British people, Trust us this one more time.

I say this to the British people. There are two sides to a deal. They gave their word; you gave your vote. They broke their word, and they don't ever deserve your vote again.

I'll tell you about the Tories and tax. They cut your taxes before an election and raise them afterwards. And they only ever give you one side of the equation: they cut your income tax, but they raise your VAT; they make you pay charges, like in the NHS on extra costs, like taxes on insuring your home. It's all a con. We all want ordinary hard-working families to pay less tax.

But the way to cut tax is to cut unemployment, cut crime, cut welfare spending – all the reasons taxes have gone up.

This is a new age, to be led by a new generation. Let me talk to you about my generation. We grew up after the Second World War. We read about fascism, we saw the Soviet Union, and we learned to fear extremes of Left and Right. We were born into the welfare state and the NHS, and into the market economy of bank accounts, supermarkets, jeans and cars. We had money in our pocket never dreamt of by our parents. We travel abroad. We have been through the sexual revolution of the 1960s. Half the workforce are now women, and the world of work has been revolutionised by science. We built a new popular culture, transformed by colour TV, *Coronation Street* and the Beatles. We enjoy a thousand material advantages over any previous generation; and yet we suffer a depth of insecurity and spiritual doubt they never knew.

The family is weakened; society is divided. We see elderly people in fear of crime, children abused. We live with the knowledge that the world – through nuclear weapons, chemical weapons and contempt for the environment – can end billions of years of evolution.

Mine is the generation with more freedom than any other, but less certainty in how to exercise it responsibly – the generation that knocks on the door of a new millennium, frightened for our future and unsure of our soul.

We live in a new age but in an old country. Britain won two world wars. We had an empire and formed a commonwealth. We invented the sports the rest of the world now plays; we gave the world some of the finest literature, art and poetry. We are proud of our history, but its weight hangs heavy upon us. Why? Because it has left us for far too long defining ourselves as a nation not by what unites us but by what divides us.

We have a class system unequal and antiquated, a social fabric tattered and torn, a politics where dogma drives out common sense – even an education system where one part of the nation is taught apart from the other. And if we do not change course we will have two classes of health service, two classes of state schools, two Britains – one on welfare; the other paying for it.

I want us to be a young country again. With a common purpose. With ideals we cherish and live up to. Not resting on past glories. Not fighting old battles. Not sitting back, hand on mouth, concealing a yawn of cynicism, but ready for the day's challenge. Ambitious. Idealistic. United. Where people succeed on the basis of what they give to their country, rather than what they take from their country. Saying not 'This was a great country' but 'Britain can and will be a great country again.'

The Labour Party believes that we are one community, one people, and citizens of one society. We make our future together or not at all. And this party will never hide, will never compromise, will never change its total commitment to the fundamental moral and political principle of racial equality.

It is intolerable that Asian and black families have to live in homes daubed with racist slogans and Nazi swastikas. It is a matter of shame that in many parts of our inner cities Asian women fear even to take their children down the street in daylight and where there have been 80,000 racial attacks in the last year.

From a speech to the party conference, 30 September 1993

Knowledge Britain

A young country must build the new economy of the future – no more bosses versus workers, but partnership at work. No more public versus private finance, but cooperation to rebuild our nation's road, rail, inner cities and regions. No more boom and bust economics, because inflation is the enemy of the stability which businesses need to plan for the future.

Above all, today we present our proposals to equip our people and businesses for new technological and economic challenges, and to change the basis of this country's thinking of the last 100 years. Education is the best economic policy there is, and it is in the marriage of education and technology that the future lies. The arms race may be over, the knowledge race has begun.

We will never compete on the basis of a low-wage, sweat shop economy. We have just one asset. Our people; their intelligence; their potential. Develop it – we succeed. Neglect it – we fail. It is as simple as that. Education does not stop when you walk out of the school gates for the last time. Edu-

Education is the best economic policy there is

cation is for life. The more you learn the more you earn. That is your way to do well out of life. Knowledge is power. Information is opportunity. And technology can make it happen. If we use it properly. Just think: there could be direct access to teaching skills from the workplace or the home, class sizes of one.

It means bringing together the private sector, government, universities, research centres and science labs to put together an advanced system of further education for the electronic age. It requires a supreme national effort. The market won't do it, a Labour government will. We have started work on it already. It will be called the University for Industry and it will transform education and skills in Britain, to make lifelong learning a reality.

But our aim must be even bolder. We have such huge advantages. Some of the finest telecommunications companies in the world. World leaders in broadcasting. The world's first language, English. Together, they could put us years ahead in education and technology and business. We should open up the markets in communications and technology. Yes, a market solution. The cable companies are playing their part, using the new technology to good effect. But we should aim for free and fair competition and end the restrictions that have prevented British Telecom, Mecury, and others from playing their part in wiring up Britain, until there is full and open competition everywhere from 2002.

This is a market with huge potential. In return, these companies owe some responsibility to the nation. We have been in discussion with BT. In return for access to the market, they have agreed, as they build their network, to connect up every school, every college, every hospital and every library in Britain. For free. They get the chance to win new markets; the nation gets the chance to succeed. That is New Labour: public and private, working together, building a dynamic economy, addressing the nation's needs and serving the nation's interests.

David Blunkett will be opening discussions with education authorities and the computer companies which supply them about how we meet the goal of ensuring that every child has access to a laptop computer. It would need new forms of teacher training. It would need a whole network of delivery. But it is possible. Think: fifty years ago their grandparents came into state schools for the first time and sat at a proper wooden desk. A Labour government provided them. Half a century later, a new way for a new age. That is what I mean by New Labour.

The Tories say that class size doesn't matter. If that's true I just wonder why so many of them spend so much buying small classes in the private sector. The Tories spend over £100 million a year on the Assisted Places Scheme. Under Labour, the scheme will be phased out. £60 million – just over half the cost of the Assisted Places Scheme – would pay for every five-, six- and seven-year-old to be educated in a class of 30 or under. That is how five-, six- and seven-year-olds will be educated in new Britain.

Stakeholder Britain

Our challenge to be a young country is not just economic. It is a social and a moral challenge. Look at the wreckage of our broken society. See Britain through the eyes of our children. Are we really proud of it – drugs, violence, youngsters hanging around street corners with nothing to do? We have to have the courage to build a new civic society, a new social order, where everyone has a stake and everyone plays a part.

Justice for all. Responsibility from all. It is a bargain between us and the people. No one pretends we can solve unemployment overnight. But no decent society can tolerate these levels of long-term unemployment with all the misery and social breakdown it brings.

We will take the excess profits of the new robber barons of Tory Britain in the privatised utilities and use it for the most radical programme of work and education ever put forward in Britain. And we will use that money too – and end up saving money – by giving single parents the chance not to live on benefit but to plan their future, organise child care and training so they can support themselves and their children. No longer the butt of Tory propaganda, they will be the citizens of new Britain who can earn a wage and look after the children they love.

With opportunity comes responsibility. It is absurd that the debate about crime has some talking of its causes and others of the need to punish criminals. Sweep away the dogma. Law and order is a Labour issue. We all suffer crime, the poorest and vulnerable most of all. It is the duty of government to protect them. And instead of wasting hundreds of millions of pounds on compulsory ID cards as the Tory Right demand, let that money provide thousands more police officers on the beat in our local communities. The truth is that the best two crime prevention policies are a job and a stable family.

A young country that wants to be a strong country cannot be morally neutral about the family. It is the foundation of any decent society. Behind strong communitites lie strong families. Go to any juvenile court and you will see. In the family people learn to respect and care for each other. Destroy that in a family and you cannot rebuild it in a country. In

68

every area of policy we should be examining its effect on the family, seeing how we can strengthen it and keep it together. In benefits, employment, education and housing we will let local authorities use the money from the sale of

A young country that wants to be a strong country cannot be morally neutral about the family

council houses to end the most telling obscenity of Tory Britain; we spend millions of pounds on slum B&B accommodation for homeless families when we could be using this money to build houses to live in.

I don't want an old social order. I want a new one, with rules for today. Don't let the Tories claim these values as their own – they are our values. You can be tough on crime and tough on prejudice too. In any young country the talents of all are allowed to flourish. There should be no discrimination on grounds of disability, gender, age, sexuality or race. In its place, tolerance and respect.

Modern Public Services for the People

A young country, new Britain, will sweep away the dogma from our public services. They need modernising, but keep them as public services and make them serve the public again, not vested interests of any kind. We created the NHS. We will save it. And we will change it for the better. That £1.6 billion in extra administration that the Tories have spent on bureaucracy, accountants and company cars could be spent on beds and patients and nurses. Let the internal market that pits hospital against hospital cease. Let our system of GP Commissioning replace the GP fundholding that has created this costly and two-tier system, and let the NHS work as a service again. Let the doctors do what the doctors should do; care for the sick, not be forced to make a business of them.

The privatised utilities will be properly regulated. We have plans for the Lottery too. The Lottery profits could be going to good causes. Camelot have six years of their contract to run. A Labour government will be seeking an efficient non-profit-making promoter so we can release more money for the benefit of good causes in Britain. We will also be seeking ways of ensuring that the views of Lottery players themselves are taken into account when Lottery panels decide how the takings are spent. It is the people's Lottery. The people should get more out of it.

Democratic Britain

Nowhere is a young country more needed than in our politics. We will change the old and dead political culture of Tory Britain. Where it is right, we will cooperate as well as oppose. I will not play political games with the peace process in Northern Ireland. The peace is too important for that.

But it is time to end the Tory sleaze, time to sweep away the quango state, to take power back from big government and share it with the people. Scotland shall have its Parliament. Wales will have its Assembly. London will be run by a directly elected authority like any other capital. And if, in time, the regions of England want a greater say in their health and education and police and transport, then that too can come.

We will rebuild local government. With it will come a change in the relationship between citizen and state – a Freedom of Information Act for central and local government – an end to hereditary peers sitting in the House of Lords as the first step to a proper directly elected second chamber, and the chance for the people to decide after the election the system by which they elect the government of the future.

Strong Britain

A young country should be proud of its identity and its place in the world, not living in its history but grasping the opportunities of the future. It is a disgrace that the Conservative Party have reduced British foreign policy in Europe to the level of a joke. Of course Europe needs reform. We have led calls to reform the CAP and the institutions of Europe. Of course, if there are further steps to integration, the people should have their say, at a general election or in a referendum. But Europe is a vital part of our national interest. To be sidelined without influence is not a betrayal of Europe. It is a betrayal of Britain. There is now a growing part of the Tory Party that would take Britain out of Europe altogether. That would be a disaster for jobs and businesses. I say this in all honesty to my country.

We can't be half in and half out for ever. This country should be leading in Europe and under Labour it will.

A young country, equipped for the future with a just society and a new politics and a clear understanding of its role in the world.

I want to make this pledge today to the whole country, and especially to those who despairing of politicians have almost given up hope of change. The party I lead will carry out in government the programme we provide in our Manifesto beforehand. Nothing more, nothing less, that is my word. We deliver what we promise. We don't promise what we can't deliver.

New Labour cannot create new Britain alone. I challenge this country: let us rouse ourselves to a new moral purpose for our nation. Let's build a new and young country that can lay aside the old prejudices that have dominated our land for generations. A nation for all the people, built by all the people, where old divisions are cast out. A new spirit in the nation based on working together, unity, solidarity, partnership. One Britain. That is the patriotism for the future. Where never again do we fight our politics by appealing to one section of our nation at the expense of another. Where your child in distress is my child, your parent ill and in pain, is my parent: your friend unemployed or helpless, my friend; your neighbour my neighbour. That is the true patriotism of a nation.

The coming election is not a struggle for political power. It is a battle for the soul of our nation.

During the 1995 VJ Day celebrations, I was on a platform with Tory ministers. As we walked down the Mall, there were thousands of people, holding their Union Jacks, and it soon became clear – to the horror of the Tories – that many of them were Labour supporters. They were waving and shouting and urging me to 'get the Tories out'. These people love this country. It is because they love this country that they look to Labour to change it. This is the patriotic party because it is the people's party.

As the Tories wave their Union Jacks I know what so many people will be thinking. I know what the people want to say to those Tories: It is no good waving the fabric of our flag when you have spent 16 years tearing apart the fabric of our nation, tearing apart the bonds that tie communities together and make us a united Kingdom, tearing apart the security of those people, clutching their Union Jacks, swelling with pride at their victory over tyranny, and yelling at me to 'get those Tories out', because they want security, because they want to leave a better world for their children and their grandchildren than they created for themselves and because they know the Tories cannot supply it.

Decent people. Good people. Patriotic people. When I hear people urging us to fight for 'our people', I want to say: these are our people. They are the majority. And we must serve them, and build that new Britain, that young country, for their children and their families. I make them this promise: I will do all I can to get the Tories out. And I will devote every breath that I breathe, every sinew of my body, to ensuring that their grandchildren do get to live in that new Britain in a new and better world.

The prize is immense. It is new Britain. One Britain: the people united by shared values and shared aims, a government governing for all the people, the party founded by the people back, truly, as the people's party. New Labour, New Britain. The party renewed, the country reborn.

From a speech to the Labour Party conference, Brighton, 3 October 1995

PART II

Our Economic Future

Social aims without economic means are empty wishes.
By uniting the two we can build a better future for
all our people.

The Mais Lecture, City University, London, 22 May 1995

9 The British Experiment – an Analysis and an Alternative

Economic theory and its relevance to policy-makers have featured in several Mais Lectures. In 1984, Nigel Lawson, then Chancellor of the Exchequer, sought to combine theory and practice in a lecture entitled the 'British Experiment', in which he set out the guiding principles that had governed economic policy since 1979. It remains one of the clearest outlines of the economic ideas that have dominated Conservative economic policy. Although much has changed since the 1980s, many of the main themes of the Lawson lecture continue to guide policy today.

I want here to examine the philosophy that has lain behind economic policy since 1979. I will say where the Labour approach agrees with the Conservatives, and where we strongly disagree. I will also outline a coherent framework for a new consensus between economists and politicians which I believe is the best way forward for Britain in the late 1990s.

Looking back over the period since the war, no one economic 'school' has ever had all the answers. Most have at different times provided useful insights into economic and financial problems, but have failed to anticipate change and to adjust to it. This is a defect, I would argue, which applies to the post-1979 economic philosophy just as much as it did to the earlier 'Keynesian' consensus. Once more it is time for change – a post-monetarist framework.

Lawson's Argument

Let's remember what Lord Lawson said in his 1984 Mais Lecture. Lawson argued that the focus and content of economic policy which has prevailed in the postwar period needed to be turned upside down.

What was the consensus in that period? It was that macro-economic policy, in the form of demand management, was the key to stimulating growth and maintaining full employment. Meanwhile, micro-economic policy – above all, various measures of wage control – was the key to low inflation.

Lawson asserted the exact opposite. He said that macro-economic policy should be responsible for controlling inflation, and should have no role in stimulating growth or creating jobs. The other side of the coin was that micro-economic policy should be concerned with promoting economic growth and jobs, but should have no role in control-ling inflation.

Furthermore, Lawson argued that, *within* both the micro and the macro area, the key instruments of policy should change. The crucial macro instrument was not budgetary policy – the variation of taxation and public spending to pre-vent recessions – but monetary policy. Interest rates should be set to achieve low inflation, and that was an end to the macro-economic responsibility of the Chancellor. Elsewhere, the private sector could be left to look after itself.

This belief in market forces governed the supply side too. According to Lawson, the government should accept no res-ponsibility to help the market function successfully through intervention. Instead, it should cease interfering with market processes wherever practicable. Deregulation and privatisation were the only instruments through which this was to be achieved. Once government was off the back of the private sector, the private sector would ensure that rapid growth and full employment were achieved.

And Lawson made one final point. The reduced role for government was to be reflected in a gradual reduction in the share of tax and public spending in GDP. Lower marginal tax rates would further increase the private sector's incentive to make the economy succeed.

This analysis in fact represented a return to the nineteenth century, when economists asserted that real (output) and nom-inal (money) variables in the economy could be determined entirely independently of each other. According to them, there was only one level of growth and employment which the economy could sustain over the medium term. They went as far as to call these the 'natural' levels of output and employment. They said that the government should look after inflation, while growth and employment should be left to look after themselves.

I strongly dispute this thinking. It probably should have had no place in nineteenth-century economics, and it certainly has no place near the dawn of the twenty-first century. Yet its appeal for many people stemmed from the failures of a period of economic management now usually known as the postwar Keynesian consensus.

Policy up to 1976

There is no doubt that some of those in the vanguard of the 'British Experiment' with economic policy after 1979 were too dismissive of the record of most postwar governments. It is too easy to forget the scale of economic and social problems that confronted Britain in the wake of the war, and the neglect of the pre-war years. Of course mistakes were made by the 1945 Labour government, but the world's finest welfare state was built, and the huge task of taking the economy off a wartime footing was accomplished. Economic reconstruction would have gone even further but for the continued need to ration scarce resources and to rearm for the fight against Communist aggression in Korea.

Conservative and Labour governments in the 1950s and 1960s committed errors too. They had an exaggerated belief in demand management, and showed too little concern for the gradual build-up in inflationary pressure which took place from one cycle to the next. Yet they provided this country with an unprecedented period of prosperity and full employment, with GDP growth averaging almost 3.0 per cent. Many historians now label this the golden age of British economic performance.

Admittedly, it seemed no golden age at the time. Growth was lower than that of many countries in Europe, but this was to be expected. The postwar period was one in which reconstruction enabled other countries to 'catch up' with the economic and technological leadership of the United States. The potential benefits of 'catch-up' to Britain were less than those to the devastated economies of continental Europe.

However, there is also no doubt that there were deeper-seated reasons for the deterioration in the underlying performance of the British economy compared with most of our major competitors. One of the most important reasons was the polarised hostility between management and unions. There was fault on both sides, but the atmosphere of trench warfare which so often existed on what was then called 'the shop floor' was unacceptable in a modern economy. Industrial action was frequent, unpredictable and crippling to industrial efficiency. This contributed to another cause of our relative failure – a lack of high-quality investment.

Whichever way we look at the evidence, two things are clear. First, the UK has invested too little in plant and equipment in the postwar era, and the quality of that investment has often been poor. Second, Britain has **Britain has neglected the impact on economic growth of investment in human capital** neglected the impact on economic growth of investment in human capital – particularly training, an area where the UK has had a poor record since the war, but an area that is of rising importance. Indeed, the increasing globalisation of the world economy means that the required levels of education and skills are now

I believe there is a strong case for introducing an appropriate fiscal incentive to increase research and development, such as is available in some of our industrial competitors. In government I will require the Treasury to review the existing fiscal framework and to examine the case both for reform and for new incentives. We must learn from others' experience. There is some evidence that tax credits for increments of research and development over a base year have worked well in the United States and seem well suited to a mature industrial economy with widely differing levels of research in different firms and industries.

From a speech to the Parliamentary and Scientific Committee, London, 21 February 1996

being set by international standards, and we continue to be left behind.

So we must encourage long-term investment. But if companies are to invest they must have a relatively stable macro-economic framework in which to plan.

I do not need to remind anyone that in the last quarter century the UK has been one of the most volatile of all the major economies. Since 1970 the British economy has suffered more recession years than other major developed economies, and the average UK inflation since 1970 has exceeded that of all major economies except Italy.

Even in the most successful years of the postwar period, governments frequently failed to provide the stable macro-economic background that companies need. In the immediate postwar period governments sought to fine-tune the economy to eliminate short-term fluctuations. However, it proved very difficult to gauge the appropriate timing of policy changes, so governments often exacerbated the next boom instead of preventing the current slump. Moreover, in trying to reduce cycles in economic activity, government policies accommodated real shocks to the supply side of the economy – wage shocks, or oil shocks, for example. The consequence of this was inflation.

The story of the breakdown of the Keynesian consensus in the mid-1970s is familiar to us all. By 1976 inflation had run out of control and Britain's external balance of payments situation was unsustainable. The Callaghan government faced a crucial decision – perhaps the most crucial in all of our postwar economic crises – on which direction to take. One possibility was for the UK to go down the path of protection, withdrawing from the world's trading system and seeking to return to a kind of wartime command economy. Fortunately, this path was swiftly rejected. Instead, macro-economic policy took an entirely new turn.

The British Experiment

In his Labour Party conference speech in 1976, Jim Callaghan sounded the death knell of the postwar Keynesian consensus when he openly admitted that the UK could no longer expect to borrow and spend its way out of recession. 'I tell you in all candour', he said 'that option no longer exists.'

From 1976 to 1979 the Labour government had a tight budgetary regime and introduced monetary targets into the UK for the first time – not, it should be recalled, at the instigation of the IMF, but through Denis Healey's own initiative. The beginnings of the 'British Experiment' were beginning to emerge. But it was not until Mrs Thatcher and Sir Geoffrey Howe arrived on the scene in 1979, with Nigel Lawson in a junior role at the Treasury, that the years of the British Experiment really began. It was then that the whole panoply of new measures started to develop, all of them based on the intellectual underpinning summarised in the 1984 Mais Lecture.

The aims of macro-economic policy became more medium-term, and policy objectives were all confined to monetarist objectives. These included money-supply targets, the rate of growth of money GDP, the exchange rate, or inflation itself.

But, if attempts to manage demand failed in an earlier period, the UK's experience exposed serious flaws in this approach too. Three reasons stand out.

First, though the ultimate objectives have stayed broadly the same, the framework for policy has been extremely inconsistent, with one regime after another failing to meet stated objectives. Since 1979, there have been at least four major lurches in the framework of monetary policy:

★ Monetarism, the primacy of the domestic money supply, or M3, from 1979 to 1983;

★ 'Lawsonomics', the mix of monetary and exchange-rate targets, from 1983 to 1989;

★ the ERM, a full-blown exchange-rate regime, from 1990 to 1992; and

★ domestic inflation targets, from 1992 to the present.

Second, the political influence on short-term monetary decisions in the 1980s, exacerbated by the effect of interest rates on the housing market, meant that policy-makers resisted raising interest rates until there was overwhelming evidence of inflationary pressure, and then tightened too much. That is the real nature of the debate between the government and the Bank of England.

The third problem which undermined the effectiveness of monetary policy during the 1980s was the failure to use monetary and fiscal policy in a coordinated fashion. In the late 1980s fiscal policy was being relaxed, with tax-cutting budgets in 1988, 1989 and 1990 at a time when interest rates were being kept high to curb inflationary pressure. That meant interest rates had to be pushed that much higher to slow down the economy and curb inflationary pressure.

The new monetary framework introduced after the exit from the ERM is still too politicised. If the public finances improve more quickly than the Treasury anticipates, there is little doubt that the Chancellor will cut taxes even if the improvement is solely due to faster than expected demand, thus repeating one of the crucial policy errors of the late 1980s. Even if they do not improve, we can assume that taxes will be cut, regardless of the economic circumstances.

Looking back at the entire period of the British Experiment, it is far from clear that the overall performance of the UK economy has been any better than it was under the Keynesian consensus:

* Unemployment has more than doubled since 1979, and there seems little prospect of it returning to 1970s levels, still less to 1950s or 1960s levels, under present policy.

* Inflation has come down, but little more than it has elsewhere in the world.

* The huge proceeds of North Sea oil somehow seem to have been squandered, without any significant improvement in domestic investment.

* Tax as a share of GDP has not been reduced.

* The growth in GDP – the ultimate judge and jury – has been under 2 per cent: around 1 per cent less than in Keynesian years.

Where the British Experiment was Right

One of the main problems with 1980s-style monetarism was that it thought there was nothing positive to learn from the successes of the Keynesian era. It threw the baby out with the bathwater. I do not want to make the same mistake in the late 1990s.

Macro-economic policy must be directed to keeping inflation low and as stable as possible. The idea that inflation can be stabilised at around 5–10 per cent, with permanent benefits to growth, is pure and dangerous fantasy. It would soon accelerate, and output would have to be cut to bring it under control.

The key elements of the 1980s legislation affecting trade unions will be retained

It is also undoubtedly true that improvements in the supply side are vital to increasing the underlying growth rate of the economy. This explains Labour's emphasis on investment in education, training and infrastructure.

There was certainly a need to change the climate of industrial relations. For example, the key elements of the 1980s legislation affecting trade unions will be retained. Indeed, if Labour's initiatives in the 1960s had been fully implemented, the 1970s might well have turned out differently in a number of ways.

Lawson was also right to stress the need to focus on the medium term. The postwar years are littered with short-term economic decisions which, taken for initially quite sensible and pragmatic reasons, have resulted cumulatively in a protracted period of decline.

Where the British Experiment was Wrong

However, despite these areas of agreement, something went very badly wrong with the British Experiment. It was put forward as laying the foundations for enhanced economic performance, but in key respects it did not. The root cause for this failure lies with mistakes in macro-economic policy, a number of which can be identified.

First, the design of the macro-economic framework itself, the Medium Term Financial Strategy, or MTFS.

The policy regime changed whenever it seemed convenient.

Sterling M3 came and went. Monetary aggregates were 'monitored' rather than targeted. The exchange rate came into greater prominence. And so on. The result was that an excessive amount of reliance came to be placed on the judgement of the Chancellor. The medium–term framework was increasingly defined in virtually any way the Chancellor chose. Herbert Morrison once defined socialism as 'anything a Labour government does'. The MTFS came to be anything that the Tories chose it to be. In the end too much flexibility became a liability, and the MTFS lost its credibility with the markets.

The second failure of macro-economic policy was the reluctance to recognise that the government has to respond to excessive imbalances in the economy even if they are produced by the private sector. The 1984 mantra was 'public sector bad, private sector good'. Because of this, the government remained far too relaxed as trade and the current-account deficits ballooned through the late 1980s. Because they reflected deficits of the private sector, the Chancellor took the view that they would adjust reasonably smoothly. In the end such a casual approach came to grief.

The trade gap had to be financed by foreigners being ready to acquire sterling-denominated assets in the UK. They would do this only if they believed the returns would be attractive. This would be the case only if economic growth was strong and as long as inflation remained low so that currency depreciation was a low risk. But if growth stalled or if inflation threatened to accelerate, a large trade deficit became a problem. The number of foreigners willing to hold UK assets and lend to UK citizens dried up. Interest rates had to be raised to extreme levels to prevent an outright collapse in the pound. The result was recession – a recession caused by the volatile behaviour of the private sector, and by the government's dogmatic refusal to worry about it until far too late.

Most fundamental of all, there was a complete failure to appreciate the interconnection between macro-economic and micro-economic policy. Since the two were deemed to be separate – again for reasons of dogma and doctrine – the

83

government failed to see that changes in micro-economic policy may need to be offset by shifts in macro-economic policy.

Furthermore, this interconnection means that macro-economic failure which allows inflation to get out of control can have long-term consequences for the real economy. And here I come to a key point. The classical split between inflation on the one hand and output or employment on the other hand turned out to be entirely false.

The failure of macro-economic policy had permanent effects on the supply side of the economy through the reduction in investment, the withering of the capital stock, and the rise in numbers of long-term jobless. This reduced productive capacity, raised the sustainable level of un-employment and reduced the trend growth rate of the economy.

Furthermore, the volatility of the economy is reflected in capital markets. In the past five years the gilt market has been more volatile than any other major bond market, putting up the cost of capital. And after every recession businesses need more and more convincing that recovery is this time 'for real'. This is why businesses have been so slow to invest in the current recovery, with the result that capacity constraints have again reappeared, with unemployment still far too high.

Despite monetarist theory, a failure of policy that affects nominal economic variables will have a disastrous medium-term impact on real ones too.

Unless the government learns the lessons of the 1980s, it will repeat these mistakes.

Lessons from the Postwar Era

So what lessons should we draw from the eventual failure of postwar Keynesian economics and the more recent setbacks for the British Experiment?

First, the control of inflation through a tough macro-economic policy framework is even more important than the Tories have said. Of course the control of inflation is vital in its own right. But what is even more crucial is that, in practice, the classical split between inflation and output cannot be maintained. Temporary failures over inflation have permanent adverse effects on the real economy – on output and jobs. The only way these can be avoided is to put in place a tough, credible and transparent macro-economic framework which will stand the test of time. This a Labour government would do.

Second, while the Tories correctly observed that both macro- and micro-economic policy measures were necessary to achieve economic success, they have failed to appreciate the extent to which failure in the former could swamp improvements in the latter. They are also wrong to see these instruments as separate or separable – they are in fact complementary. The one should support the other; the one should compensate for the failings of the other.

Third, the Tories have placed far too much faith in the benign and self-correcting nature of private-sector behaviour once deregulation has taken place. In fact, total reliance on the private sector is just as wrong as overreliance on the public sector. Deregulation alone cannot cure the ills of our economy: the public sector must accept its responsibility to act in partnership with the private sector to transform the supply side of the economy. This is a responsibility which Labour will gladly accept.

Fourth, we have learned and relearned that a cooperative attitude between workers and management at the workplace is vital. The union excesses of the 1970s were wrong, but it would be just as wrong to replace them with an attitude of worker subservience to an almighty management. The successful companies are based on partnership and cooperation, not on class war or old-style management domination.

Fifth, unemployment is not just a social problem but an economic problem as well. The Tories' indifference to the climb in long-term unemployment in the 1980s and 1990s is indefensible. We must make a clear commitment to get long-term unemployment down.

Finally, we have learned that the ability to improve public services, or to cut taxation, is derived from, and cannot be

divorced from, economic success. A low-tax economy is possible only if we first have a high-success economy.

New Labour – the Macro Framework

The first priority for a high-success economy is a tough and
coherent macro-economic framework for policy.

We must recognise that the UK is situated in the middle
of an active global market for capital – a market which is less
subject to regulation today than it has been for several decades.
Since it is inconceivable that the UK would want to withdraw
unilaterally from this global market-place, we must instead
adjust our policies to its existence.

Global capital markets have advantages as well as perils for
a British government. They provide access to overseas and
domestic savings; but capital flows, which nowadays are far
more important than trade flows in determining the value of
the currency, can swiftly move against policies which fail to
win investors' confidence.

An expansionary fiscal or monetary policy that is at odds
with other economies in Europe will not be sustainable for
very long. To that extent the room for manœuvre of any
government in Britain is already heavily circumscribed.

There is little point in trying to eliminate all the fluctuations
of the economic cycle, but getting the overall framework for
fiscal and monetary policy right is the biggest single thing that
will encourage business to invest. This in turn will enable a
Labour government to mount a sustained attack on the
country's economic and social problems.

If we get this right, it becomes possible to improve in
imaginative ways the supply side. Equally, failure will undermine other policies to improve industrial performance.

The macro framework has two elements: the monetary
framework and the fiscal framework, including the level of
tax and spending in the economy.

The Monetary Framework
A Labour government will have an explicit target for low and
stable inflation.

Controlling inflation is not only an objective in itself. It is an essential prerequisite of sustainable economic growth on a scale sufficient to attain the social and political aims of the Labour Party, including high durable levels of employment and rising living standards.

To help achieve low and reasonably stable levels of inflation, a Labour government will introduce a number of changes affecting the relationship between the Treasury and the Bank of England. The monthly meeting between the Chancellor and the Governor of the Bank of England and the subsequent publication of the minutes have been a sensible innovation. However, reform needs to be taken further, as the existing arrangements do have some drawbacks.

First, their effective working is peculiarly dependent on the personalities involved. To be fair, whatever other difficulties there may have been, so far this one does not seem to have been a problem. But it could become one, and potentially this adds an unnecessary element of instability into the making of monetary policy.

Second, the overall effect of the innovation is probably to have increased the power of the Bank relative to the Treasury, though this is not entirely clear-cut. Unfortunately, however, there has been no increase in the accountability of the Bank to the democratic process, and insufficient increase in the transparency of its operations.

How are we to move forward?

Germany's economic record and the potential role of the Bundesbank demand attention. Of course Germany's prosperity since the end of the war is based on much more than the independence of the Bundesbank, but confidence in the overall stability of monetary policy has certainly been a factor.

However, it is not always possible or desirable to transpose institutions unchanged from one country to another. The institutions themselves will to some extent reflect different cultures and traditions. For example, there is no doubt that, for historical reasons, the role of the central bank in Germany has a much greater political resonance with the electorate than is conceivable in Britain. This is reflected in the Bundesbank's position within the constitution, and differences must be heeded in any relationship between the Bank of England and the government in Britain.

Three main points should be noted from Germany's experience.

First, although its inflation record has been good, the Bundesbank has in practice shown a much greater degree of operational pragmatism – a willingness to deviate from monetary targets, for example – than its rhetoric or reputation might imply. One reason for this, of course, is its own track record. The lesson from this is that credibility can enhance the room for policy manœuvre.

Second, the operations of the Bundesbank allow it to move interest rates in small steps. This is less disruptive to business than the larger hikes that have characterised moves in Britain.

Third, although the constitution of the Bundesbank formally guarantees its independence from the political process, this is not absolute. In the aftermath of German unification, even the Bundesbank became concerned about whether its freedom of manœuvre could be guaranteed. In a democracy, political acceptance for monetary decisions ultimately has to be retained.

We have to design an institutional arrangement that fits Britain, and it may use the best practice from a number of other countries. But our objective is clear. This is to reform the Bank of England so that it can carry out its increasingly important functions in an open and more accountable manner. We will then watch the track record of the Bank before deciding what, if any, further steps should be taken towards greater operational responsibility for the Bank in interest-rate policy.

Fiscal Policy, and the Level of Taxation and Spending
The Shadow Chancellor has stated our fiscal framework. This emphasised that the ratio of public debt to GDP would be stabilised at a prudent level, and that the 'golden rule' of public finance would be observed by a Labour government. This means that public borrowing will be used only to finance investment, not public consumption. Even then it must be prudently undertaken. I want here to comment on the implica-

tions of this framework for the level of taxation and government expenditure in the economy.

Macro- and micro-economic policy affect each other, and this has important implications for taxation and spending, and illustrates the sterile nature of the debate on these issues in recent years.

For example, proper control of public spending is needed for macro-economic reasons, but if this results in disproportionate cuts in capital spending it will have a damaging impact on the supply side of the economy. Likewise the supply-side performance of the economy may be improved by reductions in marginal rates of income tax, but if badly handled this can lead to uncontrolled booms – as it did in the late 1980s. In any case, the changes that have occurred in Britain and the world economy mean that the debate over taxation and spending has to recognise a much narrower range of options than before.

The growing integration of the world economy – in which capital and, to a lesser extent, labour move freely – means that it is not possible for Britain to sustain budget deficits or tax

---

There is a higher proportion of income taken in tax today than there was even under the last Labour government. Now direct tax rates have come down but VAT and other types of tax have gone up, national insurance went up. So ordinary taxpayers, as I say, I'd like to get their taxes down. Top-rate taxpayers have increased dramatically under the Conservatives, because they brought down the threshold. You can have a policeman or a teacher that is paying top-rate tax in this country today, so we've got to be careful that we're not treading on the toes of those people. But if we have any proposals in relation to that we will put it before people, before the election so that they get an assessment of it, and all I ask of people is, Please judge us on what we're saying, not on what the Conservatives say we're saying.

From Breakfast with Frost, *BBC Television, 14 January 1996*

---

regimes that are wildly out of line with the other major industrial countries. One of the requirements of our tax structure is to attract enterprise into the UK from overseas.

I want to make one thing clear. In government, controlling public spending is a long and gruelling slog. But the alternative is far worse, as we have seen from the past, when excessive spending in the short term has had to be retrenched with painful long-term consequences for business and the public services.

The long haul also applies to taxation. No one wants a return to penal taxation, and of course the objective of any government is to lower rather than to increase the tax burden on ordinary families. But lower taxes depend on a successful economic policy.

The debate on this subject needs to become more realistic on both sides. The Right often promises to cut both taxes and spending irrespective of circumstances. The old Left was perceived as believing that higher taxation and spending are a good thing in themselves.

Neither of these is right, as the recent experience of both Labour and Conservative governments has shown. The first planned a large increase in public spending, but in the end was forced to retrench with large cuts in spending. The second promised to cut taxes, but has been forced to impose the biggest tax increases in peacetime history as the rest of its economic strategy has hit the rocks. Neither government wanted to reverse course. Both were forced to do so because economic policies as a whole failed to deliver an acceptable performance from the real economy.

An economic strategy that puts investment and economic growth at the centre of the agenda cannot ignore the implications of these objectives for the taxation of companies, savings and individual incomes. But the real point is that decisions on taxation and spending are dependent on the overall performance of the economy. And the type of spending is just as important as its overall quantity.

Economic success over the medium term will enable a Labour government to reduce the amount of spending that simply mops up the consequences of economic failure – rescue spending – and to raise the proportion that is available for renewal spending, especially on investment, education and training.

This is the opposite of what has happened under the Conservatives. In 1992–4 public spending averaged about 44 per cent of GDP. In 1995 it may fall a little, to reach roughly the same proportion of GDP as it did in 1979. But since 1979 spending on renewal areas has fallen from 13.5 per cent of GDP to just over 10 per cent – a difference of about £20 billion. Meanwhile, economic failure has meant that rescue spending, on unemployment and social security, has risen from 8.5 per cent of GDP to nearly 12 per cent. This reorientation of the type of spending within the total has been much more important than changes in the total itself.

New Labour – Micro-economic Strategy to Build Long-term Strength

So, as I have emphasised, to increase the underlying growth rate of the economy we have to recognise the importance of both macro- and micro-economic policy and the connection between the two.

In the area of micro-economic policy it is important to distinguish which areas are best carried out by government, which by the private sector, and those where a partnership between the two is the best way of raising the performance and capacity of business.

We must build Britain's long-term economic strength by cooperating with industry and commerce. New Labour would seek cooperation in seven key areas:

★ to unlock human potential through education and training;

★ to develop modern infrastructure;

★ to harness and spread new technology;

★ to encourage investment and longer-term thinking;

★ to tackle long-term unemployment;

★ to open up world markets for British business; and

★ to encourage small and medium-sized firms.

I want now to focus on three particular aspects of micro-economic policy: the flexibility of labour markets (which received particular attention in the Mais Lecture in 1984), the treatment of long-term unemployment, and investing for the longer term.

Flexibility and Employment
The British Experiment attached huge importance to the need to deregulate labour markets in the UK, which were contrasted unfavourably with those in America. While we clearly cannot ignore the recent employment record of the US, we should be wary of drawing simplistic conclusions. The benefits of deregulated labour markets have not been unqualified, and increased flexibility has not been won without costs.

The cost and price of labour are important, but 'flexibility' is not just about cutting costs. The best of our international competitors do worry about costs, but they also do much much more than that. They accept, along with their government, a responsibility to nurture and improve the skills of their workforce.

Britain cannot take the 'cheap labour' route. We will never be as cheap as the low-wage economies, and in any case most of our competition is still with other advanced industrial countries. Short-term savings may lead to longer-term costs. Deregulation may even accelerate deskilling.

For example, if deregulation leads to a large increase in part-time or contract labour, with little mutual commitment between firms and employees, companies may well be less able or willing to finance training or apprenticeships than they would be if there was a longer-term relationship with their workforce. I do not believe there is any conflict at all between sensible minimum standards at work, including on pay, and a successful labour market. Indeed, I think the one complements the other.

Labour-market flexibility should involve a new partnership between companies and workers that goes well beyond that of the buyer and seller of a commodity. Flexibility within businesses is as important as flexibility in the labour market external to the firm. The key ingredient here will be to ensure that we create a fully educated labour force conversant with the skills necessary to implement the new technology. An educated worker is a confident worker – and a confident worker is more likely to show the flexibility needed for success. This form of flexibility is increasingly important in a period of rapid technological change.

A central fault of the Tories – in this and other areas – has been that they think that deregulation is enough. It is not. We are developing plans – such as the University of Industry, the broadening of the scope of A-levels, and the improvements proposed in vocational training – to ensure that the British labour force no longer falls behind the skill levels available to business overseas.

Long-term Unemployment

Long-term unemployment is an economic as well as a social problem – for the economy as a whole and for the individual.

Between 1979 and 1986 the number of long-term unemployed rose to just under 1.5 million. This has devastating long-term effects. The longer people are out of work, the less likely they are to return to a job via the normal workings of the labour market. As the number of long-term unemployed becomes entrenched, it raises the overall unemployment rate that is compatible with low and stable inflation. An economic upturn is not enough to cut long-term unemployment significantly, and this will be reflected in the proportion of public spending taken up with what we have called rescue spending – spending on the costs of economic failure.

In our Budget submission in November 1994 we proposed eight initiatives to tackle the combination of demotivation, lack of skills and lack of opportunities. These included:

* reform of the benefits system, so that welfare payments are used to support work not unemployment;

* reform of the labour market, including a tax rebate for employers taking on the long-term unemployed; and

* reform of child-care and training opportunities, to support single parents to enter the labour market.

93

Indifference to this issue is economically and socially unacceptable. If not tackled, long-term unemployment will remain a drag anchor on our economy and its costs will squeeze out much-needed investment.

Long-termism in Finance and Industry
Much of the UK's relatively poor economic performance can be put down to a lack of high-quality investment over many years. It is much harder to identify the causes of this.

It is sometimes argued that the causes of low investment are the cost and terms of finance associated with the financial structure in Anglo-Saxon economies, which is compared unfavourably with those of Germany and Japan, for example.

The strengths of Germany are said to be the close relationships between the banks and the company sector, in which the former take long-term equity holdings and are thought to be active participants in developing long-term strategies for companies. Japan's success is put down to the 'seamless web' between government, banks and industry. Both are preferred to the Anglo-Saxon structure in which institutional shareholders are thought to focus on short-term performance of companies as reflected in stock-market prices.

This may sound compelling, but in fact the relationships between finance and industry reflect a number of different historical and cultural factors that cannot be transposed with success. Furthermore, there are a number of problems with this oversimplified view of our difficulties.

First, the Anglo-Saxon structure has not stopped the US economy being dynamic and strong.

Second, the decline in the UK's industrial performance pre-dates the development of powerful institutional shareholders, and there are plenty of examples of once cash-rich companies with household names failing because of the lack of a successful strategy within the companies themselves.

Third, the actual relationship elsewhere is sometimes more complicated than it appears. For example, there is some evidence that German firms which have supervisory boards – seen as a means of encouraging longer-term decisions – make less use of bank finance – seen by some as the key to Germany's industrial success – than those which do not.

Fourth, in continental Europe the trend may well be away from bank finance and towards a more Anglo–Saxon model. This partly reflects the need to develop financial structures able to cater for the demands for pensions from an ageing population. To this extent, well-developed financial institutions give the UK a head start in dealing with some common problems.

Having said all that, a long-term perspective does seem to be lacking in the UK financial sector. We are examining ways in which changes in the tax regime or in take-over regulations might sensibly be made to encourage a long-term mentality in industry and the City. We have already undertaken to examine CBI proposals for the reform of capital-gains taxation.

But it is a mistake to believe that short-termism stems only from the City. The behaviour of the companies themselves needs to be monitored as well. Often it is the management which initiates the expansion of a company by mergers and acquisitions rather than through natural growth. Of course it then needs to get institutional backing, but the initiative starts from within the company itself. So the UK may be suffering as much from unaccountable management as from an excessive City preoccupation with short-term profits.

I do not want to paint the picture too starkly, but it is important to develop a more fruitful relationship between the providers and recipients of finance. These issues are being actively considered in several quarters, and, provided the implications of any changes are fully thought out and considered, I believe a Labour government would in some respects be knocking at an open door.

I hope that a step-by-step approach will be adopted. Legislation might ultimately be needed in some areas, such as the information provided in company accounts, but initial progress might be made without it. For example, although it would be wrong to exaggerate the significance of non–executive directors, at the moment many are too close in a personal sense to their chairman or chief executives. We will be discussing with the major financial institutions ways of increasing the effectiveness of non-executive directors as watchdogs for shareholders. This is only one example, and its immediate impact might not be dramatic, but it is illustrative of a wider approach that over time could bring a longer-term perspective for investment decisions.

Conclusion

There is no point in arguing that everything about the British economy is awful, or that the government has done everything wrong. There is some good news, but the latest recovery has nevertheless exposed once again the persistent nature of some fundamental weaknesses – for example the re-emergence of capacity constraints and of inflationary pressures while unemployment remains far too high.

Most decisions to move interest rates involve fine judgement. But small mistakes in monetary policy can become cumulative, and over a period of months or years inflation creeps back into the system. The risk of that happening is all the greater if decisions are reached for short-term political reasons. That has been the UK's experience.

It is the structure within which policy decisions are made, rather than the merits of any particular decision, that holds the key to curbing inflation and improving the supply side of the economy on a permanent basis.

When Nigel Lawson delivered his Mais Lecture in 1984, the 'British Experiment' was at a relatively early stage. Since then, the full implications of the experiment have become apparent, including its weakness.

As in the 1970s, we now need to recognise that a new approach is needed. I have outlined the key planks of the economic approach of New Labour:

★ First, our recognition that the theoretical split identified by nineteenth-century economists and which provided the intellectual underpinning of the British Experiment breaks down in practice – largely because of the interconnection between the macro and micro economy. Failure to control inflation affects the real economy and vice versa. Short-term mistakes have long-term consequences.

96

★ Second, our belief that a macro-economic framework to keep inflation low and stable is even more important was stated in the 1980s. Far from being an alternative to Labour's long-term investment strategy, controlling inflation is an essential part of it.

★ Third, our acceptance that too much reliance has been placed on deregulation alone to improve the supply side of the economy. There is an active role for government – particularly in, though not confined to, the improvement of human capital. In a world in which education, training and skills will increasingly be tested by global standards, any country which falls behind may be faced with huge social as well as economic consequences.

★ Fourth, our belief that much of the current debate on taxation and spending is parochial and sterile. The boundaries for changes in both are much reduced, and both are dependent on the performance of the economy, not on *a priori* assumptions about the desirability of particular levels of either. The key questions therefore become not how much to spend but what to spend it on, and how to improve the performance of the economy. That is what really matters to us all.

I came into politics because I believe passionately that a fair society and a more efficient one go hand in hand. By providing long-term economic strength and by raising the education and opportunities of all our citizens, we can achieve the stronger and more cohesive society I want to see. Social aims without economic means are empty wishes. By uniting the two we can build a better future for all our people.

It is to this that our new economic approach will be applied.

From the Mais Lecture, City University, London, 22 May 1995

10 *New Industrial World*

The key to survival in the modern world is access to knowledge and information. Without it neither individuals or businesses or the nation as a whole will prosper. There is a technological revolution under way. This country must start to prepare for it together. If we don't we will not shape our future. It will simply roll over us, leaving us stranded in its wake. The changes in Asia and the Pacific Basin represent an enormous transformation in the global economy and global politics. There really is a new world being built there, and the 'old world' needs to look at its institutions, its economy and its education system to ensure that it keeps up. One of the keys to make sure the 'old world' does keep up is by realising to the full the potential of the information revolution. If we fail the consequences will be dire. The scale of the revolution is immense.

But the power of the new technologies should not divert us from their real significance, which is about transforming health care and education, enhancing democracy, and boosting wealth creation. The technology is wondrous, but its real significance is how it can change our society. Just think about the possibilities:

* bringing the world's leading medical experts into any operating theatre in the country rather than taking the risk of transporting the sick patient to the expert;

* giving the brightest children the chance to stretch their potential to the full through advanced courses with specialist teachers, and helping children who are struggling by giving them extra help tailored to their needs;

* the transformation of our economy through a new industrial revolution to make Britain the electronic workshop of the world.

A New Industrial Revolution

I have been wondering what it would be like to do the job I do today in 1980. Every time I go to Sedgefield on the train, I would be forced out of action for three hours, unable to be contacted or to contact anyone. If we wanted to do any work, it would be on paper that would have to be posted back to the office to be typed up, posted back to me for correcting, and so on. And if I arrived at the station without any cash, I would have to queue at the bank to get some, and if it was after three-thirty in the afternoon then I'd just have to go without. Without the fax, the mobile phone, the cash machine, the personal computer and everything else we take for granted, leading the Labour Party must have been a very much more frustrating job then than now. The new inventions of the 1980s – the fax, the mobile phone, the laptop, the bleeper – are now commonplace. Without them, people and companies are at a massive disadvantage.

The inventions of the last decade and the possibilities of the next have one simple subject in common: information. They communicate information faster, to a greater audience than was ever possible before; they transmit more of it; they transmit it on the move. They store more information, then make it easier to find and easier to present, easier to apply. It is because information is the currency of our economies and our societies that these technologies are so important: because they save us time, because they save us money and because increasingly they will give us an innovative edge over our competitors.

We cannot know in detail what the world will be like in 2010. But we already know the outline: that our wealth and our quality of life will depend on information. And that the job of government, therefore, will not be to second guess and thereby restrict business and technological choices but rather to create a framework both here and abroad that will give scope for businesses to develop, innovate and compete successfully.

We are entering the age of a new industrial revolution, comparable in every way with the invention of the steam engine or the development of mass production. Think back to the beginning of the industrial revolution. Consider the parallels with our own situation. Then inventions like the

99

steam engine promised to transform the economy. Raw materials were the currency of their economy. Mechanisation meant those raw materials could be made into goods faster and cheaper, and then transported further and quicker. Previously local markets became global and new products and markets emerged. Britain did very well out of the industrial revolution that followed, partly because we invented and mastered those new technologies faster than our competitors. We were the workshop of the world and the standard of living of the richest in society rose substantially.

Now fast forward to the present. Again the promise of new technologies; again a Britain full of invention and enthusiasm; again the chance to lead the world into an industrial transformation. But we have had a passive government that has not learnt the lessons of the past and that refuses to use the power of public office to bring about the public's interest. Why is it that the only time we in this country hear about the information superhighway is when we hear of or read reports of initiatives in other countries – when Al Gore popularises the term information superhighway or when he and Bill Clinton make it a central plank of their policy agenda; when the European Commission launches a vision and action plan for the Information Society or when Japan promise to give every household access to the superhighway by 2010. The Australian Labour Government has published its own agenda for change 'The Creative Nation'. It is bold and imaginative. We hear of other countries leading this race and we wonder where our government's response is.

> **Britain did very well out of the industrial revolution that followed, partly because we invented and mastered those new technologies faster than our competitors**

This is the true face of conservatism: unable or unwilling to recognise change, too arrogant or too afraid or perhaps just too conservative to take the radical steps it requires. The conservative way is to let change happen, to suffer and submit. This was the government's response to the biggest challenge to and opportunity for our competitiveness: no vision, no leadership, no change. This is a government more concerned by the size and location of their offices than whether or not government plays its full part in the competitive future of our nation.

The response of the old Left would have been better motivated. The old Left would have wanted to intervene to shape this revolution in the interest of all. But they might not have known how to do so. Misled by the metaphor, they may well have thought government should own and build the superhighway, that government should pick the technology, because the project was too important to be left to the market.

New Labour knows those means are no longer appropriate to a modern economy. New Labour knows the information superhighway should be built by the private sector. We know government has neither the duty nor the desire to choose new technologies. We know our role is not to pick winners but to create the competitive framework within which companies can compete.

New Networks and Services

In putting that framework in place, we have considered two main questions: first, what kind of networks and services do we want? Second, how do those networks affect our economy and society? Four principles underpin our answers to those questions.

First, promote effective competition. The irony of the government's position is that its aim is effective competition. But they have ended up restricting it. In trying to create protected markets, they have forbidden both incumbents such as BT and new start-ups such as Ionica from selling broadcast entertainment. Worse, the government refuses to tell our companies when their exile will end. All they will do is promise a minor review in 1998 and a major one in 2001. In consequence, every business decision these companies have to take is clouded with regulatory uncertainty. This in a market where technological uncertainty is greater than ever before and probably greater than in any other industry.

This is not about a lobbying battle between BT and the cable companies. The Labour Party welcomes the massive investment the cable companies have made. We recognise that they took risks no one else was prepared to take and we want them and their shareholders to be able to make a return on that investment. Nor is this about British versus foreign companies: many of the cable companies have floated on our stock exchange, and all of them employ mainly British workers.

Something else should be clear to everyone: that it is not government's role to tell companies which markets they can and cannot enter. The Tories may tolerate privatised monopolies: Labour will not. We will put the consumer first, so that companies make money by serving customers in a competitive market-place, not through regulatory protection. The challenge we face today therefore is how to move towards free entry and regulatory certainty for all players. Our policy document sets out how we achieve this in the interests of consumers in a way fair to all parties:

★ cable television franchises will not face new entrants until 1998, a seven-year protection period similar to that enjoyed by Mercury;

★ after 1998, there will be a franchise-by-franchise release of the restrictions, as recommended by the Trade and Industry Select Committee; and

★ that as soon as possible after the election of a Labour government all telecoms markets will be governed by effective competition, enforced by a new streamlined regulator for the infrastructure, an OFCOM to combine the powers that are currently scattered around a cluster of regulators.

I believe this framework will allow the cable companies to build their networks, and to compete against new entrants, while removing the interventionist handicaps this government has put in place of our best companies.

The second principle concerns speed of deployment. This is vital. Countries that develop networks and services first will gain two advantages: an export edge over slower competitors and a competitive edge for the domestic users of these new services. This is a race where we cannot afford to lag behind.

Effective competition will help. Low barriers will mean new entrants and new services. As supply expands, prices will fall, bringing these new technologies within reach of new customers. But this virtuous circle will not be enough to wire up less profitable areas. In return for entry into broadcast entertainment markets, we will expect a timetable from the new entrants to wire up as much of the country as is practicable. The economies of scale would in turn help private investment: the bigger the market, the more services will be viable and the cheaper the manufacturing costs will be.

Third, is to strive to achieve universality. The information superhighway should not just benefit the affluent or the metropolitan. Just as in the past books were a chance for ordinary people to better themselves, in the future on-line education will be a route to better prospects. But just as books are available from public libraries, the benefits of the superhighway must be there for everyone. This is a real chance for equality of opportunity: if instead this government allows the information haves to leave behind the information have-nots, they will further divide the nation and leave millions without opportunities to succeed.

Now, of course, as the highway develops, prices will fall and this will make it easier for people to gain access. But we must do more than simply wait for those lower prices. That is why Labour will promote universal access as soon as possible. There are thousands of buildings in this country where people don't use the television, don't have their own computer, cannot access the Internet. These buildings are schools, hospitals, health centres, libraries, citizens advice bureaux.

Labour would insist that in return for entry into entertainment markets, the network providers connect every public library, every school, every health centre, every hospital, every citizens advice bureau in this country. The marginal cost of doing this will be greatly outweighed by the social value of allowing everyone in the country to become superhighway literate. A social gain outweighed only by the commercial gain of a more confident user-base, transforming what are currently niche markets into mass consumer markets.

Fourth and very importantly, we must encourage diversity of services. People don't say: 'I just used the Royal Mail'. They say I sent mum a birthday card. They don't say I feel like using the telephone network. They say I'll just order a pizza.

They don't buy wires; they buy content, services. With Labour's proposals, anyone wanting to reach any customer will have the right to do so, for a fair price. Diversity should not mean an absence of standards. Just like the mail or the telephone before it, the Internet provides access to pornography and racial hatred. There are fears the information superhighway will ease money laundering and international crime. We won't be able to know about all crimes on the superhighway, but that doesn't mean we should give up trying to prosecute. We should concentrate on effective regulation:

★ on protecting minors, for example through PIN numbers or a kitemarking system;

★ on self-regulation by network operators, for example the successful system used by the British university network, where users sign undertakings on content and there are teams to track down abuses; and

★ on being able to investigate and prosecute where a crime is alleged. That will mean adapting existing law, particularly copyright, to new networks, and giving the police electronic search warrants – for example, in the same way they can ask for a safe to be opened they should be able to obtain decryption as part of a due legal process.

We know new technologies bring threats as well as opportunities. The job of government is to minimise those threats: these and other proposals in our document will do just that.

Wealth Creation and Interactive Public Services
The new technologies redraw the possible; it is up to individuals and businesses to make the possible real, to invent and market the information economy and society. Britain is fortunate to have potential competitive advantages here:

★ the English language, in which 80 per cent of the world's information is stored;

★ our leading information companies, from BT to Pearson, from Ionica to Reuters, from Mercury to the BBC, to name but a few; and

★ British consumers, possibly the most media literate in the world, and the fastest adopters of new technology in Europe.

We must unleash this wealth-creating potential, both within industry and for the rest of the economy. Half of us work in information industries; the telecommunications and information technology sectors are now £30 billion a year. These industries have been identified as one of the three main sources of new jobs over the next decade. Even without considering the knock-on effect, the potential for wealth creation is clear. But the knock-on effect could be enormous.

The information infrastructure is a key factor in the costs and product quality of companies all over Britain. If we lead the superhighway race, it is estimated this knock-on effect could raise our GDP by £12 billion over 12 years and create thousands of new jobs. It is sheer lunacy that the government are refusing to act on this opportunity. Of course, we know governments do not create wealth: companies, entrepreneurs, workers do. But governments can help or hinder those companies. Labour would work with businesses to turn our potential competitive advantages into real competitive products. The four principles I have set out will ensure the information infrastructure is in place: creating a competitive network, open to all service providers, available as fast as possible, to create a mass consumer base and help Britain capture the 'first mover' advantages of the superhighway race. We would then work with businesses to spread best practice, to provide the vision and enthusiasm that will galvanise companies across the industrial spectrum into taking advantage of these opportunities.

There is one area where government has a direct responsibility: public services are still 40 per cent of the national economy but here the present government's response has been lamentably slow and cripplingly fragmented. The potential for improving the efficiency and effectiveness is immense. A government of national renewal needs a radical renewal of government. The possibilities for renewing government include:

★ a University for Industry bringing lifelong learning to every workplace in the country;

105

★ a Millennium Archive available to every child, young or old;

★ an Open University of the World, combining the brand names and expertise of the BBC and the Open University, to bring education to massive new export markets;

★ electronic job centres matching skills and needs all over the country.

★ In sum, interactive public services that put the user in control.

Conclusion

In the run up to the election change will be a defining issue – change which we welcome but the Conservatives fear and don't understand. Change which we will shape in the interests of all, but which the Conservatives ignore to the detriment of all. Change, which cries out for a radical reforming government, committed to national renewal, where the Tories are content merely to manage decline. Britain has the potential to be the electronic workshop of the world, and under Labour, we will make it so.

I totally understand what anybody risks who has to work extremely hard to get a business off the ground, and if you're a self-employed laywer, as I was, that's precisely what you have to do when you're working most of the hours that God gave you in order to do it.

From 'Blair's Britain' Panorama, *BBC Television, 3 October 1994*

---

11 *New Labour, New Economy*

I am essentially a politician who works by instinct, by simple values. I share those values with those who founded my party and, I believe, with the majority of the British people. The Labour Party exists to improve and better the lot of the broad majority of people. And it believes that that is best achieved within a strong and fair society, where opportunity and power are in the hands of the many, not the few. That is what brings people to our politics: a conviction that you can combine ambition with compassion, success with social justice. These are the ends; all the rest is means.

The process of change I have undertaken, started by my predecessors before me, has been to get Labour out of outdated policy perspectives and the quasi-Marxist traditions of a small part of the party and return it to those basic values. Once freed from historical baggage, we can address the future with confidence. This we now do.

There is a new era opening up in relations between today's Labour Party and the business community. With assistance from the regional CBIs and Chambers of Commerce, I and my colleagues are currently visiting every major centre of commerce and industry throughout Britain, meeting thousands of businesspeople from every part of the country. That dialogue will continue up to and after the election.

> The minimum wage is a good policy, it's a good principle. It's wrong that employers pay people in many cases below their marginal product and that the tax system spends hundreds of millions of pounds subsidising employers through the benefit system. However, like any decent policy, it has to be sensibly introduced. If it is, it will work. If it isn't, it will cause problems. Now that is a message to my own party as well as to the public.
>
> *From 'Blair's Britain',* Panorama, *BBC Television, 3 October 1994*

This dialogue has not been established for the sake of form. It has been set up because we are serious about government. We want to exchange views and ideas. And we have found much common ground. There are also areas which are more contentious. Let me briefly touch on two issues where business and the Labour Party are often assumed to be in disagreement: the minimum wage and the Social Chapter. The charge is that these will place unsustainable burden on costs and deter inward investment. All I ask is that we deal in facts.

The Social Chapter is not detailed legislation. It is a set of principles. The real fear is that by being part of it we may in future agree to the import of inefficient practices to Britain. A Labour government will not pursue such a course. Each piece of legislation will be judged on its merits. I have no intention whatever of agreeing to anything and everything that emerges from the EU. Proposals are just that: proposals. And they will be examined, with industry, on their merits. But an empty-chair policy is not good business or good politics.

As someone once said, 'Our absence can only permit the self-interest of other nations. We paid a heavy price when others designed the Common Agricultural Policy. It would be unforgivable to repeat that mistake in industrial and financial policies. The same argument applies to the Social Charter.' And who said that? Michael Heseltine, in 1989.

As for the minimum wage, again the key is in how it is implemented. There are actually parts of business that actively support a minimum wage, and others who are reasonably relaxed about it. They understand that it is neither efficient nor fair to pay the lowest possible wage. The minimum wage has not stopped Germany or the US being competitive. Of course, much will depend on the level at which it is set. And that is why we have committed ourselves to set up, in government, a Low Pay Commission with business representation to research carefully the issues and advise government on an economically desirable level at which to set a minimum wage.

As for inward investors, they are not coming here for cheap

labour. Companies locating here generally have sophisticated management and are looking for skilled labour and developed infrastructure.

The truth – uncomfortable for parts of both Left and Right – is that the minimum wage and the Social Chapter will neither destroy nor build a better economy. They are about fair rules. But the primary means to economic strength lies elsewhere – in the new agenda I shall now describe.

Labour's Approach

I reject the rampant *laissez-faire* of those who believe government has no role in a productive economy; and I reject too, as out of date and impractical, the re-creation or importation of a model of the corporate state popular a generation ago. Today the role of government is not to command but to facilitate, and to do so in partnership with industry in limited but key areas. This is not a matter of ideology but of national interest. The philosophy of one Britain, one nation, in which we put behind us the old debates and focus on what we know needs to be done to make our country strong, is an economic as well as a social philosophy.

Our decline may not have started recently, but the news that we have slipped to eighteenth place in the world pros-

---

I think a market economy is in the public interest, but I do not think it equates with the public interest. And so I think that the means of intervention and control in the public interest should be there with us. But I think it is important that they are seen not as an attempt to abolish the market economy. I've always thought that it is much easier to make the case for intervention in the market economy provided you're credible on your support for the notion of a market economy itself. And the problem for Labour has sometimes been that it has been perceived that its desire to intervene in the market economy is really just code for its desire to get rid of the market economy altogether.

From The Revisionist Tendency, *BBC Radio 4, 18 March 1993*

---

perity league – a government league table, not ours – is a sharp reminder of the distance we need to travel.

Government should not try to run business. The days of 'picking winners' are over. But nor should government duck its responsibilities where these are necessary to fulfil the national interest.

The role of government in a modern economy is limited but crucial. It should provide a secure low-inflation environment and promote long-term investment; ensure that business has well-educated people to recruit into the workforce; ensure a properly functioning first-class infrastructure; work with business to promote regional development and small and growing firms; seek to open markets for our goods around the world; and create a strong and cohesive society which removes the drag on the economy of social costs like unemployment and related welfare benefits. If government did these things well, it would make a major contribution to the growth of the economy.

Some look for models to the so-called Asian Tigers. But the lessons are mixed. Yes, they spend less of their income through the public sector (though in Singapore there are extensive and compulsory private savings). But their public spending is intensive and productive. They have spent massively on education and on investment in infrastructure. They save more. And of course they are at a different stage of economic development – the later you industrialise, the quicker you do it. Britain – the first to industrialise – took sixty years to double its output per head. Starting in the mid-1960s, South Korea took eleven years to do the same.

Investment and savings have been the motor of economic development in Asia. In the eight High Performing Asian Economies, investment rose from 20 per cent of GDP to 30 per cent between 1965 and 1990. In the last decade the share of investment in GDP in Hong Kong has been just over 24 per cent, and in Singapore just under 40 per cent. Over the same period, the G10 countries averaged about 20 per cent, and the UK 18 per cent.

I suspect, within obvious limits, the key is not how much you spend, but what you spend on. And it may not matter whether the spending is public or private, as long as the critical investment in the future is made.

Modern Competitiveness: Which Road?

The real debate is between different visions of how a mature industrial nation like Britain can revitalise itself and achieve a stronger, more competitive economy.

Some argue that the only route to greater competitiveness is through closures, rationalisation and cut-backs. It is what one top manager recently described to me as the 'as little as possible approach': as little training, as little investment, as little research, as little commitment to your workforce as possible. It is an old-fashioned approach to competitiveness, which aims for success not by providing the best value but simply by being the cheapest.

It is always important to control costs, but I don't believe permanent corporate anorexia can bring lasting economic health. In fact it will lock Britain into low productivity, indifferent quality and poor returns for investors and employees alike. It is an approach ultimately doomed to failure. We will always be vulnerable to low-cost competitors in Asia and Latin America, where labour costs and employment standards are going to be lower than in Britain.

And − never forget − our principal competitors are still in Europe, the US and Japan. I believe Britain should aspire to do far better than seek to compete successfully with the fledgling industries of southern China, Vietnam and Indonesia. We are a mature industrial nation. We have the capability to compete with the best in the world − in the ingenuity, inventiveness and adaptability of our population. Our problem is our failure to turn capability into reality. Some of our firms in Britain are the best in the world, but too many are not. Customers in the global market-place are certainly interested in the cost of a good, but they also want quality, customised design and inventiveness.

Labour's Agenda

Our enemies are low investment, lack of skills, poor infrastructure, and short-term and blinkered horizons on the part of government as well as business.

So what should we do? We live in a global market today. There is no 'go it alone' economics. Establishing a sound and credible long-term framework for fiscal and monetary policy is probably the biggest single thing government can do to give businesses the confidence to invest. Not doing so has been an enormous failing over the years, because without confidence about future demand, investment dries up.

I am, unashamedly, a long-termist; and long-termism demands a hard line against inflation. Controlling inflation is an essential prerequisite for sustainable economic growth, as well as for the high employment and rising living standards that we want to see. That is why Gordon Brown and I have committed the Labour Party to follow a clear target for inflation. It will be set consistent with the targets of other comparable countries.

Our drive to raise the level and quality of investment will be reinforced by fiscal policy. Let me lay out some clear principles.

★ Penal rates of taxation do not make economic or political sense. They are gone for good. I want a tax regime where, through their hard work, risk-taking and success, people can become wealthy. Let me say, for the avoidance of doubt, Britain needs successful people in business who can become rich by their success, through the money they earn. I simply don't like to see them do so by exploiting a monopoly position in privatised utilities, and I suspect you don't either.

★ Similarly, companies will not invest without decent profits. We are conducting a corporate tax review dedicated to

---

I am an unashamed long-termist. Though the actions of a Labour government will be immediate, they will be aimed at the long term. If this country is to grow in strength in what is an increasingly competitive global market, it must learn the lessons of the past and move beyond its battles.

From the Mais Lecture, City University, London, 22 May 1995

---

examine not new ways to raise money but new ways to encourage investment.

* Further, despite the access to international savings, growing investment would be assisted by sustained growth in domestic savings. That requires among other things that government must keep its own borrowing on a sustainable course. We are committed to follow the golden rule of borrowing only for investment over the cycle, and will stabilise the debt-to-GDP ratio at a prudent level. We will also continue to grant tax relief to certain types of saving like Tessas and PEPs, and indeed we will look for ways to extend their scope.

I welcome the announcement of CBI studies on the Private Finance Initiative and the relationship of finance and industry in Britain. We pioneered the notion of public/private partnership. We are dissatisfied with the way the PFI is working. Recently we published proposals of how it could be improved and made more business-friendly. Similarly with short-termism. This remains a major concern, especially in the small-firms sector, and I look forward to the results of the study the CBI has announced.

But our failing in macro-economic policy has not just been boom-and-bust politics: we have continually found that capacity and skill constraints have held back our ability to grow without hitting the inflationary buffers.

Alongside stable, low inflation must come the mammoth undertaking of equipping our people and business to succeed in a new, highly competitive world market that is subject to huge economic and technological change. We must make our people a nation of ideas and excellence. A nation of wealth-creators. A creative workforce that can think and innovate for itself, where the old hierarchies of management and workforce become blurred and whittled down and replaced by a genuine partnership. In the office and on the shop floor, the workforce of the future should be thinking for itself: educated; flexible; multi-skilled.

That is why education is an economic imperative, and in particular the combination of education and technology.

Wealth and living standards in the twenty-first century will be based on knowledge and its application to the goods and services that British companies must sell at home and abroad. Today, knowledge is the currency of international business, and only if we become the knowledge capital of Europe will we become the enterprise capital of Europe.

We will never build a Knowledge Britain if significant numbers of children leave school under-educated and under-skilled. Our system has always been good for those at the top, but the education and training habit has rarely spread lower down. So we get one half as many good GCSE grades as in Germany, half as good A-level grades, and half as many workers have vocational qualifications. I don't believe we have less talented people; I do believe we fail to get the best out of them.

We have ideas too for improving our infrastructure. I believe in the power of the market to do good in many areas. But I also believe that things like transport infrastructure must be planned, by government and industry working together. For a decade or more we have had much ideology in transport but precious little strategy. Not since 1977 has central government published a White Paper setting out a transport strategy.

We need to set transport priorities for the nation – like the West Coast main line, the links to Heathrow and the flourishing regional airports, the East–West link across the North of England – and develop a strategy to achieve them.

We need greater coherence in public-policy decision-making. If you are building a Channel Tunnel, it surely makes sense to build the rail link to it at the same time. If you are spending billions to rebuild Docklands, surely it makes sense to plan effective transport provision.

We must also reverse the decline in public transport, including offering people and business greater opportunity to travel on an efficient, integrated railway system. I don't believe privatisation which splinters the industry into ninety-four separate businesses will be able to provide people with that kind of service.

Then there are a range of areas in which a modern industrial policy is essential to increasing our competitiveness:

★ in small businesses, where we have put forward again detailed proposals – warmly welcomed by the small-business community – for bringing new venture capital into small businesses and offering a better and more comprehensive range of advice;

★ in science, innovation and design, where we are world leaders, but recognised more abroad than at home;

★ in regional and local development: Labour in local government has worked closely with business to build local economic strength.

Possibly the loudest, most sustained applause during my speech at the 1995 party conference was for the announcement that the Labour Party had reached an agreement with BT to open up a market and to link schools, hospitals and libraries to the information superhighway. I made it clear at the time, but it is worth repeating: our aim is a competitive market. BT won't get monopoly status. We are in discussion with the cable companies and other providers, like Ionica and Mercury, to ensure that competition is free and fair. Our proposals on the timing and manner of BT's entry into the market are the same as those of the Conservative-dominated Trade and Industry Select Committee. This recognised, as we do, that it is foolish for Britain's largest telecommunications company to be excluded for ever from a fast-growing market. And, in return, public responsibility is discharged. That is partnership in action. Good for business. Good for Britain.

There is another area where Labour and business have common interest – Europe. We must construct a sensible policy on Europe that protects and promotes our national interests rather than being prey to every skirmish and political ambush. The young generation in this country simply cannot understand the way Europe is debated here. Nor, I believe, can British business. British business has real interests at stake in the debate on Europe and should make its voices heard on these subjects, as business does in other European countries.

Britain could set the agenda in Europe: completing the Single Market by removing barriers to trade in key sectors;

reforming the CAP both because it is right and as a necessary precondition to the enlargement to include the countries of central and eastern Europe; developing cooperation where it makes sense – over jobs, infrastructure and technology – and refashioning the institutions of Europe to make them more accountable and open. But instead we are condemned to react to the proposals of others. We need a government putting forward positive ideas of its own for the reform of Europe.

Britain must also genuinely keep its options open on monetary union. It is hard to tell whether it will proceed on the basis now planned. The Germans and French insist that it will. We shall see. I have made it clear that the test for Britain is one of national economic interest. Currency stability would have obvious and clear advantages. But we have learned sufficient from our experience with the ERM to know that such stability can only be achieved, at an affordable price, if there is genuine convergence between the economies linked together. There should be a proper and full debate about it. Unfortunately, we have a situation where, as a result of the internal politics of the Conservative Party, it cannot even be mentioned. In view of the enormity of the issues involved, that is not serious government.

> The existence of what is sometimes called an underclass – a group excluded from society's mainstream – is an economic as well as a social evil

Finally, and this may be controversial but I say it without hesitation, social cohesion – a society in which there is not gross inequality nor the absence of opportunity for a significant number of citizens – is an indisputable part of an efficient economy.

The existence of what is sometimes called an underclass – a group excluded from society's mainstream – is an economic as well as a social evil. It is an enormous drain on public spending – directly in welfare; indirectly in crime and environmental decay. It is a terrible loss of talent. And it destroys the sense of common purpose and effort essential to sustain a country as a working society and economy. That is why leading thinkers not just on the Left but also and, in some ways more significantly, on the Right are talking about the need to invest in 'social capital' – the bonds of trust and commitment that stem from giving everyone a stake in society and encouraging people to work together for common purposes.

That is why we have launched new proposals to help a forgotten generation of 600,000 under-25s, many of whom have never worked. We have also suggested over half a dozen new initiatives to help the long-term unemployed into work, including phased release of capital receipts from council-house sales to build houses; a tax rebate for employers taking on the long-term unemployed; a new partnership with the voluntary sector to provide a stepping-stone into the private economy; and a Benefit Transfer Programme to help people make work pay. We also specified precisely how they would be paid for.

These are the six key areas in which government and business have direct and common interest. Of all of them, I believe the real key is education. Get it right, and a lot else falls into place. Get it wrong, and economic underperformance as well as social decay beckon. I have said education will be the passion of my government, and I mean it.

What we now need is a supreme national commitment to succeed. To build one nation socially; to work as one nation economically. To put aside the dogma and divisions of the past. A young country willing to create a new economics for a new age and millennium.

From a speech to the annual conference of the Confederation of British Industry,
13 November 1995

12 *The Global Economy*

The driving force of economic change today is globalisation. Technology and capital are mobile. Industry is becoming fiercely competitive across national boundaries. Consumers are exercising ever greater power to hasten the pace of this revolution. Travel, communications and culture are becoming more and more international, shrinking the world and expanding taste, choice and knowledge.

The key issue facing all governments of developed nations is how to respond. I reject protectionism as wrong and impractical. If this is so, then to compete in the new global market two things must be done. A country has to dismantle barriers to competition and accept the disciplines of the international economy. That has been happening the world over, to varying degrees, in what might be called the first era of response to globalisation.

But it is not enough. To compete in the long term, a nation must also constantly be investing in new capacity and above all in the flexibility and aptitude of its people. The next era will be the creative age, where the economics of the twenty-first century will be dominated by those countries that save, invest, innovate, and above all develop the potential of the one resource that will be exclusively theirs: their people. I shall go on to argue that in this second era my party is uniquely well placed in our politics to carry through this process of change, provided we recognise – as we do – that some of the changes made by the Conservatives in the 1980s were inevitable and are here to stay.

Let's examine the impact of globalisation. It is, of course, true to say that world trade and the opening of markets have been proceeding for centuries. Globalisation in that sense is not new. What is new, however, is its pace and scope. It is as if someone has pressed the fast-forward button on the video, and there is no sign of it stopping. I also believe that the internationalisation of culture has played a significant part. In

Tokyo and London, increasingly we are sharing the same rock music, the same designer clothes, the same films and surely, over time, the same attitudes and tastes.

Some may worry that we are becoming too uniform. But the effect of this exchange of culture is to open up new possibilities in the minds of our peoples as to what can be done. New horizons have broken the limitations of one country. Consumers today demand quality, and their tastes, with global advertising, can alter with bewildering rapidity.

The Asia Pacific region of the world, as much as if not more than any other, has witnessed and participated in enormous change. One estimate is that 40 per cent of the increase in the world's purchasing power between now and the year 2000 will come in this region. Even excluding Japan and China, the countries of Asia Pacific will by the year 2000 account for 29 per cent of world manufacturing output.

The capital markets are transformed:

★ The daily turnover on the world foreign exchange market is $1,200 billion – $450 billion-worth through London.

★ The outstanding amount of international bond issues rose from $574 billion in 1985 to $2 trillion in mid-1994. Over the same period, international bank loans tripled – to $4 trillion.

★ The names Sony, Toyota and Honda are as well-known in a British home as those of Marks & Spencer and Jaguar.

★ A country like Korea or China can double its national output in ten to fifteen years, whereas in the first industrial revolution it took five times that.

★ A 3,000-mile flight costs the equivalent of a three-minute phone call fifty years ago.

★ Within a decade or two, there will be effectively limitless capacity on fibre optics capable of transporting the entire contents of the National Library in Japan in less than a minute.

★ In the world of digital technology, it costs no more to send a message – of voice, pictures, graphics or text – to the

119

other side of the world than to your next-door neighbour.

There is nothing new in countries trading with each other. But we trade more than ever before, and we trade more freely than for many years. In 1947, for example, tariffs on traded goods were about 40 per cent of the value of the product crossing the border, while the latest Uruguay Round talks take them down from 6.3 per cent to 3.9 per cent. Historically, world trade has boosted growth, and it will do so again. And in 1995 over £4 trillion-worth of goods crossed borders.

Similarly, it is not new to have an integrated world financial system. For the last third of the nineteenth century, the gold standard integrated the world economy. Capital – primarily in the form of long-term fixed-interest bonds – flowed in vast quantities from the developed economies of western Europe to developing countries. It is also not new that international finance will punish economic policy that it considers to be unsustainable. But today when sentiment turns it turns with a vicious alacrity, because at the flick of a switch or push of a button capital can be transferred anywhere in the world.

Close to 50 per cent of equity transactions for firms located in the EU take place outside the home country. In Britain, foreign firms now own 25 per cent of manufacturing capacity and employ 16 per cent of British workers. Japanese firms in Britain now achieve exports worth £4 billion a year.

Most of us, as consumers, welcome the developments globalisation have brought. We like the idea of choosing between a Japanese, British or German car, of buying Italian as well as British clothes, or choosing, as soon we will in Britain, from 30, 40 or 100 TV channels not four.

But with globalisation comes its offspring – insecurity. People feel, and are, less economically secure than ever before. Jobs for life are a thing of the past. People will change jobs several times in their career. Skills will need constant updating as technology alters. New industries can become large employers almost overnight – as with the media. Old industries, like coal mining, decline to a fraction of their former size.

The mirror image of the economic insecurity is a profound sense of social, even moral, insecurity. This is not the place to explore this issue, but I do believe that this too is linked to globalisation. Work patterns have changed; expectations have radically altered; the old cultural, social and family ties have loosened. Communities which previously changed little from one generation to the next have collapsed. Belief in religion has diminished. Crime, antisocial behaviour, irresponsibility have all increased. There is no point in taking refuge in nostalgia, but we have not yet learned how to handle and make sense of these changes.

I have argued that, in social terms, we need a new social contract between society and the individual in which rights and responsibilities are more closely defined: in which we grant each citizen a stake in our society but demand from each clear responsibilities in return.

The successful firm today works through partnership. Class distinctions are unhelpful and divisive

I would apply the same concept of a contract to the building of a strong economy. The successful firm today works through partnership. Class distinctions are unhelpful and divisive. The good company invests in its people and takes them seriously. This is not kindness: this is good business. A country is not that different. People need to know what is expected of them – what they need to give and what they require to be given to them. Both firm and country will place a high premium on flexibility, mobility and adaptability. But these qualities need to be developed, and they arise only when the self-interest and full talent of all employees are engaged.

Now let me set out the principle elements of New Labour's economic thinking.

Most countries, including Britain, have rejected the path of protectionism as a response to the new global market. We do so without hesitation. There is a growing movement towards it on the Right in Britain and elsewhere, but I believe it to be doomed. I don't doubt its political appeal, but it is standing against the tide of history. But certain key consequences flow from accepting globalisation and working with it.

Macro-economic policy must be kept tight, disciplined and

121

geared to stability. I believe low inflation is the essential pre-requisite of investment in the long term. Companies must know they can plan ahead in a stable economic environment. This has always been true. The violent swings of boom and bust in the 1980s were immensely damaging in Britain and elsewhere. Now the arguments for stability are even stronger.

Uncertainty in a government's commitment to an anti-inflationary policy is punished fast and mercilessly. The Labour Party has committed itself to setting a low inflation target, and we have reaffirmed our belief in the 'golden rule' of public finance – that the level of borrowing should only be such as to cover investment over the economic cycle. There is no room for macro-economic experiments or risk-taking in this area.

We will strongly support inward investment. We disagree with narrow or reactionary nationalism. Japanese involvement in Britain's economy is now well-established. Two hundred and twenty-eight manufacturing firms have now invested in Britain, and fifty Japanese banks are now doing business in the City. The benefits for both our countries from these links are substantial. Inward investment has become a major component of total investment. Indeed in some sectors – most noticeably cars and electronics – the arrival of new Japanese companies has totally reinvigorated the prospects of an industry.

I represent a constituency in the North-East, a region in which traditional industries like mining and shipbuilding have declined dramatically, with huge consequences for many communities. Inward investment has been a major element in the region's economic regeneration. The arrival of major Japanese companies such as Nissan, NSK, Fujitsu, Komatsu and Sanyo has shown that the region has huge economic potential. Fourteen thousand people are now employed by Japanese inward investors, with total investment of over £3 billion.

Support for inward investment is bipartisan and supported by the Labour Party. The Invest in Britain Bureau – which acts as the government's main body for marketing the UK overseas and which funds regional organisations which coordinate inward investment activities – was set up under the last Labour government. Labour local authorities have played a full and supportive role in bringing Japanese companies into the UK. Indeed, we have played a significant part in resisting calls from some on the Right for abandoning regional assistance, which has been of such benefit in easing the passage into the UK of many Japanese companies.

Britain offers much – a workforce capable of adaptability and skill; access to the EU's Single Market; the English language, which we share with your largest trading partner, the US; and an attractive legal and commercial system. Under Labour, I believe it would offer more – a better-educated and more skilled workforce, better infrastructure, a stronger, more positive voice at the EU negotiating table, and a macro-economic environment more conducive to sustained investment.

We also recognise that in a global economy our tax rates need to be conducive not merely to keeping highly skilled labour but to attracting it. Britain, rightly, has a leading role in financial services. But this sector, like others, is not fixed. It is more mobile today than ever before. Our tax rates need to be internationally as well as nationally competitive.

Workers should have basic rights to fair treatment, to proper health and safety legislation, to protection from abuse by employers

We believe in minimum standards at the workplace for employees. Workers should have basic rights to fair treatment, to proper health and safety legislation, to protection from abuse by employers. But that must not lead us to rigidity or to inflexibility in labour markets. Social costs are part of the international trading conditions today. And often the best form of job security for a modern economy will come with the skills that make a worker indispensable.

We have made it clear that there will be no repeal of the main elements of the 1980s trade-union legislation passed by the Conservative government. Ballots before strikes and for union elections and restrictions on mass and flying pickets will remain. Trade unions will be treated with fairness but no special favours. We will not meet the challenges of the future by rerunning the arguments of the past.

It will be obvious, therefore that I do not see the role of a

Labour government as switching the clock back to the 1970s. We have frankly admitted that we took far too long in the 1980s as a political party to face up to the need for change. Much of the change was to do not with ideology but with the altered circumstances of the world economy. Governments of Left and Right in the 1980s abolished exchange controls, cut top rates of tax, and deregulated trade, just as governments of Left and Right in the 1960s and 1970s pursued different policies. The top rate of tax in Britain was 75 per cent under the Conservative government of the 1970s, which also pursued price and income controls. Changing these types of policy was the first wave of activity by governments to meet the challenge of globalisation.

But now a new approach, a second era of change, is needed to take up and build upon what has already been done. It is here that I believe that a rejuvenated and modern Labour Party can make a distinctive contribution and, in the course of doing so, improve both Britain's competitiveness and its attractiveness to inward investors.

The aim is to create a viable modern partnership between government and industry Knowledge, infrastructure, technology – these are the well-springs of national prosperity today. They do not come easily. They come from investment – long-term investment, by committed partners from finance, industry and government. The whole of our economic policy is geared to promoting stability, saving and investment.

To this end we have put forward a range of policies for partnership between public and private sector to revitalise our infrastructure, our transport system and our inner cities. We have proposed measures to encourage small businesses and self-employment and to boost science and research. The aim is to create a viable modern partnership between government and industry, not based on government running industry or government in the pocket of industry, but limited to key specific objectives it is in the national interest to obtain. We have proposed substantial reform of our welfare system and new ways of encouraging saving and investment.

But above all, in a world where capital and technology are mobile, people are our key resource. It is their intelligence, aptitude and skill that will make a difference. This is accepted. Yet it has not been acted upon with anything like the rigour and urgency we need. It is this upon which I wish to concentrate now.

To develop our human potential in the way we require demands a revolution in thinking and policy no less great than that of the 1980s. Britain has long boasted an excellent élite education system. Our top universities rank among the best in the world, and now one in three eighteen-year-olds goes into a higher-education sector made up of some eighty universities. The students coming out of these universities will make up the core of a skilled and adaptable workforce for the next century.

We are proud of our traditional strength in basic scientific research, and will seek to exploit it better. We are proud too of the engineers and scientists whose work is known around the world. But the challenge for any country seeking to make its economic way in the twenty-first century is to spread educational excellence throughout the population. Every pair of hands working in a factory needs to be directed by an active and thoughtful brain, contributing imagination and skill as well as effort to the production process. The economic race now goes to the cleverest and most innovative, not simply to the fastest or the cheapest.

Knowledge is the currency of international business. Only if Britain becomes the Knowledge Capital of Europe will it become the Enterprise Capital of Europe.

Our educational agenda is based on what I believe is a new and important insight. It is that the revolution in business of the 1970s and 1980s – the revolution that reorganised companies away from mass and uniform production for mass markets of undifferentiated consumers and towards flexible and specialised production for small markets of diverse and demanding customers – will over time take place in education too. We will move away from a system that assumes that every child of a particular age moves at the same pace in every subject and will develop a system directed to the particular talents and interests of every pupil, fashioning education and learning to suit their aptitudes and interests.

125

Of course, not everything will change. The foundations of a successful system are still good schools with good teachers and strong support from families and the community at large. But there are new challenges and new opportunities too – the need to make education a lifelong process; the need to forge a new alliance of education and new technology.

We have put forward a new platform of policy to improve dramatically our educational standards. We are committed to the creation of a new General Teaching Council to promote the ability and professionalism of teachers, and to a new grade of Advanced Skills Teacher to reward those excellent teachers who decide to use their talents in the classroom and not in management positions.

We are developing plans to make out-of-school study easier, to demand more of parents in relation to their child's schooling through home–school contracts, and through the work of Associate Teachers working part-time under the direction of the class teacher and bringing expertise from business and the wider world to the classroom, to use the experience of the wider community to improve our educational standards. We will set tougher targets of school achievement, and back them up with new methods of enforcement.

All this is good. But it isn't enough. Our entire attitude to educating our people must change.

First, education must be lifelong. That does not mean a lifetime sitting behind a desk, but it does mean lifetime opportunities to update old skills and develop new ones. This is important for people to stay in employment and also to move up in employment. Two proposals we are working on embody the spirit of ambition and excellence to which my party is committed. The development of individual learning accounts for every worker would provide the basis for training in and out of work across the life cycle. And we are committed to creating a new University for Industry for the twenty-first century, to bring the benefits of workplace education to every business in the country. The UFI would not only promote new opportunities but would provide the national infrastructure for the development of common standards and rigorous courses.

Second, education – its curriculum and its organisation – must respond to the opportunities afforded by new technology. Children can now learn about ancient rock formations by visiting the Grand Canyon on the information superhighway; they can have their work marked as they do it by computers that help identify their strengths and weaknesses; and they can work with children on the other side of the globe by communicating through the Internet. All these things are made possible by the power of new technology. We are constructing a programme with British Telecom and the cable companies to combine free and fair competition with the public interest to guarantee access for every school and college in Britain to the benefits of the information superhighway. That means more technologically literate pupils coming out of schools. It means children achieving higher standards earlier. And it means students laying the basis for working lives that will increasingly be dominated by new technology.

Third, education must be understood in its broadest sense. A learning society is a thinking society – a country of innovative people, not a nation of automatons. That is why I say **This new era of opportunity must not divide our societies** the next stage of change must be the creative change. Information alone is not enough. It must be used, and used creatively. Our education system is still too narrow. That is why, for example, we are committed to broadening the educational experience of 16–19-year-olds, offering every student the chance to combine academic and vocational study – science and business studies; languages and engineering – rather than choose a narrow and specialised academic stream or a low-esteem vocational alternative. Our aim is not just an educated nation but an intelligent one.

I also believe passionately that this new era of opportunity must not divide our societies – a relatively secure and prosperous top part and an unskilled, under-educated bottom part whose prospects and ambitions are thwarted. What is striking about the way Japan has educated its people is not just its commitment to basic numeracy and literacy, and the huge numbers that go on to advanced education, but also its success in pulling up the lower-achievers, raising standards for all.

I believe in what I call one-nation politics: that social cohesion and fairness to all are essential conditions of both a decent and an efficient country. Only in this way can we persuade our people to live and thrive in the new global economy.

There are two final aspects of globalisation which I should mention, where the British Labour Party has a clear and distinctive contribution to make.

We believe Britain must be a leading player in Europe, and, moreover, that such a role is not in contrast to but complementary to our role in the rest of the world. The European Union is a market of 370 million people and is crucial to Britain's economic future. Already around 60 per cent of our trade is with the rest of Europe. We are well aware too of the importance of Britain in Europe to potential inward investors.

The EU has helped bring peace. It has created a vast market. It acts as a major force in world trade. And Britain has much to bring to Europe. A policy of perpetual isolation would be disastrous to Britain and to the EU, and my party has strongly rejected it.

We have played and will continue under a Labour government to play a key role in driving through the Single Market – in energy, transport and telecommunications, for instance. We have advocated fundamental reform of the CAP. We are keen to welcome into the EU those former Communist countries in the East. We have supported changes to the institutions of the EU to make it more open, accountable and democratic.

On the moves to a single currency, we have laid down the test of Britain's national economic interests. For it to work, there must be real economic convergence in the main countries. It is essential, after the problems of the Exchange Rate Mechanism, to get this issue right. At present, neither the economic conditions nor the political consent for such a move exist. If it could work, however, a single currency would have benefits in terms of trade, stability and costs.

We reject the notion of an insuperable constitutional barrier to our joining a single currency, and we understand why other countries are keen to see currency union happen. But, as I have said many times before, it cannot be forced in defiance of the economic facts.

We take a different view to the government on the Social Chapter, believing it is best to be part of discussions that can lead to legislation rather than have an empty chair. But it should be stressed that many of the social costs in EU countries are the result not of Social Chapter legislation but of legislation indigenous to the individual countries.

Finally, global financial markets bring new opportunities, but also new responsibilities for governments – working together – to ensure the world financial system remains solvent and stable. We need to acknowledge that mistakes have been made – and learn from them. The sad story of Barings shows the importance of vigilant supervision, clear early-warning signals and closer cooperation across national borders. The US Savings and Loans crisis demonstrated the importance of tougher setting and monitoring of internal management practices and financial controls.

I have no time for living in the past. Many of the political struggles of the twentieth century will seem odd to the children of the twenty-first century. In recent years I and my predecessors before me have put through a transformation of the British Labour Party. Our constitution, our policy-making, our membership, our culture and our relations with the unions have all undergone radical change. We have done this because without changing our party we could never have claimed the chance to change our country.

The vision I have of Britain is of a confident, young, clever country; an outward-looking nation that is unafraid of the new economic challenges, because it is preparing itself to meet them, equipping its people for change. The economic policy of a future Labour government will be modern, progressive and utterly committed to shaping this new future.

From a speech to the Keidanren, Tokyo, 5 January 1996

13 New Labour and the Unions

There is no bigger threat to people's quality of life today than insecurity in employment. Many millions of people will still work in traditional secure employment, but the level and spread of insecurity are greater than ever before. Teenagers leave school with little chance of finding a career with prospects. Graduates find qualifications are no longer a passport to a good job. Those in work fear for their jobs or are working under poorer terms and conditions than before.

In part these problems are derived from the recessions we have experienced. But we are fooling ourselves if we do not see that in part this insecurity derives from fundamental insecurity in the labour market and the economy.

These problems require a radically different approach to the labour market – one that centres on the individual within it. The answer is not to resist change – which is impossible – or to ignore it and have a market free-for-all with no attempt to respond to the change – which will result in precisely the insecurity we face. The answer is to empower the individual to survive and prosper through change.

I want to set out clearly the Labour Party's approach to this new labour market. It is not to try to re-create a labour market which is gone. Neither is it the new Right's approach of stripping away all rights and protection for employees and operating a labour market based on fear and insecurity. It is instead to empower workers to adapt to change and to guarantee a labour market that works within a sensible framework of rules and standards.

That approach, I believe, represents the best option for a competitive economy. It is in the interests of employers to have a flexible workforce. It is in the interests of employees to have choice and flexibility throughout their working lives and to acquire the skills to help them adapt to change. What neither employees nor employers want is the fear and insecurity which result from the Right's approach to these questions.

The last fifteen years have seen profound changes in the way people work:

★ More of us than ever before are working part-time, are self-employed or have a temporary contract. Four out of ten of us in the workforce – almost 10 million people – now fall into one of those categories.

★ Low-skill jobs are disappearing, and new ones are being created which demand new and different skills. Some industries are employing ever fewer people; other, new, industries are expanding.

★ Year by year the number of women in the labour force grows – a million more in 1994 than in the mid-1980s, and soon probably as many women as men.

The revolution in working life has destroyed the old certainties about career patterns, about what is men's work and what is women's work, and about income.

The Tories are content merely to abandon people to the effect of global change in the labour market. No minimum wage, no Social Chapter, no minimum standards. They call it deregulation, but this is a complete misnomer. It is instead a deliberate strategy to ensure that employees have no rights and the labour market has no rules. And the result is a low-wage workforce, poorly motivated and badly trained, combined with long-term mass unemployment.

Labour, by contrast, seeks both to reduce unemployment and to help those who are in work adapt to the new labour market. While the government is trying to shift people from one benefit to another, we are determined to get people off benefit altogether and into productive work. It is absurd, for example, that when a man loses his job his wife often has to give up her job – particularly if it is part-time – or the family will lose so much benefit it makes no sense for her to continue working. We want to build second-generation welfare, which gives people a hand-up and not just a hand-out, which pro-vides child care as well as child benefit, training as well as unemployment benefit, and which – most importantly of all – will be a springboard to success, not just a safety net to cushion failure. The Commission on Social Justice addressed this problem in its report by recommending a Jobs, Education and Training plan to tackle long-term unemployment and to take people out of what in too many parts of Britain has become 'Giroland'.

We know that many of those who are in work welcome flexibility in the way they lead their working lives. When people are juggling the responsibilities of work and family life, and when more and more people want to go back to college or to retrain, it makes sense for individuals as well as for industry to have flexibility in employment. But flexibility should not mean stripping away of employment rights or a trend towards discrimination against people who choose to work part-time or are on temporary contracts. Unlike the Tories, we believe genuine flexibility will work only in a labour market which has rules and standards.

Labour will not simply press the rewind button when it comes to union legislation – ballots before strikes and other measures to improve the internal democracy of trade unions are here to stay. The issue today is not law or no law, but fair or unfair law – a positive framework of right which ensures that people who work hard and play by the rules get a fair deal at work.

If more people are choosing to work part-time, why should that result in a loss of rights? The same question applies to temporary work. And where a majority of employees want to organise in a trade union then employers should have a legal

> Industrial relations should not be a battleground. The vast majority of employers and unions work together harmoniously in their common interest for the vast majority of the time. When harmony does break down or interests conflict, there must be a framework for resolving disputes that is fair, and seen to be fair. The objective is to secure, on the broadest possible basis of consent, a new settlement in industrial law – one that lasts.
>
> *From a speech to Sedgefield Labour Party, 18 December 1989*

duty to recognise those unions and to work with them.

And of course a crucial rule in today's labour market should be a national minimum wage. It is both just and efficient. A minimum wage will stop the taxpayer having to subsidise low pay through the ballooning family-credit bill. It will decrease employee turnover, encourage investment in training, and help motivate employees.

But the case for the minimum wage must be fought and won among the public. I believe we have to go out and campaign on the principle of a minimum wage, to show that it is both efficient and just, and really to make it a winner for Labour. And if we are going to do that we should not make the mistake of getting bogged down in a discussion of this figure or that figure at this stage.

These are some of the rights Labour will guarantee to all employees. But government cannot and should not do it all. As John Prescott has said, 'We should be creating a fair framework in which all parties can coexist. And leave them to get on with sorting their relationships out for themselves.'

That means unions themselves have a responsibility to adapt to the new circumstances:

★ they have to speak out as effectively for the part-time woman in the new labour market as they have done for the full-time man in the traditional labour market;

I want to be quite blunt with you about the modern relationship between today's Labour Party and the trade unions. There was a time when a large trade union would pass a policy and then it was assumed Labour would follow suit. Demands were made. Labour responded and negotiated. Those days are over. Gone. They are not coming back. Today, trade unions will of course be listened to. So will employers. But neither will have an armlock on Labour or its policies. We seek to govern for the whole nation. Persuasion is in. Demands are out.

From a speech to the Transport and General Workers Union conference,
Blackpool, 10 July 1995

★ they have to ensure that they take trade-unionism into new sectors, and recruit and represent members in areas where unions have traditionally been weak; and

★ they have to play a positive role in creating the partnerships at work which can help Britain become a more successful and competitive economy.

These are major challenges for trade unions. The new environment is not an easy one for them. But, just as political parties have to change if they are to survive in the modern world, so too do unions if they are to represent their members effectively.

There are already signs of optimism that unions are rising to the challenge.

The UCW have just led a successful and imaginative campaign to defeat Post Office privatisation and to blow a massive hole in the government's legislative programme. They didn't just go through the motions of producing a few leaflets, holding protest meetings or calling a stoppage. They ran a campaign

---

I think trade unions are necessary in a democratic society. I think that there are problems that people are facing at the workplace today that make it all the more important that you have trade unions able to represent their members properly at the workplace – and able to go out and win new members too. The idea that either the trade unions or the Labour Party have become historically redundant has been disproved by what has been happening at the workplace up and down the country over the past few years. What I do believe, however, is that that relationship must be democratic, and that's why I support the reform of One Member One Vote. I don't believe it's possible for the Labour Party credibly to go out and make the issue of democracy a big campaigning issue unless we can turn round and say our relationship with the trade unions is one based on democratic principles.

From Walden, *London Weekend Television, 26 September 1993*

---

to defend a highly popular public service. They highlighted the essential role the Post Office plays in communities up and down the country, and built maximum public support for the sensible case of keeping the Post Office in the public sector but freeing it up to face the challenges of increased competition. They have every right to be proud of their well-organised and successful campaign. It showed that unions can operate in a tough environment and can win.

And that has not been the only progress unions have made. United Biscuits, a company with a long history of financial donations to the Conservative Party, have announced an agreement with the GMB to establish a works council, making a mockery of the government's opt-out from the Social Chapter. They did not have to reach such an agreement, but they realise it is in their own interests to have a workforce which is involved in how the company is run.

This shows yet again just how out of touch this government has become. While the Tories leave Britain on the sidelines in Europe, and in an increasingly weak position from which to influence future events, both industrialists and unions realise we have nothing to gain from such posturing and seek instead to exercise real influence in the mainstream of the debate.

Let me quote in support of our case the Business News section of *The Times*. Commenting on the United Biscuits move, it argued cogently, 'It gives a strong incentive to plan continuously, rather than manage by crisis, or grandly operate as portfolio managers rather than business managers. And that

> If, as a country, under a future Labour government, we are to obtain a settlement in industrial law that endures, we must demonstrate – in contrast to the Tories – that industrial relations are not merely about the balance of power between employers and unions but are rooted in the individual rights of people at work ... If we are genuinely to take individual rights seriously, the ability to organise collectively should be in fulfilment of, not at the expense of, individual civil liberties.
>
> *From a speech to Sedgefield Labour Party, 18 December 1989*

could help raise the performance of industry as a whole.'

And we will continue to press for the adoption of the Social Chapter on grounds of both justice and efficiency. There is simply no reason why working people in this country cannot have the same basic rights as working people in every other state in the European Union – rights which are also supported by each of the four newest member states.

Unions have been active at both a British and a European level in their support for the Social Chapter, and in pressing for real improvements for working people. They have taken the Home Secretary to the Appeal Court and successfully exposed the yawning gap between his rhetoric of concern for victims of crime and the seedy reality of his illegal changes to the Criminal Injuries Compensation Scheme.

For some time now the GMB have been campaigning for a better deal for members of occupational pension schemes. They have launched a helpline for the many people who have been victims of poor advice on personal pensions, some of whom have lost a great deal through ill-advised transfers from occupational schemes to personal schemes.

And the T&G's new 24-hour legal helpline means that all T&G members have access to initial legal advice whatever the time of day, which will be of real benefit to union members.

These are real, concrete examples of unions making a positive difference for their members and for working people in general. But there is a great deal more to be done. And I hope that, working together, we can argue the case for productive economic investment, for increased employment, for education and training, and for social justice.

There is a bond of belief between Labour and the unions that is more than a few lines in the rule-book. Unions know and accept that from a Labour government they can expect fairness not favours. But fairness will be a big advance on the open hostility they have had from government in the past fifteen years.

It will give unions a fair chance to adapt to the new world of work. It will give them an opportunity to work for new members and in new areas, and to campaign for the future in new areas of concern to people at work.

Government will provide the framework. It is up to unions themselves to take advantage of the opportunities that that framework provides.

From a speech to the Unions '94 conference, London, 19 November 1994

The people of this country want healthy, free trade unions capable of representing properly the interests of their members. But they do not want them confused with the elected government. That government – any government – must speak for the whole nation. And we will. It is as simple as that.

From a speech to the GMB conference, Brighton, 7 June 1995

PART III

Equality and Opportunity

The end we seek is a society where every individual is able to develop their talents to the full, and where wealth, power and opportunity are in the hands of the many, not the few.

From a speech to the 'Hearing from Women' consultation, London, 13 February 1995

14   Social Justice

The Social Justice Commission report is obviously important for the future of the welfare state. But it is also important because it shows the degree to which the left-of-centre is coming to dominate the battle of ideas in British politics.

The report is not, and is not meant to be, a manifesto. It is the work of an independent commission. Commissions write reports. Parties write manifestos. That is now our task. But, both in its description of Britain's deep-rooted problems and in the issues it raises, the report is **Insecurity does not just affect the poor and the unemployed** undoubtedly the most significant and comprehensive analysis of the welfare state since Beveridge. It is a remarkable piece of work.

The political context should also be clear. In 1979 Mrs Thatcher came to power promising to cut unemployment and reduce welfare dependency. In the fifteen years since then, the numbers on income support trebled and more people became dependent on benefit than in the whole of the period 1945 to 1979. This is despite all the changes to the benefit rules, the harsher political climate, and the much-trumpeted assaults on dependency.

We can start by understanding that the Tories in Britain, like the new Right elsewhere, have failed.

There is a significant minority of people cut off, set apart from the mainstream of society. Their lives are often characterised by long-term unemployment, poverty or lack of educational opportunity, and at times family instability, drug abuse and crime. This problem has got worse, not better.

Secondly, insecurity does not just affect the poor and the unemployed. Even with a semblance of recovery in the economy there are large numbers of people afraid for their jobs, working with much less secure conditions, wondering whether their children will have the same start in life as they had, and anxious for their elderly relatives and their own old age. There is a crisis of opportunity which extends far beyond what some call the underclass.

Thirdly, this waste and lack of opportunity has an economic as well as a social cost. Indeed the social cost is an economic cost. For far too long both the Left and Right have treated these issues as merely social ones. The Right pays lip-service to compassion but claims it has nothing to do with the efficiency of the economy. The Left – or some part of it – has tended to view the problem as simply one of inadequate benefits.

The welfare needs of today are not met by the welfare state of fifty years ago. We face some very difficult choices – on pensions, child benefit, health and education, for example – and we must show that we have the courage to tackle these questions and apply new thinking to them so that the welfare system actually improves people's lives rather than deepens their dependency.

The issue today, therefore, is not whether the welfare state needs reform. It does. The dividing line is between Labour that wants to modernise it and the Tories who fundamentally do not believe in it and are undermining it.

Second-generation Welfare
Beveridge created the first generation of welfare for this country fifty years ago. His was a world of the nuclear family, full-time male employment, and national planning. Beveridge's first-generation welfare state was designed to pick up the pieces when things went wrong, when people were unemployed, sick or old.

But Britain today is not Beveridge's Britain:

* women now make up nearly half the workforce;

* long-term unemployment has become structural and endemic; and

* in 1991, 37 per cent of all marriages involved at least one divorced partner.

I want to build second-generation welfare:

* Second-generation welfare is about giving people a hand-up and not just a hand-out. It means services and not

142

just cash: child care as well as child benefit, training as well as unemployment benefit, care in old age as well as a pension. Welfare should be a springboard to success and not a safety net to cushion failure. It should provide the stability within which families and communities can cope with a world of change.

★ Second-generation welfare adapts to the changing patterns of family life, where work and parenting are shared, and where retirement can last twenty or thirty years. Welfare must promote change by offering security in place of fear.

★ Second-generation welfare understands that citizenship is founded on responsibilities as well as rights.

★ Second-generation welfare does not hand down commands from government on high, but encourages local decisions, public/private partnerships, and local innovation by local people.

★ Above all, second-generation welfare attacks the insecurity of middle-income Britain *and* the poverty of low-income Britain.

We know that the concerns of the poorest – jobs, crime, education – are also the concerns of those squeezed in the middle. There is common interest in a united society – one nation – that prospers together because it works together.

We reject the failed dogma of the Tories. But we also move beyond the traditional policies of the old Left. So this report is not just born out of a need for a new politics for Britain, but is part of reconstructing a new politics for the left-of-centre.

New Dividing Lines on Welfare
Labour has always been the party that cared for the casualties of our economy and society – the unemployed, the sick, the disabled, the disenfranchised, the homeless. And we will never as a party do anything less. It is part of what makes us democratic socialists, and we are proud of it.

But, because we were anti-poverty, we were portrayed as

143

anti-wealth. Because we were concerned with lifting up the less successful, we were seen as attacking those who aspired to do better.

Because we campaigned for adequate benefits, we were said to be unconcerned about the working poor who were taxed to pay for benefits. Because we wanted to defend the welfare state, people came to assume that we did not think it could be improved. We were seen as interested more in protecting the gains of the past, rather than building on them.

Pensions

There are more than 4 million more pensioners in Britain today than in 1951. We all pay contributions while we work, and receive a basic state pension when we retire. Increasing numbers of people are also able to call on occupational and personal pensions. SERPs is the state alternative for the second-tier pension.

Since 1980, the basic state pension has been linked to prices and not earnings. It was worth 20 per cent of male average earnings in 1977/8; it was worth about 14 per cent in 1994. It will be worth 9 per cent in 2020 if present policies continue. The result is that the basic pension is anything up to £15 per week below income support levels.

About 1.5 million pensioners rely on means-tested income support to top up their basic pension. Nearly 600,000 are entitled to income support but do not claim, because of the stigma attached to it, or because they do not know they are entitled to it.

So we face the following situation. More than 3 million pensioners live in poverty. Nearly two-thirds of pensioners have too little income to pay income tax. And the top third or more of pensioners have seen their income rise significantly since 1979.

Our top priority has always been, and remains, the abolition of pensioner poverty. We have always opposed means-testing the basic pension – rightly – and we will continue to do so. We have always believed that the basic pension is the foundation on which all should be able to build for retirement. Labour is committed to a basic state pension available to all.

In the past, we have seen across-the-board increases in the state pension – for all, irrespective of circumstance – used as the only weapon for attacking pensioner poverty. But it had two problems:

* First, it could be inefficient. The increase is of no value to the poorest pensioners, because income support would be reduced, pound for pound, as the pension increased.

* Second, it can be very expensive. It would, for example, cost £9 billion to raise the basic pension to £80 per week.

The Commission has come up with an alternative. Its key proposal is to establish a pensions guarantee which would offer higher pensions at manageable cost. The guarantee would build on the basic pension, taking those dependent on income support out of the crude trap of means-testing. It would merge public and private provision and attack pensioner poverty.

The pension guarantee is a pledge to individuals. It would integrate taxes and benefits for pensioners – a radical step – and use the potential of new technology for greater efficiency.

Its advantage is that it abolishes the means-test for pensioners and guarantees them a decent income by mixing public and private provision. The claim is that it would radically reduce pensioner poverty. We must now test that claim to see that it stands up and determine whether it is indeed a better way to improve pension provision.

The Commission also addresses the issue of second-tier pension provision. At the moment, everyone must invest in a second pension – either SERPs or a personal or occupational pension. I do not underestimate the value of SERPs, but we will look further at the idea of a switch from pay-as-you-go to funded, contribution-based provision for all, and at the claim that the National Savings Pension Plan, set out by the Social Justice Commission, offers the possibility of an effective public-sector contribution to choice in retirement.

Child Benefit

There are three issues here:

* child poverty is a blight on our country;

* child benefit is an efficient way of getting money to mothers, but it makes no discrimination between rich and poor parents; and

* children need time, care and education as well as money.

The Commission backs child benefit as an important means of investing in children. It rightly points to its high take-up, and to how it is a platform for people to move into work. But we have to ask ourselves, as the Commission asked itself, whether everyone, irrespective of income, should receive the same level of financial support for their children.

The Commission's proposal is that the benefit should continue to go to all. But it suggests that top-rate taxpayers should pay tax on the benefit, raising £300 million, with the gains used to improve the lives of all other children. This is clearly a significant change to the way we regard child benefit. The detail must be considered carefully, but I endorse the principle that it is now right to examine how we use the resources paid through child benefit effectively to open up new and better opportunities for our children.

Welfare to Work

The true divide here is not between the Tories who believe that welfare spending is too high and Labour which believes it is too low. It is between Labour which provides opportunities for people to get off benefit and the Tories who have doubled welfare dependency by failing to provide opportunity. That is why the Commission's emphasis on full employment, and the need to smooth the path from welfare to work, is so important.

The Commission makes proposals for increasing the demand for labour, creating a fairer distribution of work, and increasing the reward for work. It highlights for special attention the problem of long-term unemployment – the worst curse of economic failure.

Further, the Commission suggests reforms to benefits. At the moment, we have a rigid benefits system which clashes with the flexible labour market and changing family structures. The old model of full-time, lifetime work for men can no longer be the foundation of the benefits system.

I am sure it is right to say that tackling long-term unemployment is the place to start. And also that we should remove, so far as can be financially possible, hindrances to work in the benefits system. At the moment, it is too often neither secure nor worthwhile for unemployed people to take up work.

I applaud the attempts of the Commission to root out the discrimination against women that exists at the heart of our welfare system. For example, it seems absurd that the wife of an unemployed man has to give up her part-time job because the family is better off on benefit.

And if anyone is still in doubt that the minimum wage is essential to make welfare reform cost-effective, I urge them to read the Commission's report. A minimum wage is needed for social reasons – to prevent exploitation at work. But it is also needed for economic reasons.

First, we must save the taxpayer from subsidising exploitative low pay. Today, the ballooning family-credit bill – now over £1.3 billion – is the price we all pay for not having a minimum wage.

Second, low pay increases employee turnover and therefore deters investment in training. It is bad economics.

And, third, every good manager will tell you that the key to success is that the workforce is motivated to work well with a stake in the company.

Today, the Tories announce plans to move people from one benefit to another, from unemployment benefit to jobseeker's allowance and means-tested income support. Our objective is not to shuffle benefits, but to move people from benefit to work.

We will look at all the Commission's ideas, and try to improve on them. This is a complex area, where small changes can have a big impact. But the goal of updating our benefits system to meet the realities of labour-market and family change should command wide support.

Citizens' Service

Now take the issue of responsibility. The true divide is not between the Tories' belief in personal responsibility and Labour's belief in social responsibility. The divide is between Labour which offers opportunities and demands responsibility in return and the Tories who don't understand that giving people a stake in society helps to create a responsible community.

I applaud the Commission's proposal for a Citizens' Service. It has great potential to provide a sense of worth, discipline and responsibility to many of our young people. It would promote personal development, and I hope it would act to break down social barriers.

I also want to look further at the discussion of family responsibility that the Commission rightly puts on the agenda. It is in families that we first learn respect for others, and it is on strong families that the strength of our communities rests.

Education

Education is an area where there is the clearest link between economic and social policy.

The real divide is between free-market Tories who believe social justice is a barrier to economic success, and so deliver economic decline and social decay, and Labour which believes social injustice denies us economic prosperity.

For example, an education revolution would boost economic prosperity and social justice. We must make high standards in every school the birthright of every child, with good discipline, high expectations, and partnership with parents. Quality nursery education is an important foundation for children. Broader A-levels are already party policy.

And the need for learning throughout life, to cope with economic change, should also be widely accepted. We all need new skills for new jobs. Politicians too. And that requires more and better higher and continuing education.

The problem today is fourfold:

★ lack of funds prevents expansion of the higher education system;

* there is gross inequality between full- and part-time students;

* middle-class parents have to pay thousands of pounds to support their children at university; and

* students are still poor.

The choice before us is to increase student grants for the increasing number of students or to introduce the recovery principle – i.e. that students themselves should, after they graduate and when they are in reasonably paid work, make a contribution to the system.

The Commission says that the way to expand the system for people of all backgrounds is to recoup the cost of student maintenance and a fraction of the cost of tuition fees from students once they become taxpayers. As they earn more, they will be better able to pay back some of the cost of their higher education.

The risk is that such a system of recovery may deter young people, especially those from poorer backgrounds, from entering higher education. It is for this reason that the Labour Party has always rejected it. But, as with all the Commission's recommendations, we will examine it.

The Commission takes seriously the need to expand adult education, and suggests new and innovative ideas in this area.

The Commission says that a Learning Bank, funded by a partnership of public and private sector, would run the system, allowing people to save and borrow to finance education and training, just as people save and borrow to finance a home now. In the future, it should be as natural to invest in education as part of a salary package as it now is to get a company car.

This is radical thinking. Some of it fits in with other proposals developed by the Labour Party, including the University for Industry.

In the future, it should be as natural to invest in education as part of a salary package as it now is to get a company car

We will address the Commission's proposals. We should discuss difficult issues, and not duck them. But one thing should be clear above all others: we will sanction no change that breaches the most fundamental principle of all – that education should be based on ability to benefit and not ability to pay.

Putting Principles into Practice

It should be clear to anyone with eyes to see that £80 billion-worth of social-security spending does not guarantee social justice. In fact, in Britain today it is evidence of economic failure.

A more just society should allow us to invest in the areas we wish to spend on and cut the areas of spending that are merely the consequence of social decay. Social justice can be extended within existing levels of spending. It is a matter of getting the strategy right, the system right, the priorities right. Then we will get the return right.

A successful economic policy combined with effective modern welfare would mean a reduction in the benefits bill. That is the prize for middle-income Britain and for those who are poor and unemployed.

One thing should be clear above all others. This report is a central challenge to the governing philosophy and ethos of the last fifteen years. And it is a signal of growing confidence on the Left, not just because the government is failing but because we are addressing the concerns of British families.

The British people want a new direction for our country. And the Left has the ideas to take us forward. This report is evidence of that.

I applaud the Commission's diagnosis. I share its ambition. Social justice is not a matter of altruism. It is about self-interest and common interest.

Social justice is about building a nation to be proud of. It is not devoted to levelling down, or taking from the successful and giving to the unsuccessful. It is about levelling up.

That is our pledge in opposition. It will be our practice in government.

From a speech at the launch of the Final Report of the Commission on Social Justice, London, 24 October 1994

15 *Hearing from Women*

The issue of women's politics can no longer sensibly be regarded solely as an issue of discrimination against women. Nor as some easy shorthand that allows the question to be conveniently sidelined under a heading 'women's issues', to be swiftly passed over in favour of mainstream politics. In fact, the change in the economic and social position of women in society raises fundamental questions that are in the interests of all of us to confront.

The central question is this: Do we try to turn the clock back and re-create the Britain of fifty years ago, in order to avoid these questions, or do we accept and indeed support progress in the economic, social and political position of women, and say our task is both to extend that progress and to meet its consequences in a planned and sensible way? We favour the latter course.

My argument is that we cannot resolve the issues of work and family without addressing the issue of community – of the creation of strong social ties and structures within which families and individuals can flourish.

None of the questions facing women – work, family, crime, health – can be satisfactorily answered except through structures that enable women and men to share both freedom and responsibility. Leaving these to chance will mean the allocation of freedom and responsibility is random and unfair. We need to think these questions through together as a society of people with a common objective.

Our challenge is to develop a policy agenda that speaks to the common *and* specific priorities and needs of women. Some priorities they share with men – investment in long-term prosperity, the rebuilding of the social fabric, the fight against crime, the democratisation of the quango state, and the restoration of our reputation abroad. Others are issues in which they have a particular interest, be it in employment, welfare reform or public services.

A good deal of progress has been made towards equality between men and women, though there is still some way to go. We will not be complacent until equality is achieved. But the changes brought about over the last fifty years themselves raise new questions for individuals, for government and for employers – questions about the shared responsibilities of men and women at home, about the role of government in

We will not be complacent until equality is achieved

expanding choices through public services, and about the provision for flexibility and security at work by employers.

We are at a turning-point. The vast majority of British women today, whatever their age or education or current circumstances, would say without much hesitation that they are better off than their mothers were. The problem is that they fear that their daughters will be worse off than them. The key challenge we have to address is how we make sure that does not happen, and how instead the women and men in the next generation can continue to make progress.

Labour's Challenge

The Labour Party was, of course, founded predominantly by working men, but it is clear that throughout its history Labour has been at the forefront of campaigns for sexual equality. We are proud of our achievements:

★ support for the successful campaign for suffrage, culminating in 1918;

★ the first woman Cabinet minister;

★ the postwar Family Allowance Act to provide a child allowance irrespective of means, and the National Insurance Act to provide security for widows and pregnant mothers, as well as the introduction by Barbara Castle of SERPs and the best-twenty-years'-earnings rule which was of special benefit to women until the government halved the value of the scheme;

★ the Equal Pay Act in 1970, and the Sex Discrimination Act in 1975.

152

But, as long as society is dogged by inequalities and prejudices, we cannot be complacent. And Labour in particular has
no reason to be complacent. In the 1992 general election there
was a 9 per cent gender gap against us.

When I first came into Parliament – not that long ago –
there were only twenty-three women MPs altogether. Now
there are thirty-eight in the Labour Party alone. But we can
hardly call ourselves a proud representative democracy when
less than 10 per cent of MPs are women.

After the next election, I hope to have at least double that
number working with me. Not only will this reflect the composition of the electorate more closely, but it will undoubtedly
change the culture of the party and the House of Commons.
That can only be a good thing. Debate is an essential part of
politics, but it does not have to be petty, personal and squalid.
Confrontation for confrontation's sake is what turns people
off politics. There is, of course, no guarantee that increasing the
number of women MPs will change the House of Commons
culture. But my judgement, and that of many others, is that
it will.

I remember the Labour Party conference in the mid-1980s.
There was scarcely a women's face to be seen in the hall. At
the 1995 conference there were over 500 women delegates.
The chair of the party is a woman; half of the National Executive
Committee are women. How many boardrooms can boast
fifty-fifty?

In the parliamentary party too we have increased the number
of MPs, and we will go still further at the next election. We
have already selected forty-one women to stand in winnable
seats at the next election. I look forward to the day after the
next election when I have eighty or ninety women MPs with
me on the Labour benches. It will signal a dramatic change in
the culture of politics in Britain. The Labour front bench already
contains more women than ever before: nineteen now hold
front-bench posts or are in the whips' office.

From a speech to Opportunity 2000, 31 October 1995

The New Context

We are living in an era of unprecedented economic, social and political change. I would say that, for my generation, the revolution in the lives and aspirations of women has been the biggest agent of change in our society. Assumptions about education, work and politics that would have been heresy for my mother's generation are the assumption of my daughter and her classmates.

In all three areas of change – economic, social and political – women are in the front line. And because these changes involve enormous changes in the lives of women, they imply big change for men too. The changes are a huge challenge to the way we have traditionally done things, and how we cope with them will define our future as a nation. Do we stand back from change, leaving ourselves to be blown this way and that, or do we see how we can equip our people not just to cope with change, but to manage it and shape it to their own advantage?

The campaign for women's equality, and for equal choices for women in shaping their lives, is a central part of our campaign for social justice in Britain. The extent of injustice was graphically illustrated by the February 1995 Rowntree report:

★ Since 1979 Britain has become more unequal – in relative

British men work the longest hours in Europe – hours that have gone up in the last decade against the historical trend – but low- and middle-income British women struggle to make ends meet with two, three or even four part-time jobs. I believe it is essential to create a framework where all employers follow the practice of good employers and properly value all workers. In the 24-hour global economy, we are all part-time workers. Only one in four of the workforce now work a five-day week, nine to five: we all have to be flexible workers, and employment laws must reflect this.

From a speech to Opportunity 2000, 31 October 1995

---

and absolute terms – more quickly than any other industrialised country.

★ Inequality in Britain is now greater than at any time since 1945.

★ The theory of trickle–down economics on which the Conservatives were elected in 1979 has been shown to be a comprehensive failure.

★ And social division and inequality damage not just the lives of the poor but the quality of life of the rest of us.

Injustice has always been a moral issue. Today it is an issue of self–interest as well as common interest, of rationality as well as morality. Because the fact is that unjust Britain is poor Britain:

★ When we waste the talents of the unemployed, we are poorer.

★ When single mothers are trapped at home for lack of child care, we are poorer.

★ When women are discriminated against in decisions about promotion because employers think they are going to get pregnant, we are poorer.

★ When mothers return to work after having children but find themselves down the job ladder – typically spending fourteen years in a lower-paid job after an eight-year career break, according to the Equal Opportunities Commission – we are all poorer.

★ And when we fail to provide child care, we are all worse off, because the evidence of the world-recognised High Scope programme in the US shows that for every dollar invested in child care for disadvantaged children more than seven dollars is returned to the taxpayer by way of savings in the cost of juvenile delinquency, remedial education, income support and joblessness.

Social justice is a majority issue, because we are all worse off in divided Britain. Our task is not just to put social concern back on the political agenda. That is slowly happening. It is to show that the diverse interests of not just the poor but also the anxious-but-comfortable point to the need for a government committed to enabling the talents of all to flourish.

That goal is not a pipedream. There are no easy answers in an age of change. But there are answers.

Labour's Agenda

First, we say there is no going back to a mythical halcyon age. We do not want to see women chained to the sink, just as we do not want to see men unable to see and care for their children. The social change we have witnessed since the war will not be reversed.

Second, we do not seek to play male off against female, just as we do not seek a situation in which women see as little of their children as men traditionally have.

Third, we respond to the new situation by returning to our core insight – that individuals prosper only when supported by a strong community. Individual and family are not the antithesis of community, as Mrs Thatcher said, but dependent on it. And the great power of community – of what we do together – is to make more equal our opportunity and ability to develop our talents to the full.

The freedom to choose is not based on the absence of restraint, as the Tories insist, but on the ability to decide, as Labour believes. And that ability to make decisions crucially depends on the society in which we live – the opportunities it makes available, the services we provide. It is that approach which will inform any Labour government I lead, and it has very practical consequences.

> Half the workforce are women, but the benefits system still assumes they are dependent on men. Part-time work is more and more common, but part-time workers are still treated as second-class citizens. Parents try to work out new ways to share responsibilities at home, but a leading government minister scoffs at paternity leave.
>
> *From a speech to Opportunity 2000, 31 October 1995*

Look at the balance between family and work. Women are working in ever greater numbers. We welcome that. But we are living in a world where the assumptions of the forty-hour work week are a thing of the past. There is no going back to the world of full-time jobs paying men a family wage, with lifetime security, a guaranteed pension and a carriage clock at the end of it.

What we want to do is make flexibility work for people in work, so they can make choices about how to balance commitments to themselves and their employer and responsibilities to their partners and their children. This is why we want to see new choices for men and women at the workplace – for example through education and training. It is why we support the introduction of proper rights for part-time workers. It is why we support a minimum wage to help make work pay.

As for those out of work who want to get in, we know what they need above all. They need a fully developed system of child care and nursery education for their children, and that is why such a system will be a top priority for a Labour Secretary of State for Education. They also need training and employment advice to get them into the labour market, which is why we are committed to making training work for the unemployed. They need a benefits system that rewards properly every step they take towards financial independence, rather than penalising them as the current system so often does.

It makes sense to be able to recruit from 100 per cent of the pool. It makes sense to retain skilled workers by offering proper maternity leave. It makes sense to keep women workers by offering decent child care. Midland Bank have seen the number of women returning from maternity leave double since they introduced flexible work arrangements. Rank Xerox has saved £1 million over five years through savings in recruitment, retraining and lost productivity by changing the work culture.

From a speech to Opportunity 2000, 31 October 1995

The ideas I have been discussing – social justice, opportunity, social solidarity – are essential to my political project. The struggle for equality for women is an essential part of my vision of the values and ideals of the new Labour Party. That means a commitment to equal treatment for all human beings – men and women.

From a speech at a 'Hearing from Women' consultation, London,
13 February 1995

16 Realising Our True Potential

The title is taken from Labour's new statement of aims and values, the new Clause IV of our constitution. It was included with a very clear purpose in mind – to signal the historic but also enduring belief of the Labour Party that education has the potential to liberate us personally as individuals and collectively as a society. This is summed up in a favourite quotation of mine from Archbishop William Temple. He said, 'Morality demands that you treat people as they have it in themselves to become ... and raising people from what they are to what they might be is the work of education.'

This was the insight that motivated the ground-breaking campaigns for free primary schooling, for secondary education for all, for the expansion of further and higher education, and for the Open University. Today I want to apply our faith in education to the modern world – the new world of change, competition and innovation that we see around us.

It is time to learn from our experience of the comprehensive system and distinguish what is right and what should change. What is right is not dividing children into failures and successes at the age of eleven; but this should not mean uniformity or levelling down, but rather providing children of differing aptitudes and interests with the high-quality education they need. It is time to end dogma and bring in common sense. Modernisation in Labour thinking applies to comprehensive education too.

I want to move the argument on, from the structure of schooling to what actually goes on in the classroom. Let me be blunt: I want a Labour government to lead a drive for educational improvement in Britain, modernising the comprehensive system to achieve its goals of high standards for all.

I will repeat what I have said before – that education will be the passion of my government. That means national leadership. But leadership should be the basis of partnership with all parts of the education system, not dictatorship over it. And partnership should extend to the research community, so that we root education policy in research fact, not political prejudice.

It is absolutely vital that we get away from the culture of blame and short-termism that has marred our education system for too long. Government, teachers, parents and administrators are joint partners in the most important economic and social task facing this country, and it is time that we behaved like partners, with a joint mission to give our children the best start in life.

Where We Stand

There is some good news in our education system. Enter almost any school or college in the country and you will see something to admire. Enter most schools and colleges and you will find many things to admire:

★ skill and commitment in primary and secondary teaching practice;

★ a better performance at GCSE;

★ higher participation after sixteen, though more limited signs of increased attainment at seventeen and eighteen; and

★ a doubling of higher-education participation, with much greater adult participation.

But there is bad news too. Research shows that 3,000 schools are poor or failing. That is one in eight schools. Yet I am sure we all believe that one failing school is one too many. At twenty-one, one in five people has trouble with maths, and one in seven has trouble with reading. When it comes to meeting the standards of our neighbours, or preparing for the challenges of the new global economy, our deficit is stark. Overall, our performance is simply not good enough.

★ At GCSE, the percentage getting grades A–C in maths, national language and one science is 29in the UK, compared to more than twice that in France and Germany.

★ At advanced level, at eighteen or nineteen, about 36 per cent get two A-levels or the equivalent, compared to more

160

than 60 per cent in Germany and France and 80 per cent in Japan.

★ And catching up requires that we improve at a faster rate than other countries, because they are improving too.

Look for the reasons for these statistics, and some obvious problems suggest themselves. We tolerate a situation where less than half of our three- and four-year-olds receive education of any kind, despite the overwhelming evidence of its social, educational and economic benefits. We recycle silly quips from a Bernard Shaw play about those who can doing and those who can't teaching, when in fact teaching is probably the single most important profession for the future of our nation. And we accept a system of post-sixteen education and training that excludes two-thirds of pupils from 'gold standard' A-level study, and then tolerates the fact that of those who actually start A-level courses 30 per cent will not successfully complete their studies. Little wonder the Higginson Committee described our education system as an obstacle course designed to weed out all but a small minority. The question is why it should be so. I believe we need to look at both our national culture and our attitudes to education as well as national policy.

Poverty of Aspiration

On the Left, low performance was often blamed on socio-economic factors. This neglected the fact that schools clearly make a difference to a child's education, and different schools with similar intakes can produce markedly different results. On the Right, meanwhile, excellence for the few and mediocrity for the many was seen as a natural corollary of the distribution of ability. But that ignores the reality that other countries achieve high basic standards for all: France, for example, is apparently set to meet the target that 80 per cent of eighteen-year-olds should reach baccalaureate standard by the year 2000.

Ernest Bevin, Labour's Foreign Secretary in the 1945 post-war government, put the undervaluation of education down to 'poverty of aspiration'. Its source is a potent mixture of class snobbery and economic élitism that belongs to the nineteenth

161

century not the twenty-first. Put crudely, Britain's class system stemmed social pressure for mass education, and Britain's early industrial revolution obscured the need for education and quality training for all.

Today the old attitudes live on. Too many people at the top say that the search for more excellence will lead to less of it – 'More means worse' in the appalling phrase. Too many at the bottom say education is 'not for me'. Too many children are written off. Too many talents are wasted. We need to break out of this vicious circle, but to do so we need to challenge some of the preconceptions about how we teach and learn – and above all about how we promote and value good teaching and good learning.

Pressure and Support

For me, as an MP and not an educationalist, it is alarming to find almost unanimous agreement among educators and researchers about what creates a good school, but then great difficulty in universalising those conditions, particularly in disadvantaged areas. We know the characteristics of a successful school: effective leadership, high expectations, discipline and commitment, continual staff development, continuing parental involvement, good links with the local community. The question is why we find these characteristics so difficult to replicate from one school to another.

I have discussed widely the relationship between pressure and support in the education system. Of course education is not only a matter of carrots and sticks: learning is a creative enterprise, and the sheer thrill of learning is motivation in itself for many bright-eyed children. Pressure means targets for improvement, publication of meaningful performance data, proper school inspection and teacher appraisal, rigorous pupil

---

A politician who does not try within their principles to do the best for their child is a politician who is in danger of losing touch with humanity.

From Daily Mirror, *26 January 1996*

---

assessment, and intervention when schools are failing. Support means finance, professional development, extracurricular support, follow-through from inspections, community involvement and national leadership.

In Britain, the Left has traditionally argued for support. It became taboo to say that bad teachers had to go. Meanwhile, the general public and most teachers understood the common-sense position that to question the ability of a few teachers is not to attack the whole profession. In fact the opposite is the case. If we are honest with ourselves and with the public about the minority of poor teachers, we can talk more proudly of the good job that the vast majority of teachers do.

But there has been dogmatism on the Right too. They have traditionally argued for selection at eleven as a way to overcome educational disadvantage. They claimed that the 'sponsored mobility' of one third of pupils, picked to succeed and provided with the facilities to do so, provided the incentive to high aspiration for people of all classes. But I am convinced that any return to the eleven-plus would be retrograde. We will not overcome the limitations of schools as they currently exist by going back to schooling as it used to exist. The UK's educational problem is not and never has been a failure to educate the élite.

For some on the Left, to talk of pressure on schools, teachers and pupils is to sell the pass. For me, this typifies the reasons why the Left has been losing general elections for the last sixteen years instead of winning them. The people who suffer from lack of pressure are not the well-off and the articulate. Instead, the losers are precisely the people who most need a hand-up in life because they were not born with natural advantages. It is traditional Labour voters who lose out when teaching is poor, discipline is non-existent, and the culture is one which excuses low standards on grounds of background or disadvantage. Little wonder that Labour lost their votes. What these parents want is the best possible education for their children. The fact that they are less deferential in asking for it is all well and good. My case is that they are right to demand more than we currently deliver. We urgently need the combination of both pressure and support to lever up standards for all.

New Ideas in Education

My argument stands on the belief that school pupils are capable of achieving much more than they currently do. Our challenge is to bridge the gap between what our children could achieve and what they currently do. I want to discuss how we can help bridge that gap through three sets of measures: two that provide support, one that offers pressure.

Primary Schools

There is a lot that is good in primary education: commitment, innovation, skill. But for a long time primary schooling has been seen as a poor relation in the education system, when in fact it is the foundation of a successful system. Research shows that it is essential for children to get the basics right early on: performance in primary school is a good predictor of success at GCSE, and it is expensive and difficult to put things right later on. Children never get a second chance at their first chance, and we need to ensure that as many as possible achieve all that they can.

Children start school early in this country, but their attainment does not reflect this. Far from being a time we can afford to waste, it is a time we must exploit. Rigour and high expectations are as important in primary school as in secondary school.

Children should learn to read, write and count. They must learn how to learn. And they should be educated in a disciplined environment that teaches responsibility to self and to community. Responsibility is what I call the fourth R that is essential to successful schooling. And children should be

Responsibility is what I call the fourth R that is essential to successful schooling

stretched at school. There is nothing worse than the feeling that your child has a talent for maths or music or science or drama or sport but is not developing it.

To provide these opportunities, what we need above all is a valued and well-supported teaching profession on whom high demands are placed and by whom high performance is

164

given. But we also need to attack the barriers that prevent children forging ahead in areas where they are strong.

First, lack of pre-school provision. Nursery education promotes educational development and has long-term educational and social benefits. It is a national disgrace that, more than twenty years after Mrs Thatcher promised nursery education for all, half our three- and four-year-olds still lack nursery opportunities.

The government is now showing interest in the idea again, which is good. We will welcome any increase in the quantity of provision, but we will also be watching carefully to ensure that the quality of provision is assured. If the newspapers are right, the government believes vouchers are a panacea because of the choice they offer parents. We favour that choice: public, private and voluntary providers all have a place. But vouchers are a mechanism, not an answer. They are not directly addressed to the question of quality supply of nursery education. They may not cover the cost of quality provision, and so may lead to a system based on personal income. They can provide subsidies for people who are already investing their own money in nursery education for their children. And they can be bureaucratic and inefficient, as the pilots in the 1970s showed.

I stand by my party's commitment to make the extension of nursery education to every three- and four-year-old a priority. I believe that we can learn from the huge range of local initiatives that is taking place, the central lesson being that education and care should be brought together to ensure a quality offer for children while also meeting the needs of working parents.

Second, we must as a country help every child tie down the basics. Inability to read or write is a terrible thing to admit, and unless children learn early they are condemned to fall further and further behind. Language is the currency of a person's freedom, so we need to get much closer to the goal of all eleven-year-olds having sufficient language skills to take advantage of their secondary schooling.

The third barrier to high achievement in primary education is rigidity in curriculum and school organisation. The two keys here are the ongoing assessment of children and meticulous planning of the curriculum. 'Baseline' assessment of five-year-olds is being pioneered in a number of LEAs, taking an initial view of strengths and weaknesses and shaping teaching accordingly. Baseline assessment can be used for early-intervention programmes and the tracking of progress. It is time for the development of national guidelines for this sort of work.

We know our objective: to maximise opportunities for children to develop themselves

Then we need to use the information gleaned to good effect. We know our objective: to maximise opportunities for children to develop themselves. And we know too the two extremes that we must avoid – divisive selection on the one hand and teaching to average ability on the other. The key, I believe, is flexibility in teaching method and class organisation. There is no one right method to teach every child through their school years. We need to combine formal whole-class teaching with targeted help for individuals and small groups. Good teachers already do this.

Differences in capability do need to be addressed, and 'setting' in different subjects as children proceed through the primary years – or 'target grouping', as they call it in Nottingham – has a role to play and we should not shirk from this. 'Target groups' can consist of those particularly good in a subject, those with a special interest in science (in Nottingham there are special science lessons for girls), and those who have missed parts of the curriculum as well as those with particular difficulty at school.

We can expect to see startling results. In June 1995 eleven-year-olds in Birmingham sat GCSE maths exams. According to all reports, they were not fazed by the experience, but instead thrived on it. In the last ten to twenty years, businesses have been moving from systems based on mass production to those based on the needs of those they serve. A similar revolution is overdue in education. We must escape the obsession with rigid linkage of age and progress – whether at eleven, sixteen or sixty-five. People should be enabled to succeed in education at the time that suits them best.

New technology can help here. It can help motivate chil-

166

dren by allowing them to make progress at their own pace; it can challenge students to improve on their best performance; it can allow students literally from across the world to work together to solve problems; and it can make learning more fun. I know from my own children how much greater is their facility for technology than mine. The potential is enormous:

* on-line bulletin boards of frequently asked questions answered by top teachers;

* e-mail link-ups with mentors in business, the arts or sport;

* immediate feedback on pupil strengths and weaknesses;

* multimedia products on CD-Rom that take students to NASA labs or the Hermitage museum;

* a conferencing facility in every staffroom to promote wider professional debate beyond the individual school.

Computers are no substitute for teachers. And personal contact with a machine is no substitute for social contact with other children. But equally we do need to recognise the potential of new technology to transform the educational process throughout people's lives. Pilots for new integrated learning systems in the US – 'smart' computer-based tutoring systems – show children making up to twenty months' progress within a six-month period.

Reform of A-levels and Vocational Qualifications
The second big issue we must confront is our culture of low expectations at sixteen-plus.

Our aim can be stated simply: a system of post-sixteen study that allows every young person to combine academic and vocational study according to aptitude and interest. In the very long term, that may even lead towards a modular system of courses leading to a single school-leaving qualification at eighteen. In the meantime, we need to broaden the academic track, we need to upgrade vocational alternatives, and we need to develop compatible curriculum structures and common principles of assessment that promote not just flexibility between academic and vocational options but a combination of academic and vocational study.

The choice, flexibility and high performance that we seek demand common approaches across the academic/vocational divide. No one can expect a student to combine A-levels awarded according to exams after two years with GNVQ packages assessed according to coursework on a unit-by-unit basis. But when assessment and curriculum organisation are more compatible – as they are becoming in Scotland, where in effect some of Labour's ideas are being piloted – combination of academic and vocational study does take place.

In the long term it must make sense to aim for a coherent 14–19 system of education and training provision, taking pupils from teenage to a range of opportunities in college and in work. We know that the demand can be stimulated – the response to the expansion of higher education is testimony to that. We can create a culture of high expectations. What is more, our institutions have shown the capacity to deliver high-quality education.

Further-education colleges, for too long a neglected part of the system, are delivering cost-effective education and training responsive to the needs of some learners. FE's flexibility has been and continues to be its enduring strength. Incorporation

---

The concern about league tables is that the information is often too crude, but people should have, in my view, as much information as they possibly need about schools. Indeed, there is a case for saying that you should have more information rather than less – and that includes academic performance, it includes truancy, it includes information from the school about discipline, about the types of changes that the head is foreseeing over the next few years to improve the school. So I'm all in favour of information. The problem has been that people sometimes felt that league tables on their own can be somewhat crude, but the information that is in them is information that should be available to people.

From 'Blair's Britain', Panorama, BBC Television, 3 October 1994

---

and independence have been a big challenge, and now we need to look closely at the future path of reform.

Teaching and Learning

Some American towns have taken to posting signs on roads leaving town saying 'We thank our teachers.' That is a symbol of the esteem and value put upon teaching in that community. Symbols don't make up for poor pay, floods of bureaucracy or overstressed conditions of work – but they usually signal that those things are taken care of too.

However, when I speak to teachers in Britain, they use words like 'excluded', 'misunderstood', 'misrepresented', 'undermined'. They feel that for too long government has refused to listen. A symbol of change under Labour will be the establishment of a General Teaching Council. The existing multitude of teacher unions, and the factions within them, means that teachers do not speak with one voice. That is why our proposal is so important. For the first time, teachers would have an organisation representing their professional status, committed to raising the stature and quality of teaching, and committed too to maintaining and raising professional standards. Teaching is not just a profession but a consuming and personal vocation that should be honoured by the community.

At the moment, many dedicated teachers resist the blandishments of money and status associated with school management and stay in the classroom, imparting their knowledge to new generations of pupils and fellow teachers alike. I want to see government recognise these special teachers who sparkle in their profession.

I am interested in the structure of the teaching profession. In 1994 I launched a proposal for the development of an Associate Teacher grade – people from the community who offer expert input in the classroom under the guidance of the class teacher. Today my concern is that exemplary teaching is not recognised. Many teachers – perhaps one or two in every school – achieve outstanding results on appraisal, get top marks in school inspections, show impressive capacity for innovation, and act as mentors to younger teachers. They do not want to go into management, yet they feel their achievement is not recognised. That is why David Blunkett and his team will be investigating the establishment of an Advanced Skills Teacher grade in the profession. It would be designed to recognise the teachers who we all feel are a credit to the profession and should be encouraged to stay in the classroom.

Let me finally turn to issues of teacher performance. I want to focus on the role of head-teachers, because they really are the linchpin of a successful school. All the studies show that the quality of leadership is the single most important determinant of school effectiveness. Some schools succeed despite their head, but it is very rare indeed to find a good head running a bad school.

All heads do an immensely difficult job. Those running schools are responsible for budgets of up to £2 million or even £3 million. Some college principals run budgets of £20 million. They lead a team of dedicated professionals and support staff, all with experience and expertise. They carry with them the hopes and trust of hundreds of parents and children. And they are central figures in the local community.

It is worth reminding ourselves that anything up to 500 secondary heads and 2,000 primary heads are appointed every year. That affects 10 per cent of schools in the country. Appointing a head-teacher is probably the most important thing that a group of school governors will ever do for their school. But the National Commission on Education found genuine problems with the current system: selection processes that are arbitrary, selection panels that show signs of patronage, governor training that is poor.

The Commission referred to a number of reforms, including standard application forms, better references, and the development of mentoring programmes for experienced heads to take new heads under their wing. But it also mentioned the system that currently operates in the United States, where potential heads have to undergo sufficient training to prove their capacity to take on the responsibilities of leading a school. I think we should look at introducing such a system in the UK.

I referred earlier to the difficulty we have in replicating the characteristics of successful schools. Yet all new heads want that for their schools. We therefore need a map of school-improvement processes – not just characteristics – which can help develop a virtuous circle of success. It is extraordinary that there is no infrastructure of support for heads to enable them to address management issues with peers and colleagues and develop management capability. For example, heads need the chance to focus on schools in comparable circumstances but with different outcomes. That argues for a national network for school improvement.

There is also the question of what we do to monitor, review and improve the performance of head-teachers once in post. This is an essential part of the effective management of a school. Head-teachers can go stale. They can get out of touch. Mistakes can be made in selection. It is legitimate for governing bodies to ask questions about the performance of head-teachers – particularly in failing or struggling schools. Head-teacher appraisal – which is not the same as school inspection and at the moment is not informed by it – should set targets and time-scales for school improvement and the head's contribution to it. I am very keen that we establish a dialogue with representatives of head-teachers on this issue.

The Passion of My Government

I have been told that the test for me is not whether I promise to be an education Prime Minister in opposition, but whether I am still claiming it after several years in government. That is a fair point.

I know that good education confers enormous privilege, and I passionately want that privilege to be extended much wider than it has been extended up to now – extended into the roots of our society, so that we banish once and for all the deadening culture of low expectations that is so damaging to us all. This requires a commitment to a long haul. And in education policy, as in much else, I am an unashamed long-termist.

When I look around Britain today, I can say without hesitation that unless we improve our education system we will not reverse our economic and social decline. What Labour will be offering at the next election is not a quick fix but a programme over time to lever up standards and achievement for all. We will reform what the government has done, not reverse it. And we will prepare all our pupils with the knowledge and skills to succeed in the new worlds of work, leisure and community that will face them in the next century.

A Labour government will lead a national drive for higher standards, and I hope everyone will join it. We could not have a more important task. That is why education will be the passion of my government.

From a speech at the Institute of Education, University of London,
23 June 1995

17 *A New Vision for Comprehensive Schools*

The grammar school system – grammar schools for the minority, secondary moderns for the majority – was a response to the needs of a vanished society which required a small educated class and a large number of manual workers. It is no longer the appropriate model for a world where most jobs require educated men and women. But the excellence grammar schools provided and the ladders of opportunity they formed are the things we want to preserve.

New Labour is committed to meritocracy. We believe that people should be able to rise by their talents, not by their birth or the advantages of privilege. We understand that people are not born into equal circumstances, so one role of state education is to open up opportunities for all, regardless of their background. That means we need to provide high standards of basics for all, but also recognise the different abilities of different children, and tailor education to meet their needs and develop their potential.

We believe in the comprehensive school system. To return to the 11-plus, as the Prime Minister wants us to do, would be a mistake of monumental proportions for this country. Who can really justify settling a child's fate by one exam at eleven? Do we really want the majority of children going to secondary moderns? But equally the comprehensive system is not working as well as it should and we want to refine and redefine it not in response to political or educational dogmas but in the light of what actually works.

It is essential for this country to have both a good education for all *and* an education system that stretches our best brains. It is not a choice between the two. We need both if we are to thrive as a nation in the next century. Equality must not become the enemy of quality. True equality means giving everyone the education that helps them achieve all that they can. That implies special help for those who need it, a challenging education for the average pupil and the full extension of the capabilities of the intellectually gifted. In other words, an equally good education – whether you are brilliant, average or slow learner – is not learning in the same classes for everyone but the experience best suited to you as an individual with your own particular needs. That is why I argue for a flexible system of grouping pupils within comprehensive schools to ensure that everyone can get the education best suited to their needs.

We must establish that level of expectation and put behind us the low expectations which have, in some schools, led to performance far below what children and young people are capable of. Every pupil should leave primary school literate and numerate. It is scandalous that so many 11-year-olds are unable to read at the level expected for their age. Instead of the constant war of attrition between government and teachers, the two need to work together to meet ambitious new targets for all 11-year-olds to reach. Government must challenge the deeply embedded and destructive British cultural attitude which holds that success, by definition, is only possible for a minority. The evidence from the most successful schools shows that this it false.

The Conservatives are delving deeper and deeper into the failed policies of the past. We want to address the challenges of the future. Take for example the Prime Minister's idea of a grammar school in every town. This would mean spending large amounts of public money on schools which at best would provide for one child in twenty. It would be yet another policy designed to benefit a tiny minority at the expense of everyone else. It would also be a dangerous distraction from the central issue of raising standards for all children. It would unsettle and demoralise existing comprehensives in the same locality.

In many parts of the country, especially in suburbs, in rural areas and small towns, the record of comprehensive education has been successful. There are also some shining examples of success in disadvantaged inner urban and outer rim estates. It is also clear that though social conditions can of course affect a school's performance, it is absolutely wrong to say that because a school exists in a poor or deprived neighbourhood, it cannot succeed. It can. The task may be harder, but there

174

has been nothing more damaging or short-sighted than the counsel of despair that says poor social conditions lead to poor schools. On the contrary, one of the most important ways of turning round poor social conditions is high quality schools and it is our mission to make that happen. If one believes, as we do, in social justice, there can be no greater social injustice than giving a child a bad education.

> Though social conditions can of course affect a school's performance, it is absolutely wrong to say that because a school exists in a poor or deprived neighbourhood, it cannot succeed

Overall, there has been progress. More children are doing better than ever before. This is a tribute to teachers in comprehensive schools which still educate over 90 per cent of our young people. But, as we have seen, it has not enabled us sufficiently to raise standards for the average and below average. Comprehensive schools have not yet, in Harold Wilson's words, universalised what was good about grammar schools: high standards and a ladder up for bright children from poor families or deprived backgrounds.

Mixed ability teaching is for some people as much of an ideology as the principle of comprehensive admission itself. It works in some cases – when done by the best teachers with proper support and a well-motivated and cohesive group of children. But mixed ability teaching makes heroic assumptions about resources, teachers and social context. While an overly rigid system of streaming can lead to the same problems as the 11-plus, not to take account of the obvious common sense that different children move at different speeds and have differing abilities, is to give idealism a bad name. The modernisation of the comprehensive principle requires that all pupils are encouraged to progress as far and as fast as they are able. Grouping children according to their ability can be an important way of making that happen.

It is not of course up to central government to prescribe classroom organisation in 25,000 schools. Professional judgement according to local circumstance is important. At the moment setting tends to be adopted most among older pupils, but in fact it can do as much if not more good early on. Interestingly, in maths and science, where progress is most easily measured there is the least use of mixed ability teaching. If setting is best in these measurable subjects shouldn't it be applied too in less easily measured subjects like history and English?

In government we will start from a general presumption in favour of grouping according to ability or attainment unless a school can demonstrate that it can meet the heavy demands of a mixed ability approach. Every school needs to justify its approach to grouping pupils and show how it stretches all pupils to achieve their best. There are a number of ways in which this can be done.

The use of new technology, support staff like associate teachers and flexibility in timetabling will make it possible to move beyond the traditional debate of mixed ability versus the 11-plus. Some schools now have individual learning programmes which set targets for improvement for each pupil. Other schools have achieved timetable flexibility that allows them to vary their approach to pupil grouping, with special provision for high flyers, for girls interested in science, for pupils who want to take lessons at a local FE college. Still other schools provide enrichment activities before and after the formal school day to challenge those capable of achieving more and support those who need help. And still others have shown how accelerated learning — not taking a pupil out of his or her year group but making it possible for them to progress beyond their own year group's study — can retain pupil interest and promote achievement.

This is the way to ensure that children with aptitude in a subject advance as fast as possible and children with less talent receive the help they need. In the vision that is unfolding the current debate about selection by school, promoted so vigorously by the Prime Minister, will be revealed to be the anachronism it is. Unlike the 11-plus, children will not be stigmatised by one make or break exam. They will move up depending on how well they achieve. Adding these strategies to a general policy of grouping by ability, we can ensure the excellence and mobility for all pupils and not just a few.

From a speech at Didcot Girls School, 7 June 1996

18 *The One-Nation NHS*

I want to explain my conception of a One-Nation NHS, not one divided, demoralised or fit only for those who can afford private care but a genuine health service for the nation. Modernised, of course, but true to its founding principles. These are the principles of such a service: That good health and a modern NHS are essential foundations of security in a more insecure world. Second, the NHS needs reform and not upheaval and those reforms must centre on the patient instead of on structural revolution. Third, we want resources put into front-line services not unnecessary paperwork, which is why we believe in

For the first time a generation of people — my generation — is growing up uncertain as to whether their children will have a better life than they had

cooperation not competition. Fourth, health care in the future will need to adapt to make the most of changes in technology and the changing expectations of patients.

Fifth, there is now a clear dividing line on health. It lies between a Conservative Party that will preside over the decline of the NHS until it ends up as a safety net service — a fall back for those who can't go private — and New Labour that wants a national service which can provide access for patients whatever their background and whatever part of the country they live in.

Insecurity

Meeting people from all backgrounds — teachers, doctors, small businessmen, the unemployed, managers and young mothers — I become more certain each day about what is wrong with Britain. It is a simple yet precious thing: we have lost our confidence as a nation and lost our security as individuals. For the first time a generation of people — my generation — is growing up uncertain as to whether their children will have a better life than they had.

That anxiety is reinforced in people's daily lives. People

feel more insecure about their jobs, higher taxes, educational standards, negative equity, rising violent crime. And more and more people are insecure about their health care. They fear that the NHS is undermined. They fear, too, illness from new threats – the food they eat, the air they breathe, the return of killer diseases such as TB that are associated with poverty.

No one believes we can guarantee a life free from insecurity. But if we let change become our master, only those who are already powerful will prosper. In a world that is changing rapidly people need a government that will help them cope with change. They want the building blocks for a more secure life: the NHS is one of those key building blocks.

We believe that the principle of the NHS is still the basis of the best health care Britain could have. In a more unequal society, it is still part of what binds us all together, what makes us one nation. We must keep to that founding principle that health care is based on need and not on ability to pay. For New Labour, the NHS is the proudest creation of a past Labour government and the embodiment of our belief that we can achieve more together than we can alone. Labour created the NHS. New Labour will give it a new lease of life as a public service that can respond to the changing needs of the population.

The Strong Community

Good health is about more than the NHS. It is about how we live. It is about what kind of country we are. People who are poorer can, on average, expect to live 8 years less than the richest. When I meet people who have lived on benefits for many years, in poor housing, with bad health, I know that what will transform their lives is not just a better hospital nearby or more regular visits to the doctor. It is a job, decent housing, a sense of hope. So I believe the way to improve the nation's health is by starting to build a more inclusive society – a society in which everyone has a stake and in which everyone has a sense of security. Security means action to tackle health inequalities. It means action to tackle unacceptable variations in treatment between people who live in similar circumstances. It is unacceptable that fifty per cent more people die from breast cancer in north west Surrey than in south west Surrey.

Labour will create a Minister for Public Health with the job of coordinating across Whitehall departments policies to improve the nation's health and reduce health inequalities. And we will make sure that we give health authorities new responsibilities for meeting health-of-the-nation targets and targets for reducing health inequalities.

I believe that improving the nation's health is a joint project between the individual and government. Let me give two examples: First, it is up to an individual whether they smoke or not, but it is simply not true to say government can do nothing to affect that choice. We have made it clear that we will initiate a ban on tobacco advertising and focus on programmes that help pregnant mothers give up. Second, government should provide individuals with information and protection on the food they eat. The recent scare over beef and baby milk in particular – and the government's incompetent handling of it – has left people more anxious about what is safe and what is not.

There is an overwhelming case for an independent Food Standards Agency. It should be free from the conflict of interest between agriculture and food safety that comes from them both being under the same roof at the Ministry of Agriculture. It should be a consumer agency with the remit of giving the public the best possible protection. It should provide all advice in public and should ensure all food products have clear labelling of ingredients.

While prevention is always better than cure, it is to the NHS that people look for reassurance when illness arrives.

The Universal Principle
The first and overwhelming impression I get walking into a hospital is how dedicated the staff are, and how difficult the job is. It is the mixture of 'humanity and science' as Sandy Macara of the BMA calls it that is so striking. And it is clear that managers as much as clinicians are dedicated to the NHS. It is therefore tragic that many in the NHS feel demoralised about the direction the service is heading.

179

It is no longer a right-wing fringe but senior members of the Cabinet who want to turn the NHS into a rump service. It is not hard to see why there has been a 35 per cent increase in individuals taking out private medical insurance in the last fifteen years. They are reluctant refugees from the health service. They are going private not because they want to but because they fear for their health and that of their families. Our opponents say that patients going private is good for the NHS because it relieves some of the pressure. I believe this is the road to reducing the NHS to a poor safety net service that no one in the end will be able to rely on.

For the first time since it was founded the principle that health is about need not ability to pay is being seriously undermined by this government. More and more people are being hit by a double tax on health – paying once out of their pay for the NHS and paying again for private treatment if the NHS is not there for them when they need it.

If things continue as at present and more people reach for their cheque books to pay for private insurance I genuinely believe that the NHS will cease to exist as we know it. A decade ago if you had said to people that in parts of the country there would not be NHS dentists, only private ones, they would have thought you were joking. **More and more people are being hit by a double tax on health** But as other countries have discovered a market in health care does not work because health should be based on need not purchasing power. Those who enter the market with little or no money end up doing worse. We know from the US where 37 million people have no health cover, and many of the state-run hospitals are poor, that this is no route for Britain to follow. It is both inefficient and unjust. I believe in a universal health-care system paid for by taxation that gives every citizen the best health care based on need not ability to pay.

Reform not Upheaval
The second message I have received loud and clear from those who work in the NHS is that no more major upheaval is wanted. Nor is permanent revolution believed to be in the

interests of patient care. I am not someone who believes in changing things out of dogma or because I am sure that everything I will inherit is bound to be wrong. The NHS needs stability as well as modernisation and change. Our priority will be to make changes that are in the interests of patient care and not start making organisational change where it is not needed. Change will not be foisted upon the service without consultation. I will not be making political appointments to trust and health authority boards but enforcing the Nolan recommendations to ensure that merit is the sole criterion for any appointment.

Cooperation not Competition

Health care is about team work, integration and sharing of information. How perverse then to have set up a market system which makes team work so difficult. What the market fails to appreciate is that two-thirds of health care is treating on-going illness such as multiple sclerosis and not one-off operations. On-going treatment does not lend itself to the simple contract. It leads to a proliferation of contracts and rising costs. Treatment of on-going care depends on cooperation and more flexible commissioning.

The one thing that everybody I speak to in the NHS is agreed upon is that many of the transaction costs of the market are unnecessary. Until recently only five per cent of the NHS budget was spent on bureaucracy. It is now 16 per cent. The BMA put the costs at more than £1.5bn a year extra. The market is bad for patients and it worse for taxpayers.

The NHS needs to be well managed. And there are many dedicated and good managers. What concerns me are the excesses of the market and not the fact that we need skilled management to run the service. The NHS is a big organisation using £40bn of taxpayers' money. The public need to know that the money is being spent wisely. Public services must have public support. The public will not accept a system which tells them there is no intensive care bed for their child, that they will have to wait on a trolley for 12 hours, that their elderly mother will have to wait in pain for 12 months for a hip operation, when they see hundreds of extra millions of pounds going into administration.

Most importantly of all, competition is not the best way of organising health services which rely as they do on the creativity and dedication of all those in the service. Trust is a fragile thing. It takes years to build up; it can take seconds to destroy. Crude use of market mechanisms threatens to undermine that trust. If doctors feel their clinical judgement is second guessed by accountants then trust breaks down. It is ironic that at a time when trust relationships are being eroded in the NHS, many businesses are trying to take what they see as the dedication, loyalty and trust of the NHS and recreate it in the business setting.

So Labour aims to replace the internal market that sets hospital against hospital, doctor against doctor and results in ballooning red tape. In its place will be a system based on cooperation and efficiency. We will combine quality and value for money with devolved decision-making and collaboration. That is why we want to move to long term agreements between commissioners and providers. It is important that the health needs of people locally are properly assessed and the provision of services to meet those needs are properly planned. It is also important that health services, the hospitals, clinics and primary care services are properly run. With Labour the planning of health and delivery of health care will remain distinct responsibilities. They will be kept separate.

Keeping the NHS Close to Patients

When people think what's best about the NHS, they think of their local hospital or their family doctor. Decisions should be taken as near to the patient as possible. Primary care under the NHS has been the envy of the world. It deals successfully with nine out of ten health problems. Our task must be to strengthen it by ensuring that more services are delivered to a higher standard in primary care. We must help the best GPs get better and deal with the problem of low morale and recruitment as well as raising standards.

There are many more important issues facing primary care and the exciting ways in which it can respond to the needs of patients. But they need to be put in the context of a system in which all GPs have equal access to hospital treatment. I know that fundholders recognise that as things stand the system is bureaucratic and costly and has resulted in a two-tier system of care. That is why we want to move forward by combining the patient-sensitive approach of GPs with the population-sensitive approach of the health authority in a unified system that is flexible enough to respond to local needs.

We will give all GPs equal say in shaping hospital services for their patients by replacing GP fundholding with a flexible GP commissioning model. I believe that this is the best way forward for all doctors and all patients.

To make local services effective we must make care in the community work. That means we must ensure that there is a continuum of care between health, housing and social services. It means we must have a moratorium on closing mental health beds.

Modernisation
The world has changed. The technology, medical break-throughs in genetics and new treatments, an ageing population, different work and family patterns mean that health services have to adapt to meet those changes. There is no place for nostalgia. I believe that the NHS is responding to these new challenges but is being held back by the market from making them widespread. The key is to put the patient at the centre of any change. When the patient becomes the focus of policy, the focus of every GP, every manager, every consultant, every nurse, then I believe a revolution in care unfolds before our eyes:

★ Same day medicine that gives individuals tests, X rays, scans on the same day and the results as well;

★ Tele-medicine that enables patients to get the best opinions in the country beamed into a GP's surgery or even the patient's own home;

★ Regional centres of excellence. One of the ways that we can modernise the service is by having expertise in specialist

183

centres and sharing that knowledge with hospitals and GPs
– in many cases through new technology;

★ More information and involvement of patients;

★ Better guarantees that the treatment a patient receives has
been clinically proven to be effective.

These are some of the new ways forward that are being
developed on the ground. They will revolutionise the quality
of care given to patients.

But there is one current problem that is perhaps the most
pressing. That is the large increase in emergency admissions.
The result is that in some hospitals patients are waiting many
hours between the decision to admit and ending up in a hospital bed. For many patients the consequence is a long period
in pain waiting on a trolley. There are many reasons for the
growth in emergency admissions and NAHAT has been at
the forefront of finding solutions. Many of the ways forward lie
in changing the way things are planned and do not necessarily
require more resources.

The best practice that is emerging includes: First, the use
of admission wards which will give patients – particularly
urgent cases requested by GPs – the chance to go straight into
a bed. Second, there should be a redeployment of some senior
managerial staff to become senior bed managers given authority by hospital trusts to organise beds to maximum efficiency
responding promptly to GPs and minimising disruption to
elective admissions. Third, in conjunction with the Royal Colleges and other professional bodies, there needs to be a reassess-
ment of the roles of professionals to see whether the potential
of staff can be used in different ways. Nurses, for example,
with the appropriate training and support could take on much
greater responsibility.

In government we will set up a task force to report urgently
on how we can end trolley waits in the NHS for good and
how we can make sure that the NHS can cope with the extra
pressure on emergencies. I do not see why people should have
to wait on trolleys for hours in a modern NHS.

As with any government, we can only spend, of course,

what we can afford and it is not right or possible for an opposition party in this or any other area to write detailed spending plans whilst in opposition. We understand and share the concerns about resource difficulties but we must also see, first, whether existing budgets are well spent – and the unnecessary form filling is removed – second, that existing treatments are based on the best evidence and money is not being wasted on ineffective treatment. Only after these two stages would a Labour government look at whether there was still a funding gap that needed to be bridged.

The Choice
Facing those who use the NHS and those who work in the NHS there is a stark choice. You can continue down the road towards a scaled down NHS, where the decline is managed, people lose faith in its ability to provide a comprehensive service and more and more hard-working families spend money on private health insurance. Or there is a future for the NHS as a part of a health policy that believes in the NHS as a modern public service that could give the quickest and best service to patients and that responds to the new demands of the population.

New Labour offers the second future, and is proud to do so. The NHS is not just safe in Labour's hands but will get a new lease of life as a patient-centred, innovative and modern public service.

From a speech to the NAHAT annual conference, 20 June 1996

19 *The Age of Consent*

Let us be clear about the issue involved in the age of consent for homosexual sex. It is not at what age we wish young people to have sex. It is whether the criminal law should discriminate between heterosexual and homosexual sex. It is therefore an issue not of age but of equality.

By supporting equality, no one is advocating or urging gay sex at sixteen, any more than those who would maintain the age of consent for heterosexual sex advocate that girls or boys of sixteen should have sex. It is simply a question of whether there are grounds for discrimination.

At present, the law discriminates. There is no doubt about the personal misery that such discrimination brings: to young people frightened to admit their own sexuality and of the fear of imprisonment, and to any man who is homosexual and who knows that the criminal law treats that in a different and more incriminating way.

The argument – and the only argument – advanced to justify that discrimination and its attendant tragedy is that it is necessary for the protection of young people. Without it, it is said, young men unsure of their sexuality may be preyed upon by older homosexuals and induced to become homosexual when they otherwise would not.

The overwhelming evidence – scientific or indeed merely experience of life – suggests that being homosexual is not something that people catch, are taught, or are persuaded into, but something that they are.

It is not against the nature of gay people to be gay; it is in fact their nature. It is what they are. It is different, but that is not a ground for discrimination. The vast bulk of evidence suggests that, at sixteen, boys and girls, particularly nowadays, are aware of their sexuality and that that sexuality is normally developed with those of their own age, not with predatory elders.

However, let us assume for the purposes of argument that

there is a small minority that fits into the last category. How would use of the criminal law assist such a situation? How would that deal with vulnerable young people of whatever sex? For those who are confused about their sexuality, how does the criminal law help to resolve that confusion? Indeed, it merely complicates it. It deters many from seeking the information, advice and help that they need.

If we are in any doubt about that, let us listen to organisations that deal day in and day out with the problems of young people, such as Save the Children Fund and the National Children's Bureau. They say that the real danger is not young sexually uncertain men being preyed upon by older men, but young boys and men who are gay but who are afraid to seek the advice and help that they may desperately need. That is the evidence that was given by the British Medical Association, which backs up that view on the ground of better health education.

There is talk about predatory older men. That happens – if it does happen – not just with young men but with young girls, yet no one would advance that as a reason for raising the age of consent. Moreover, where such predatory conduct takes place – let us assume for the purposes of the argument that it does – it takes place in circumstances that we all know: in parts of our inner cities and around some railway stations late at night, where young boys and girls sell sex for money and shelter. Surely the question that we should ask is why those young people are in those circumstances when it is not the criminal law but a roof over their heads, a decent family and home and a chance of a job that will help them.

The practice in other countries has been raised. The point is not that we should follow what happens in other countries; nor should the fact that the majority of other countries in Europe do not discriminate mean that we necessarily blindly follow their path. The point is, first, that many of those countries are usually among the most conservative in such matters, which makes their decision on equality all the more telling, and, secondly, and most important, that there is no evidence to suggest that any of the adverse consequences forecast as attending a move to equality here have happened in those countries – none, not a single shred of evidence, not anywhere.

On practical grounds – and even accepting that there is a small percentage of cases in which there is a fear of predatory conduct – can it be said that the fear that, without the sanction of criminal law, there might be an unquantifiable number of young men who will engage in homosexual relations who otherwise would not is a reason for perpetrating discrimination against all homosexual men when we know that the vast majority of young people are not in that situation, when, if anything, the protection that they need is the removal of the stigma attached to their sexuality, when independent organisations that deal with young people want it removed, and when equality is the norm in neighbouring countries without any of the adverse consequences claimed for it?

The real objection to equality is not reason but prejudice

That is why the real objection to equality is not reason but prejudice. In the end, all the concern, however ostensibly objective – let us assume that some of it is genuinely motivated – is traceable to that very subjective prejudice. Let us be clear that people are entitled to think that homosexuality is wrong, but they are not entitled to use the criminal law to force that view upon others. That is where the real practitioners of political correctness lie – not in those who merely seek equality of treatment but in those who insist that the law must discriminate in favour of their view of the conduct of others. That is why, also, the so-called compromise of eighteen is misguided. What is the rationale behind maintaining the stigma but at a different age? It is an issue not of age but of equality.

Because this is an issue of equality, and because it concerns the equal rights of our citizens, this is an issue not just for those who are gay but for all of us who are concerned about the type of society in which we live.

Yes, it is the case that any strong society needs good and decent principles to sustain and motivate it. But it should be a society that makes sense of the passage of time, that learns from and evaluates its progress, that has confidence to build its own future, not one that takes refuge in the prejudices of the past because it is afraid to change them. A society of genuine standards and principles allows individuals the freedom to develop to the full. A society of prejudice and discrimination can merely make them conform.

That is the choice. We should seek the best of the old and the best of the new. Some change is good; some change is bad. We should distinguish between the two. I deplore, as we all do, for example, the greater lawlessness in society, the increased violence, and the abusive behaviour of today. I should like to return to a better time when those issues were less urgent. But I have no desire to return to a time when women were inhibited from going to work, when sex could not be openly discussed and debated, when young people were not taught at school how life is given and created, and when gay men hid their sexuality in fear.

Some change is indeed progress. Let us recognise it when it happens. After all, 100 years ago there was no universal suffrage for men and no votes for women. Fifty years ago there were no laws against racial intolerance. Each change was fought for but resisted by prejudice wrapped in a coat of reason.

The point is not that, over time, our basic values should change – of course not. But it is through experience and thought that our understanding of what those values should encompass has been enlarged. Indeed, I go further: the most basic civilised value is the notion of respect for other people. That is what creates and sustains any decent society. That is why crime is wrong; that is why violent and abusive behaviour is wrong; that is why racial abuse is wrong. It is also why it is wrong to treat a man as inferior because his sexuality is different.

A society that has learned, over time, racial and sexual equality can surely come to terms with equality of sexuality. That is the moral case for change. It is our chance to welcome people – I do not care whether there are 50,000, 500,000 or 5 million; it matters not a damn – into full membership of our society, on equal terms. It is our chance to do good, and we should take it.

From a House of Commons speech on the 'Criminal Justice and Public Order Bill', 21 February 1994

189

20 *Housing*

Housing policy has long been a touchstone for many voters. Slum clearance was an early demand of the Labour movement. One of the few pieces of legislation passed by the first short-lived Labour government in 1924 was John Wheatley's pioneering Housing Act. In 1945 housing renewal offered upward mobility to millions of voters. In the 1950s and 1960s Labour and Conservative governments traded promises about the number of houses they would build. And in 1979 Mrs Thatcher identified the Conservative Party with the aspirations of a whole generation of voters who wanted to own their own homes.

I understand the aspirations of those voters. They wanted control over housing to get control of their lives – the chance to make improvements and changes, to get on in life. In the 1980s many of them identified with the Conservative Party. The Tories used to call themselves the party of the home-owner in Britain. Today this claim would be a sad joke. Far from defending home-owners, they are reduced to defending the excesses of the few at the top. They have lost touch with the insecure majority. But Labour is back in touch – the party of social housing, but the party of private housing too.

The growth of insecurity has made life's choices much less certain. Most people still want to own their own homes, though of course there are some for whom that is not the best option. But the ability to make the choice to buy a house is greatly weakened in an economy where insecurity is rife and families are more anxious than for generations about what the future holds for them.

Our approach is basically very simple. Labour supports the aspiration of the majority of people to own their own homes, but also wants a healthy, properly run social and private rented sector for those who either cannot afford to buy or who choose not to.

Poor housing strikes at the heart of the good society. It

makes it more difficult to hold a family together. It makes it more difficult to bring children up in a healthy environment or to ensure they do the best they can at school. Decent homes give people a basic sense of their own security. And, in housing as elsewhere, the combination of a stakeholder economy and a one-nation society is the partnership we wish to create.

There will be an enormous demand for new houses in the future. As well as looking at the types of tenure and financing for new housing, we must also consider its location. It is important that we think sensibly and plan future development so as to meet the need for new housing while protecting the countryside from being paved over unnecessarily and looking at the scope for revitalising the derelict and run-down areas of our cities.

The Tory Failure of Home-owners

The millions of people who bought homes in the 1980s now feel let down, abandoned and betrayed by the government in which many of them placed their trust.

A brief housing audit of John Major's premiership sums up the picture. According to the Halifax Building Society, in 1992 prices fell by 5.6 per cent, in 1993 they fell a further 2.9 per cent, in 1994 they rose by 0.5 per cent, but they dropped a further 1.4 per cent in 1995.

Ministers keep talking up the market but the truth is that, having been stung once, home-owners don't believe them. And no wonder, when the slump has left 1.7 million living in houses with negative equity – a cold technical fact beneath which lie millions of stories of disappointment, frustration and anxiety about the future.

In addition, there is a continuing crisis of mortgage arrears and repossessions. In 1992 the Prime Minister told us that 'We've stopped . . . the repossessions, just before Christmas.' Yet in 1995 alone there were 50,000 repossessions, and they are still running at almost 1,000 a week. Three hundred thousand households have lost their homes through repossession since John Major became Prime Minister – an average of one for every two minutes of every working day in his time in office.

The Tories are not the party of the home-owner: they are the home-wrecker's party – the party of negative equity, repossessions, broken dreams and falling house value; the party which encouraged people to buy their own homes then turned on them once they had done so. The collapse in the housing market is not just a knock-on feature of the wider economic recession – it has been fed by deliberate and specific government policies.

The first blow the government dealt to home-owners was to cut MIRAS – to 20 per cent in 1993, then a year later to 15 per cent. Then the government went one further by also cutting income support to home-owners who had lost their jobs. Each of these moves was a betrayal of people who had supported this government throughout its time in office.

And the betrayal was added to by the tax rises which affected the whole population. Not surprisingly, the effect of all these measures was to add to insecurity, to destroy confidence in the housing market, and to make people much more wary of buying and selling homes.

I fully understand the very human aspiration to own your own home. But many of the people who have tried to fulfil their dream have been let down. Home-owners kept their side of the contract. The Tories just tore it up.

It was in part a failure of competence, but it was also a failure of understanding. The Tories have simply been left behind by the enormous changes taking place in the economy and in society as a whole.

Labour's Approach

The truth is that any successful housing strategy must begin with an understanding of the enormous extent of insecurity in today's economy. Since the last election 8.7 million people have experienced at least one spell of unemployment. Half of those currently unemployed were in their last job for less than a year. Britain stands twentieth in the league of major industrial countries for its record on job creation since 1979. And a recent Council of Mortgage Lenders survey found that a quarter of home-owners were unwilling to move because of job insecurity.

New Labour wants to draw a line under the failed policies of the Conservatives and to re-establish a relationship of trust between government and the people which ensures that people once again have the confidence to buy and sell and to exercise choice over their housing. That means building an investment-based economy which looks to the long term and seeks to lift Britain from eighteenth place in the world prosperity league. An economy which takes no risks with inflation. An economy which helps people develop the skills and education to adapt to change and in which everyone has a stake for the future.

We do not want a return to the damaging cycle of boom and bust which has characterised the Tory years. What is needed now is steady and sustainable growth in the economy and in the housing market to help those in negative equity and to restore the shattered confidence of home-owners and those who want to buy.

Today I want to outline a series of measures which I believe would help both home-owners and those in rented housing, but all of them have to be seen against the basic requirement of reducing insecurity and giving people confidence about the future once again.

Lenders, as well as government, have a direct interest in adapting to a more insecure world and working to restore confidence to the housing market. And there ought to be a partnership between government and lenders to get the market moving again.

The first thing we need is mortgages which suit the way people live their lives. Is it really appropriate against the sort of employment patterns which now exist to assume that when people are buying a house they should have a mortgage which requires a constant monthly repayment over twenty or twenty-five years? Or should mortgages suit the flexibility with which people lead their lives? I am glad to see that a number of lenders are starting to offer 'lifestyle' mortgages – for example with provision for payment holidays to cover the birth of a child or a temporary loss of income – and I hope this is a development which more lenders will take up as traditional working patterns continue to evolve.

I also believe lenders have a key role to play in reducing

repossessions. It is impossible to overstate the distress and hardship caused to families who lose their own home. And the flow of 1,000 repossessed properties coming on to the market every week undermines recovery and keeps prices down for everyone else. I believe there is real potential to make flexible tenure schemes which mix owning and renting work better than in the past.

Individual lenders have shown what can be done. For example, the Bradford and Bingley Building Society, in partnership with the English Churches Housing group and Circle 33 Housing Trust, has rescued over 1,100 borrowing members. Their scheme is based on helping people with serious mortgage arrears in negative equity. The building society lends the housing association the funds to buy the property, and the occupiers stay on as tenants. This kind of scheme shows the potential for imaginative solutions to problems of serious debt, and that alternatives to repossession can be developed. And it shows that the stark divide between renting and owning ought to be a thing of the past.

A more flexible approach to housing tenure would give people a hand up to home-ownership and could help further to reduce repossessions. Already housing associations in many parts of the country operate shared-ownership schemes which allow people to pay a combination of rent and mortgage on

---

The problem of homelessness is one of the most telling indicators of the social and housing crisis Britain is suffering. The Tories have neglected housing in this country. Since 1979 they have halved the budget for investment in housing, while the amount paid out on housing benefit has rocketed – in 1994 alone it will have cost £11 billion.

In Tory-controlled Wandsworth, this absurd situation means that in 1993 the council had 435 families in bed-and-breakfast accommodation at a cost of over £7 million a year, yet in that year they built just one new house.

From the Evening Standard, *21 December 1994*

---

the property. In economic circumstances where some people may be more wary of buying outright, the potential of shared-ownership schemes in years to come could be considerable.

Giving hope to those with negative equity is of course a key issue. We want to discuss with lenders expansion of schemes to allow people – but only, and I stress this, in strictly defined circumstances – to borrow more than 100 per cent loans against their new home, so that in effect they would carry their negative equity with them and transfer it into a new mortgage. Of course lenders would rightly want assurances that the borrower had a good repayment record, that they were in stable employment, and they could meet the new repayments which would result. It is not a scheme suitable for everyone, but it could be a further mechanism which would help get the market moving again.

For some people, buying their own home will be the biggest single investment they will make. It is crucial that the pros and cons of different types of mortgage are explained fully to prospective home-buyers and that buyers' rights as consumers are properly protected. People should know exactly what they are buying and how much it is costing them. There is a clear case for more disclosure of commission and other charges. Lenders have nothing to fear from letting their customers know exactly what the costs are for the services they provide. They should publish full information on charges and commissions so that consumers know where they stand.

I welcome the publication of a consultation paper and a draft code of mortgage-lending practice by the Council of Mortgage Lenders. Agreement to such a code would demonstrate a commitment to high standards by responsible mortgage-lenders. However, a voluntary code may not be able to guarantee the sort of advice and information that consumers should be able to expect. That is why we believe there is a strong case for making the selling of mortgages subject to the same requirement to give best advice as is currently required for other financial services, like pensions, under the Financial Services Act. But we will obviously consult on this further with the Council of Mortgage Lenders and others.

A group of home-owners who need particular help are

leaseholders. Despite all the government's promises in this area, it has consistently failed to bring forward meaningful reform. Year after year we hear of abuses by some landlords who levy huge charges on leaseholders who are effectively powerless to do anything about it. Our proposals include:

★ simplifying the enfranchisement rules to enable more lease-hold flat-dwellers to exercise their right to buy the freehold or to obtain an extension of leases;

★ giving leaseholders the right to manage as a really effective sanction against rogue landlords; and

★ introducing commonhold as a new form of tenure to enable flat-dwellers to own the freehold of their flats and to own collectively the freehold of the shared parts of their build-ings such as stairways.

Rented Housing

I now want to turn to rented housing, which has been and will remain the best option for millions of people. A healthy social housing sector which offers homes at affordable rents and decent rights for tenants is a central part of our vision of the one-nation society.

One of the most senseless policies the Conservatives have pursued is to prohibit councils from using the capital receipts they have raised through people exercising the right to buy. This means that councils are sitting on funds they could be using to invest in housing. So we will lift the ban on the use of these funds and allow their release on a phased basis so that councils can start to build and reverse the neglect of recent years. The effect would be to provide more new housing, to improve existing stock, to reduce homelessness, and to provide much-needed jobs in the construction industry. I am the first to acknowledge the successes of the right to buy, but I also believe the funds raised from it should be used for new invest-ment in housing.

And to increase investment we will also encourage new public/private partnership initiatives, including local housing companies. Such partnerships will need to bring together all those who must be involved in the regeneration of areas of substandard housing and in the construction of good-quality new homes. Of course, to be successful these companies must command the confidence of everyone involved – including tenants, who will rightly expect a real say in the way in which the company operates.

While the Conservatives have been obsessed with the privatisation of council housing, Labour, by contrast, sees the local housing company as an exciting new option which will bring together tenants, local councils and the private sector in a genuine three-way partnership.

Social housing is not just about investment. It is also about how that investment is used. Many parts of our country have housing estates facing huge problems of multiple deprivation. The war on this deprivation has to be led not by government or councils but by tenants themselves. The state will play a role, but the tenants must take the lead. It is only by empowering the people who live in them that deprived urban estates can be turned around. These are not hopeless places. They are places facing huge challenges. And the decent people who live there have to know we are on their side in the fight to improve them.

Tenants should be involved at every stage of design, building and maintenance. Many Labour councils have made great strides in involving tenants in recent years. York City Council, for example, has worked with residents on the Bell Farm estate to turn around what was known locally as a problem estate. Together, the council and local people developed an estate agreement to ensure an ongoing partnership committed to the health of the area. They involved the police, the local health trust, social services, education and housing. Standards of service are now monitored regularly by a panel of residents and service-providers, and a recent study hailed the scheme as a 'ground-breaking' venture in empowering local residents to manage their own affairs.

Of course, local authorities are not the only providers of social housing. This country has a rich mix of housing associations building around 30,000 houses a year with a long history of meeting need – often for specific groups of people. Associations have pioneered the involvement of local communities in the building and management of their own homes. Some have led the way in care-in-the-community provision; others have achieved remarkable results in energy-efficiency schemes. In recent years housing associations have been the main providers of social housing, working in partnership with private investors to lever in funds to invest in new rented housing.

I want housing associations to continue to develop their role as providers of social housing, in partnership both with the private sector and with local authorities. In the use of council capital receipts I hope there is a close dialogue between associations and councils to make the best possible use of housing investment. And in government I am firmly committed to encouraging the housing-association movement and in ensuring a diversity of providers in rented housing.

Part of that diversity must also be to encourage the private rented sector. Changing career patterns make the flexibility of renting in the private sector the right choice for an increasing number of people. When people leave college or university and take up a job for the first time, very often private renting is the ideal option. Yet this sector has been in long-term decline. I want to see that decline reversed. I very much welcome the relaxation of the rules governing investment trusts which are intended to facilitate investment in private rented housing by both individuals and institutional investors. The housing investment trusts which may be created as a result must be kept under review to assess both their impact and their potential, but they could help attract investment into this sector.

And whatever sector people live in – owning, renting or a mixture of the two – they have a right to expect reasonable behaviour from their neighbours. We have been quite clear about this. Tolerance and respect are essential in any decent society. And there can be no excuse for antisocial behaviour which makes life a misery for others.

It is also any government's duty to make sure that available funds are spent in the most efficient way possible. Roughly the same amount of taxpayers' money is being spent now on housing as was being spent in 1979, when the Tories took over from Labour. The difference is that in 1979 two-thirds of the housing budget was invested in building new homes. Now investment accounts for only half the total – the rest is going to meet the £11 billion housing-benefit bill, which is leaving more and more people caught in the poverty trap.

Not only is this benefit bill growing but it is being fuelled by fraud. The House of Commons Social Security Committee recently received evidence that up to £2 billion may be being claimed in fraudulent housing-benefit claims. Housing benefit should go to those in genuine need, not to crooked tenants or landlords. There has to be far greater cooperation between individual councils and between councils and the DSS to tackle housing-benefit fraud and to stop this waste of taxpayers' money.

Our housing policy must also, of course, tackle head on the problem of homelessness. There are 120,000 families registered as having nowhere to live – and thousands more single homeless people who are not officially registered. Homelessness leaves a deep scar on our society, and its effects can be seen in every part of the country – in rural as well as urban areas.

Homelessness

A new Labour government will launch a determined attack on homelessness. A measure of our commitment to building one nation and healing the divisions of the Tory years will be our determination to do everything in our power to end the scandal of homelessness, to tackle the spectacle of people sleeping rough on the streets and to end the waste of families sleeping in bed-and-breakfast accommodation.

We have already begun that battle with our fight to prevent the current government proposals to water down the obligation on local authorities to provide permanent accommodation for homeless families – a proposal which is not only anti-family but will result in a further growth in the housing-benefit budget as people are forced into the private rented sector. But there is more that could be done.

Maximum use must be made of existing housing stock, too much of which is lying empty. There should be a determined effort to reduce the number of empty homes. Some local authorities have made great strides in this area, not only bringing their own empty properties into quicker use but also encouraging the letting of empty private properties. The government itself could do a great deal more to reduce the number of its own empty properties and to make them available to reduce waiting-lists and ease homelessness.

Our plans to increase investment through the release of capital receipts will have a direct impact on homelessness. And we will encourage more schemes like the Camberwell Foyer, which, like many similar projects, is doing an excellent job combining the provision of accommodation with training and employment.

Housing does not occupy a world of its own. It is part of the wider economic picture. Tackling the current problems in housing – either in the private market or in the rented sector, or indeed among the homeless themselves – is directly linked to tackling the insecurity which is such a characteristic of the British economy today. After seventeen years of bust, boom, then bust again, it is New Labour which is best placed to rise to the challenge of creating the stakeholder economy and the one-nation society which can provide security in a changing world.

From a speech to a Labour housing conference, London, 5 March 1995

PART IV

Security and Responsibility in a World of Change

A society based on strong values has, at its heart, respect for others, mutual responsibilities, obligation to more than oneself. That is why a crude individualism — social or economic; of Left or Right — won't work.

From a speech to the Newscorp Leadership Conference, Hayman Island, Australia, 17 July 1995

21 Security in a World of Change: The New Politics of the Left

Let me give you some facts that sum up the breathtaking pace of change. You can take your pick as to which ones you consider to be significant but what nobody can do is deny that the rate of economic, political, industrial and social change is quicker than at any time in our history. Much of that change is happening in the Asia Pacific region, with profound effects for the rest of the world.

By the turn of the century 400–500 million people living in East Asia will enjoy living standards as high as, or higher than, those in Europe.

The fastest growth in market capitalisation is in Indonesia, which is 10,000 per cent bigger than it was in 1985.

Korea spends 20 per cent of its GDP on education. India has 60 million people with the equivalent of a university degree.

An estimated 1.3 billion people will be added to the work-force in Asia, Africa and Latin America between 1995 and 2020.

Change in the media world is even more dramatic, with a communications revolution transforming business, entertainments, education – virtually every aspect of work and home life.

More facts. A transatlantic flight can now cost the equivalent of a three-minute phone call fifty years ago.

Within a decade or two there will be an effectively limitless capacity on fibre optics, capable of transporting the entire contents of the British Library in less than a minute.

By the year 2005 there will be 10 million people working in computer software in OECD countries.

The turnover through digital channels of foreign exchange each week equals the US national debt of $4 trillion.

All this – and yet so much of the world is still blighted by the eternal evils of poverty, squalor and ignorance.

Change presents opportunities but dangers too.

What is called globalisation is changing the nature of the nation-state as power becomes more diffuse and borders become more porous. Technological change is reducing the power and capacity of government to control its domestic economy free from external influence. Free movement of currency means free movement of capital which seeks the highest return worldwide. New names from the Far East have become part of the Western consumers' vocabulary – Sony, Toshiba, Hitachi. BT and ICI now have listings on the New York and Tokyo stock exchanges.

The economic role of government, in this world of change, is to represent a national interest, to create a competitive base of physical infrastructure and human skills to attract the capital that will produce the wages for workers and the profits for investors.

Foreign firms own 25 per cent of British manufacturing capacity and employ 16 per cent of British workers. Japanese firms alone churn out exports from the UK worth £4 billion a year.

The challenge before developed economies and newly industrialised economies in equal measure is not to slow down the pace of change and so get off the world but to educate and train and retrain for the next technologies. So, instead of protecting older industries which face competition, Asia Pacific countries are liberalising their economies and freeing their trade to international competition in order to make their economies more efficient and more internationally competitive.

The media are, of course, at the heart of the technological revolution.

Labour will phase in full competition between cable companies and telecommunications groups such as BT and Mercury. And under our new plans we are constructing a new partnership with companies entering the market, who will cable schools, hospitals, health centres, citizens advice bureaux and libraries as part of the licensing process.

This is the mass-multimedia society. The aim should be to create as much choice and diversity as possible, and the best way of achieving it is by an open and competitive media market – though the special place that the media have in the dissemination of information means there is a need, of course, for a proper framework of rules. We have already laid out the principles which should govern this area: diversity of content; plurality of ownership; regional strength; quality of programme-making; and the avoidance of excessive dominance by any one company.

Change and the Left-of-centre

The twentieth century will be regarded as the century of transformation. A revolution of politics, technology, science, culture, communications, travel and thus of society has taken place, and it will continue. With the disappearance of the old certainties has come enhanced opportunity, but massive instability and insecurity too. Universal suffrage has become the norm. Knowledge and education are far more widely available. Prosperity for the broad mass of people has increased beyond the dreams of previous centuries.

But jobs are displaced through advances in technology and global competition. Traditional values are displaced by rampant mass culture and universal media. The family unit – the bedrock of stability – is, at least in parts of the West, almost collapsing.

The central question of modern democratic politics is how to provide security during revolutionary change. That is what people look for from the governments they elect. And I don't just mean economic security. They want social stability too. They want some sense of rules, boundaries, parameters, reorganised and accepted by society as a whole, and enforced. It is not just the economy, stupid.

The task is to combine the preparation of a nation for economic change with the re-establishment of social order. The disillusion with much of politics and politicians in modern democracies is in part that this task is immense in size and complexity, but in part because politicians have failed to ignite the honest debate needed about the nature of the society we

205

want to live in and the values it is built upon. Yet the moral challenge is every bit as pressing as the economic challenge. Indeed, at critical points the two are linked.

The old-Left solutions of rigid economic planning and state control won't work. What is more, during the 1960s and 1970s the Left developed, almost in substitution for its economic prescriptions, which by then were failing, a type of social individualism that confused, at points at least, liberation from prejudice with a disregard for moral structures. It fought for racial and sexual equality, which was entirely right. It appeared indifferent to the family and individual responsibility, which was wrong.

Moreover, as the influence of some of the traditional supporters of the Left in Labour and working-class organisations waned, there was a real danger – occasionally realised – that single-issue pressure groups moved into the vacuum. Women's groups wrote the women's policy; environmental groups wrote the environmental policy; and so on. This was the same elsewhere. I remember the telling intervention of a speaker at the Republican convention of 1984in the USA asking rhetorically, 'When was the last time you ever heard a Democrat say NO?' It was too close to the truth for comfort.

It is interesting to note that these latter developments were an aberration peculiar to that period. Look back to the first heyday of the Left in the 1930s and 1940s and you will find heavy emphasis on responsibility, self-improvement and the family.

What of the new Right? It led the changes in politics in the 1980s. It held the political initiative. The Thatcher/Reagan leadership symbolised it. And it got certain things right – a greater emphasis on enterprise; rewarding not penalising success; breaking up some of the vested interests associated with state bureaucracy. In that sense Mrs Thatcher was a radical, not a Tory. But I want to suggest that in the end it was a project more successful at taking on and destroying some outdated attitudes and prescriptions than it was at building and creating.

Some economic problems were tackled, but others – levels of investment in capacity and people; infrastructure; long-term unemployment; the quality of education; crime; welfare – were not.

Socially, the Tories were far too slow to recognise the signs of social breakdown, and when they did recognise them they appeared to offer little by way of solution. What is more the Right developed a type of economic libertarianism which often lapsed into greed, selfishness, and social and moral irresponsibility.

My case, therefore, is that neither old Left nor conservative new Right can provide the framework for the solution of the central question. If – and I accept this is the real challenge – the Left can liberate itself from outdated preconceptions and strip its essential values out from the means of their application relevant to another part of history, then a modern left-of-centre is best able to provide security amid change.

Let me now make that case, and in doing so demonstrate also why this new left-of-centre is not simply an accommodation of the Right but tries to move the political debate beyond the old boundaries between Left and Right altogether. The claim that 'new Left' is just a fancy way of saying 'Tory' is false.

Economic Change

First, the left-of-centre will act to organise and prepare a country for change. The choice is not between resisting change and just letting it happen. Nor between the state trying to run industry or some rather crude version of *laissez-faire* liberalism.

Investing in education and skills; putting in place a system of life-long learning; a partnership between public and private sector to renew a nation's infrastructure; help with small businesses; ensuring a country is at the forefront of science and research; regenerating run-down inner-city areas and regions facing industrial restructuring; above all, creating the right framework for the harnessing and development of the new technologies – the common theme is that they all require an active, purposive government.

That does not necessarily mean government from the centre. It may be a mix of public and private enterprise. It may not be government at all but the private sector, given a strong competitive framework in which to exist; or the voluntary sector, a potential third force that can deliver services in a far more imaginative and creative way. But, without a government that both recognises the scale of the challenge and has some sense of urgency in acting to meet it, change will end up being perceived as an enemy not a friend, a threat not an opportunity.

Social Change

Secondly, the left-of-centre is the true position of moral purpose today. The only way to rebuild social order and stability is through strong values, socially shared, inculcated through individuals and families.

This is not some lurch into authoritarianism or an attempt to impose a regressive personal morality. It is, in fact, about justice and fairness. The strong and powerful can protect themselves. Those who lose most through the absence of rules are the weak and the vulnerable. The first casualties of social breakdown are often the poor and disadvantaged. That is why the Left should treat it seriously.

And why is the new Left able to tackle such disorder? Because a society based on strong values has, at its heart, respect for others, mutual responsibilities, obligation to more than oneself. That is why a crude individualism – social or economic; of Left or Right – won't work. The family is important because it is in the family that self-respect and respect for others are learned. It is in the family that the limits of freedom are first experienced and the roots of responsibility grow. The family is the antithesis of narrow selfishness.

Of course, elements on the Right, at least in theory, would assert notions of respect for others. But this should be more than not mugging your neighbour. If it is to work, it must find its social dimension too. From the family, we build out into broader society. I believe in a moral obligation to help those worse off or weak or unemployed. Yet this makes no sense outside of a belief in society and in the nation as a community of people as well as families and individuals.

Here is where the traditional values of the Left, applied sensibly and practically to the modern world, are its strength. It can fashion a new moral purpose for the nation which

208

combines individual and social responsibility and which can assert the importance of social rules and order, because through its belief in social justice and mutual respect it has some chance of achieving them. It has the moral authority to enforce the rules because it sets them within an active and strong community. That is why a communitarian philosophy, again applied with common sense, allows us to move beyond the choice between narrow individualism and old-style socialism.

A True Meritocracy

Third, as part of this, the Left should reclaim the ground of the anti-establishment. Many of those who supported the British Tories during the 1980s were not really Tories: they were anti-establishment. And they saw part of the Left as well as the Right running that establishment. But, unfortunately, many of those Tories never really wanted to bust the establishment: they wanted to buy it out.

We have, in many ways, changed the personnel but few of the attitudes. We still have hereditary peers voting on legislation in the House of Lords. Our legal system is a nest of restrictive practices. The old-boys network is much in evidence. The intake at Oxford and Cambridge from public schools has barely shifted in thirty years. The system of divided education itself is a pretty poor reflection on a modern country. Our parliamentary system is hopelessly outdated in many of its practices and attitudes. There is, believe it or not, still prejudice against success in trade and business. We are light years from being a true meritocracy.

The left-of-centre should be the meritocrats of the twenty-first century, and the establishments – new and old – should be opened up. I suspect, meanwhile, the Conservatives will return to their more traditional role, with a small as well as large c.

Britain Looking Outwards

However, there is one other advantage of the left-of-centre over the politics of the Conservative Right. The Conservatives are in danger of becoming narrowly and insularly nationalistic. There is no future for that in a world of change. I am not saying it does not have popular appeal. It does. But it is not serious politics.

Ten years ago, who would have believed that Labour would be the party of Europe and the party of free trade? The Right argue that further integration in Europe would lead to the loss of Britain's separate identity, sovereignty and freedom of action. Britain, they say, should retreat from Europe and be a separate player and base its strength on its relationships elsewhere in the world – the Commonwealth, the US. This argument has popular appeal, but it is based on delusion.

Historically, while being a European power, Britain has been special in having an empire and a global role. This has led us to think of ourselves as apart from Europe. But if we want to maintain that global role now we must be a leading player in Europe. We no longer have an empire, and although the Commonwealth gives us valuable links around the world it is not an alternative to Europe. The transatlantic relationship will continue to be important – particularly in the security field – but the Americans have made it clear they want a special relationship with Europe, not with Britain alone.

Our road to maximum influence leads through Europe. If we are to be listened to seriously in Washington or Tokyo, or the Pacific, we will often be acting with the rest of Europe. If we want to influence trade negotiations, we have to act as part of the EU, the world's largest trading bloc. If we want to attract inward investment, it must be clear we are part of Europe.

The so-called Euro-sceptics argue that we can retain the economic advantages of membership without the loss of sovereignty by reverting to membership of an EFTA-like body. But this is not a serious option – which is why Sweden, Finland and Austria have gone in the opposite direction, precisely so they can have a say in the decision-making process.

The real patriotic case, therefore, for those who want Britain to maintain its traditional global role, is for leadership in Europe. And, to revert to domestic politics for a moment, the position I have outlined is where any government – Left or Right – would in the end be driven. You can have it honestly under New Labour, with some chance of influencing the process; or you can have it larded with anti-European rhetoric about 'defending Britain to the death', and arrive there in any event with the Conservatives. But in their case without influence – where Europe is something that happens to us, rather than something we shape.

None of this means that Britain would slavishly follow whatever idea originates in the European Commission. Why should it? Other countries don't. There is a clear agenda for reform in Europe, including in the European Commission, fundamental change of the CAP, enlargement of the EU to the East, completion of the Single Market, cooperation on infrastructure, science and technology. But there is a far better chance of achieving that reform through constructive engagement rather than mindless negativity.

I also find, certainly among the left-of-centre parties, a growing consensus that the next stage of European development should not be more powers to the EU but making sure that the powers already in existence are exercised wisely and democratically. Britain, if viewed as a true partner in Europe, could therefore cut with the grain in advocating sensible reform.

The hard issue is economic and monetary union. The argument of the Right and some on the Left is that by losing control over the exchange rate we might be locked into a currency union with countries more economically efficient, resulting in recession and unemployment. If we were to join a single currency without real economic convergence, that might well be so. I can't resist pointing out that this is in effect an argument for the freedom to devalue, and reflects somewhat poorly on the Right's economic management since 1979. And if devaluation were the answer to Britain's problems we would have solved them a long time ago – the pound having halved in value in relation to the Deutschmark since 1979.

But the determining argument should surely be our national economic interests. To rule out a single currency for ever, now, would be folly. Again, however, other European countries are far less anxious to rush into currency union than our Euro-sceptics pretend. Britain, fully participating in any such discussions and respected in Europe, can ensure that it is

211

rational economics that govern these questions, and any proposed timetable, not politics.

More than Europe – the Asia Pacific

So Europe is vital for Britain. But there is a danger that Europe
envelops our foreign policy. Britain's role in the world is not
confined to Europe. We have always sought out opportunities
abroad. We have heavy investments in America, Latin America
and Asia – and not just in former British possessions like India,
Pakistan, Malaysia, Singapore. Britain is the largest European
investor in China.

Because of our colonial and Commonwealth links, our
commercial interests in Asia have traditionally been much
stronger than those of other European powers. But these
powers are alive to the opportunities in the region, and we
should build on our lead rather than cede it.

British strength in design and construction, power plants,
water treatment, airports, ports, telecoms and transportation
will help Britain participate in building much-needed infrastructure for East Asia.

The greatest promise for economic growth and therefore
for investments, trade and services in East Asia is China. It
is therefore important after 1 July 1997 that Britain enjoys
constructive relations with China, with, I hope, the present
problems properly resolved. Britain also favours building links
between Europe and East Asia, as the Asia/Europe Leaders'
Meeting in 1996 indicates. Ties between the two regions
should be strengthened. Asia Pacific has institutional links with
America and should have links with Europe. Again, Asian
countries will be more interested in increasing ties with Britain
if we have influence in Europe. A Britain without influence
in Europe is a Britain less valuable as a partner.

So the Labour government I hope to lead will have its sights
set firmly beyond as well as within Europe. But it will be
outward-looking, internationalist and committed to free and
open trade, not an outdated and misguided narrow
nationalism.

Conclusion

There are two final reflections on the changing nature of politics. First, the culture of politics should start to catch up with its reality. There will, inevitably, be overlap between Left and Right in the politics of the twenty-first century. The era of the grand ideologies – all-encompassing, all-pervasive, total in their solutions, and often dangerous – is over. In particular, the battle between market and public sector is over. There will be boundary disputes but not war (apart, possibly, from the more extreme manifestations of the Right).

This should start to reflect itself in a more open, more pluralistic style of government, with a more healthy market in ideas across Left/Right divides. The value systems and the objectives will differ, but there will be some policy convergence and we should be relaxed, not tribal, about this.

Secondly, though this may seem unwise for a politician to say, politicians should explain these challenges more honestly to the public and in the process challenge them. Part of the disaffection from politics is the belief political parties tend to foster that government can do it all – 'Vote for us and we'll cure it' politics.

At an early stage of political development – and, remember, this century was almost three decades old before there was universal suffrage in Britain – people really did look to government for all the answers. But, partly in the face of the change revolution, governments are less able to fashion entirely the destiny of their nation. Partly, too, the problems are deeper and more diverse. But most of all, as a result of economic and social progress, government does not have the power over its citizens simply to enforce the change it wants. It cannot just direct and insist. There are a myriad of individual choices that go to make up the economic and social life of a nation.

This is a good development, but it means we need to start sharing responsibility with the people, enabling desirable consequences to be achieved but not pretending they can be achieved without the people working for them too. You cannot legislate for family life. You cannot direct moral purpose. You can have all the police you want, but they won't cut crime on their own. Devolving power, pushing it down to local communities, can help. But there is no substitute for the active will of the people, and politicians should be far stronger in their leadership in asserting the need for such a will to prove itself.

From a speech to the Newscorp Leadership Conference, Hayman Island, Australia, 17 July 1995

22 New Community, New Individualism

Politics this century has alternated between the ideologies of crude individualism and collectivism. What is required today is to define a new relationship between citizen and community for the modern world. The task for the Labour Party and the left-of-centre is to make itself a credible expression of that relationship.

I don't link the Left to this task just because I am a member of the Labour Party. The phase of politics we are in now – which recognises the limitations of crude individualism – is one naturally suited to the Left. The country now wants and needs a confident, revitalised left-of-centre. Perhaps the most frustrating part of being in opposition is the instinctive belief that the Left could, if only it wanted to, shape the politics of the next generation. But that can be achieved only if the failures of the past are properly faced and a clear modern identity is established in which people can believe.

The first fifty years of this century saw huge and necessary social change. The century began with no welfare state, no universal suffrage, trade unions barely able to function legally, and a class structure in which the upper, middle and lower ranks were sharply delineated. The majority were without their own homes, without suitable or well-paid employment, and had little or no education. They saw their only hope in collective action: what they could not achieve alone they could do together. Economic forces of mass production were pushing them closer together anyway. So trade unions sprang up, and soon trade unionists wanted their own political representation to protect and advance their interests.

The state grew as the instrument of intervention to bring increased opportunity, to guarantee the basic amenities of life and – through better housing, employment, health and education – to allow people to prosper. The state became powerful – as indeed it was intended to be. It employed a lot of people.

215

It raised taxes to carry on its work of intervention. In time, living standards increased and the fruits of growth were much more widely shared.

There is a myth that at some point the nature of the people themselves then changed: they were collectively minded and became selfish. In fact, if you speak even to miners in County Durham about voting Labour in 1945, never mind the south of England, they weren't voting for everyone else or for some abstract notion of the public good: they were voting for a collectivist government because that government was going to do good by them. They would get on in life as a result, and their hope was that their children would not spend their lives underground in the way that they were forced to.

People didn't change. Society changed. Alongside the vested interests of capital and wealth sat the vested interests of the state and the public sector − not always faithfully delivering what they were supposed to. What's more, an increasingly prosperous electorate was paying more taxes to fund the state. They became consumers, anxious to participate in the luxuries of life which the better-offs had always taken for granted. A conflict was born between the desire of the individual to consume and the necessity for us all to invest. Moreover, the old base of the economy was breaking up − and with it notions of 'class' based on a static view of the processes of production.

In retrospect, it is easier to see that these changes were actually taking root in the 1950s, but their political focus was blurred. By the 1970s that focus had become sharper. There was an antagonism towards the institutions of the collective − a perception, rightly or wrongly, that rather than making people free they were holding people back. Thatcherism caught this mood. It pitted individual enterprise against collective action, and set about dismantling collective power in the name of individual freedom.

It is probably too soon to judge, but it may be that even those on the Right will eventually decide that Thatcherism was better at destroying than creating, better at plucking out weeds than in planting new seeds.

Today, however, we are in a new phase of development.

216

The supposed changes of the Thatcherite revolution have turned out to be less enduring and more questionable than its supporters wished. In particular, the fragility of our economic position has become painfully transparent. There is no desire in the country to go back; but no wish to stand still either. People do not regret that collectivism in its old form was challenged, but they do not have much faith in the crude individualism that replaced it.

It is not that people now want to see the end of a market economy, any more than, even during the heyday of Thatcherism, they wanted an end to the welfare state. But they recognise that the problems we face cannot be solved by the market alone. Economically, we are not competitive because we lack sufficient capacity and skilled labour. We have failed to invest in building and modernising our industry over a long period of time, and are poorer as a result. Our public

---

The founding principle, the guiding principle of the Labour Party is the belief in community and society. It's the notion that for individuals to advance you require a strong and a fair community behind you. Now that founding principle – the power of the community to advance the individual, breaking down vested interests that hold them back, granting opportunity to people – is as relevant now as it's ever been. In my view, the trouble with not just the Labour Party but indeed most of the left-of-centre parties, whether it's in Europe or indeed the Democrats in the States, was that that founding principle got confused at a certain point with particular policies for particular ages or generations. And what is necessary is to retrieve that notion of community action to further the individual and apply it anew and afresh to the age in which we live. And I don't think that means a ditching of our ideology or a ditching of our traditions. On the contrary, I would argue that you're actually fulfilling them – that it's not in fact simply a new revisionism: it's actually a new radicalism.

From The Revisionist Tendency, *BBC Radio 4, 18 March 1993*

---

services are bad and in urgent need of improvement. At work, many people remain badly treated and underpaid, in need of proper union representation. Socially, we are severely divided, with the growth of an underclass that may be a minority but is frighteningly large. The notion that the less the government does the better for the country just seems outdated. There is an inchoate but perceptible belief that we have lost our way – that we need, but have not got, a more clearly shared sense of community. The word 'community' is used in many different ways, and not always happily, but for me it expresses the mutuality of both interest and obligation that rises above a narrow view of self-interest. It allows a more enlightened and actually a more rational idea of self-interest, and by placing the individual within society, rather than apart from it, recognises that people need to cooperate as well as compete.

There is therefore a desire to regain our identity as a society, to advocate and use social action once again – but only in a way that learns from the excesses and failings of the past and does not repeat them.

What, then, should the new relationship between society and individual consist of?

First, it involves a new concept of citizenship, in which rights and responsibilities go together and where we cease to posit an entirely false choice between social and personal responsibility. As is so clear the more you examine the rise in crime and social disorder in Britain, the problem has been that the Left has tended to undervalue individual responsibility and the Right has ignored the influence of social conditions. Indeed, to the Right, talk of the link between social conditions and crime is to excuse crime. So the obvious common sense – namely that children who are brought up with no chance of a job, poor education, family breakdown, and in bad housing, are more likely to drift into crime than those who are not – is denied.

A modern notion of citizenship gives rights but demands obligations, shows respect but wants it back, grants opportunity but insists on responsibility. So the purpose of economic and social policy should be to extend opportunity, to remove the underlying causes of social alienation. But it should also take tough measures to ensure that the chances that are given are taken up.

This means that constitutional reform becomes integral, not peripheral. The fundamental rights of the citizen should be guaranteed, with the ability to challenge the state or the

Labour's commitment to a Freedom of Information Act is clear. We want to end the obsessive and unnecessary secrecy which surrounds government activity and make government information available to the public unless there are good reasons not to do so. And we want to open up the quango state and the appointed bodies which will of course exist under any government but which should operate in a manner which exposes their actions to proper public scrutiny.

The Act would also be of practical use to individuals. In recent years we have finally been allowed to have access to our medical records, thanks in large part to the efforts of the Campaign for Freedom of Information. But why should we stop there? Why should what is held on other personal files also not be available for us to see? At present we have a mishmash of rules which allows us to see some files and not others, partly dependent on whether they are held on computer or held manually. But I believe there is a strong case for taking a consistent approach to giving people access to what is held on file about them — subject, of course, to some obvious exemptions.

The Act could also contain provisions similar to those outlined in the Public Interest Disclosure Bill which is designed to protect those who reveal evidence of serious malpractice provided they are acting in good faith and have raised the matter internally first. This is not so different from the requirement in the new code for civil servants to report 'illegal, improper or unethical' activity in government where they see it. Again, what is important is to protect the public interest.

From a speech at the Freedom of Information Awards, London,
25 March 1996

government. Local government – heading for dereliction – should be reborn so that decisions are taken closer to where people live. The process and machinery of government should be opened up and made accountable.

Secondly, this new relationship between society and individual needs new principles of public intervention and action. Economically, it requires the creation of a genuine partnership between public and private sector, the purpose of which is to intervene to enhance individual economic opportunity and rebuild the economic base.

We need new instruments of public intervention. In this, the voluntary sector has a central role to play. The Left has for too long misunderstood this sector's role as being nine-teenth-century charity, while the Right uses it as a convenient way to relieve government of its own responsibilities. In fact the voluntary sector can often provide services more effectively and more creatively than either public or private sector. The voluntary sector today is of course made up of much more than 'volunteers': the vast majority of those who work in charities are paid to work. But there are many thousands who do 'volunteer' in the traditional sense, and people who volunteer to give service to our community should be praised for the work they do.

Local government is also utterly central to a regeneration of the principles of government intervention. The destruction of local government is one of the most foolish – almost wicked – dogmas of the Thatcher years. The stupidity of one or two councils has been used as a cover for the wholesale dismantling of a large part of our machinery of government. Yet, properly harnessed to clear public policy objectives, we should be seeking to do more, not less at a local level.

Binding all this together is the notion of rebuilding a modern view of community, where interdependence and independence are both recognised, where the existence of a strong and cohesive society is considered essential to the fulfilment of individual aspiration and progress. To use the old language, we need collective action that advances individual freedom and is not at the expense of it – a fusion of cooperative action and individual expertise.

So we come to the second part of the argument: the Labour Party as the credible expression of this new relationship between society and individual. It is here that the economic and social changes in the country meet the need for political change in the Labour Party. As the former changes happened, support for Labour declined, from a peak of over 50 per cent in 1951 to just under 27 per cent in 1983. Yet it is Labour, because of its historical commitment to social action, that is best placed to take up the challenge the country now faces.

The most basic belief of the Left is that people are not individuals in isolation from one another but members of a community and society who owe obligations to one another as much as to themselves and who depend on each other, in part at least, to succeed. It is from this ideological core and the idea of using the power of community or social action to advance individual liberty that all notions of democratic socialism or social democracy stem.

The reason Labour lost in 1992, as in the previous four elections, is not complex, it is simple: society changed and we did not change sufficiently with it.

The changes in social composition, the breakup of the old class structure, mean that to form a new electoral majority the Left has to reach out beyond its traditional base. This reaching out has to be based on an appeal about the values and nature of our society, not on a snapshot of its economy.

Most important of all, such a reaching out – creating a basis of support that is 'value'-based, not simply 'class'-based, certainly in the traditional economic sense – is not a jettisoning of principle. The principles of the party surely *are* its values. It is the means of their implementation that will and should change with each generation. To tie ourselves to the policy perspective of one era is to chain ourselves to history rather than learn from it. Nor does changing mean abandoning traditional support for the poor and unemployed, because this strategy of change is precisely what is required to win power, and it is the absence of power and the impotence of Opposition that is the real let-down for them.

The process of what is called 'modernisation' is in reality, therefore, the application of enduring, lasting principles for a new generation – creating not just a modern party and organisation, but a programme for a modern society, economy and constitution. It is not destroying the Left's essential ideology: on the contrary, it is retrieving it from an intellectual and political muddle.

From the Charities Aid Foundation tenth Arnold Goodman Charity Lecture,
London, 8 July 1993

23 Our Common Environment

The essence of the left-of-centre is that it believes that the individual prospers best within a strong, cohesive society and that such a society has to be built around a sense of mutual responsibility. Our relations with each other are not simply market-based: they require social and moral principles to underpin them. This is what the concept of stakeholding is about. We have to balance the interests of all – not just the producer, but the consumer; not just economic growth, but the environment.

So the left-of-centre, I believe, is the natural home of those concerned about the environment. Such concern is founded on mutuality, on what is around you, not just on you as an individual. That mutuality extends not merely between people in one generation but between generations.

I believe the important thing is not that the country goes green from time to time, or that there is a resurgence of green politics. What is important is the notion that the environment is a fundamental building-block of a stable community.

I think it is important to look at the environment broadly. Sometimes people don't talk about the environment directly but about their quality of life, about the countryside, or about what the future will hold.

Consider these facts:

* over two-thirds of the population in the UK use recycled or ozone-friendly goods;

* there are over 800,000 members of the Royal Society for the Protection of Birds;

* there has been an explosion in the health-food industry.

What conclusion should we draw? I believe it is that people from all backgrounds and all parts of the country care about the air they breathe, the food they eat, the other species that live alongside us on this planet.

The British public are ahead of the game. They don't need

politicians telling them that the environment is important. They know it is. They are telling us that it matters. And they don't like those who damage it.

For these people it is not the economic case for protecting the environment that drives them on, though there is a powerful one, but the moral case. I understand the power of that moral case. And so do the people who protest against the pollution of our rivers, those outraged by French nuclear testing in the South Pacific, those who are angry at the destruction of bird life, marine life and coastline in South Wales. These are people who care passionately about the world around them. And they want government to provide a stronger lead.

But the environmental debate is about more than the countryside and our immediate physical environment. It is now linked in the public's mind to our most pressing concerns, such as crime, health, the welfare of our children, and the quality of the air they breathe and the water they drink. Most significantly of all, environmental concerns are tied up with fears and hopes for the future – what kind of Britain and what kind of world our children will inherit. For the environment stretches far beyond national borders. It encompasses issues of global pollution, climate change, resource depletion, declining biodiversity, and massive population increase.

Our Changing Environment: The Facts
We therefore depend on the integrity of the environment for our survival and that of generations yet to come. It is important not to become too doom-laden or panic-stricken about the pressures on our environment – governments and people can

---

The EU can make an important difference to the lives of our people on the environment. By acting together Europe can take the lead in action to clean up the toxic legacy of Communism in the CIS and central and eastern Europe. European-level cooperation to achieve this will be essential. Pollution is no respecter of frontiers.

From a speech to the Friedrich-Ebert Stiftung, Bonn, 30 May 1995

---

and do act to preserve it. But the problems do need to be faced. No government can ever promise to do everything that the environmental lobby wants. It would not be responsible to do so. It is not just that there will always be hard and stark choices: there need to be fine judgements too. The responsible course is to analyse the facts and incorporate them into decision-making, rather than ignore them and hope they will go away.

One of the most serious problems we face is that of climate change. There can be no absolute certainty about climate change until it has happened, but the 2,000 scientists consulted by the Intergovernmental Panel on Climate Change concluded that the new evidence indicates 'a detectable human influence on global climate'. Their conclusions mean there are risks of further deforestation, further damage to human health, and changing rain patterns. The fact that major insurance companies are setting up projects to examine the effects of the so-called greenhouse effect perhaps tells us something about the risks we may be running.

Another problem is human population growth. Since 1930 the world population has more than doubled, to 5.8 billion. By 2025 the prediction is 8.5 billion. Environmental degradation, especially of land quality, contributes to increasing famine and poverty.

The story nearer home is not much better. We are continuing to pollute our seas and rivers. Only recently we saw the tragedy – according to many an avoidable tragedy – of thousands of tonnes of oil leaking into the sea from the *Sea Empress*, damaging miles of coastline and smothering hundreds of birds in oil.

Industrial and commercial development and modern farming are continuing to have a profound impact on our countryside and wildlife. Species of once common farmland birds such as the lapwing and kestrel have declined sharply over the past thirty years. According to the Council for the Preservation of Rural England, we are losing rural land to urban development at the rate of 11,000 hectares a year. The impact of development, roads and traffic is eroding the tranquillity – the peace and quiet – of our countryside. At the same time many areas of our inner cities remain derelict.

Labour's Approach

One of my first acts as leader of the Labour Party was to rewrite the party's constitution. Many of us felt that the old Clause IV no longer reflected the goals of the Labour Party, and we wanted to replace it with a modern statement of our values. As I attended meetings up and down the country to discuss our aims and values with party members, some of the most compelling speakers for change argued that the old Clause IV was inadequate precisely because it did not refer to environmental protection. For people of my generation it is as natural to think of including a reference to the environment as it is to equality of opportunity as a core element in our values. It is for this reason that our new constitution states that we will work for a dynamic economy, a just society, an open democracy and a healthy environment which we protect, enhance and hold in trust for future generations.

Labour has, of course, always believed that good government means good environmental government. Keir Hardie's first Labour manifesto included the reforestation of Lancashire as one of its ten proposals! The 1945 Labour government was recognised across the world as a great reforming government, setting up as it did the National Health Service and the welfare state, and rebuilding the British economy from the rubble of the war. But what we must not forget is that in the midst of this social and economic reform the government was also addressing the most pressing environmental concerns of the day in half a dozen pieces of legislation. The Water Act in 1945 regulated the supply of water to our towns and cities; the National Parks and Access to the Countryside Act in 1949 created Britain's National Parks and introduced new rights of access to the countryside for people throughout Britain. The government of the day recognised, as I do, that the environment was not just a middle-class issue, but one critical to all people's quality of life.

> Our new constitution states that we will work for a healthy environment which we protect, enhance and hold in trust for future generations

The new Labour Party is founded on a determination to apply traditional values to new conditions in new ways. We

226

now have access to more and better science and information about the world round us. We must take stock of the transformation wrought by increasing globalisation, the opportunities and challenges thrown up by massive social change, and the cynicism and apathy about government and decision-makers. I want Labour to be at the fore in shaping the evolving debate.

New Problems, New Solution, New Thinking

Our current policy statement on the environment, *In Trust for Tomorrow*, was a very important document, for it helped to demolish two myths. It argued that environmental protection and social justice could be achieved together, and it stated that high environmental standards could improve rather than damage our competitiveness. The party is now in the process of setting priorities and translating the contents of *In Trust for Tomorrow* into a programme for government.

The arguments now centre on the idea of sustainable development. Like many other people, I am persuaded by the Brundtland Commission's definition of environmentally sustainable development as being 'development that meets the needs of the present generation without compromising the ability of future generations to meet their own needs'. Social and economic development need to take place within the limits of the environment's capacity to produce resources, regenerate itself, and absorb the effects of human activity.

But many in the environmental movement know that to take people with them there have to be social and economic benefits too. Friends of the Earth have launched a campaign on the links between good environmental practice and jobs and health, the World Wide Fund for Nature one on jobs and the environment. 'Forum for the Future' has been launched, and the 'Real World' initiative will for the first time in the UK bring together environmental, development, social-justice and democratic-renewal organisations. I welcome the fact that so many environmentalists now recognise that for lasting change to come about we need to explore the common ground between social justice and the environment.

The coalition for change stretches further. Businesses are beginning to recognise the economic benefits of integrating

227

environmental consideration into their strategic decisions.
Bodies such as the CBI and the Advisory Committee on
Business and the Environment are placing an increasing
emphasis on the need to integrate the environment into
business decision-making. And government is learning slowly
that environmentalism is not a fad which will go away.

Mr Gummer is not winning the argument on the environment within the Conservative Party. The government has
published very worthy reports on sustainable development,
but many recommendations remain unfulfilled. The second
report of the Panel on Sustainable Development notes that
the government's commitment to targets has been 'patchy',
that the panel is 'disappointed that proposals relating to pollution of surface water, sulphur emissions and the use of sol-
vents have so far been delayed'. Most significantly, the
government has still failed to respond to the Royal Commission
on Transport and the Environment in 1994.

So how is Labour pushing the agenda forward? I believe
that our response must be threefold:

★ to show clear leadership internationally and integrate
  environmental considerations into decision-making;

★ to seek new solutions which promote economic efficiency,
  social justice and environmental sustainability together;
  and

★ to encourage community action and local democracy.

Leadership
No nation is immune from the changes to the world climate.
Likewise, pollution is not restricted within national boundaries. We must act together on an international basis. Of
course there will be dispute about the changes which we are
now experiencing, and we must use the best scientific evidence
available on which to base our decisions so we can take the
appropriate action.

That is why Labour is committed to taking action to reduce
so-called greenhouse gases. The reason the government is on
track to meet its target of reducing CO_2 emissions to 1990
levels by the year 2000 is not through a comprehensive pro-

gramme to reduce emissions. In fact it has cut the scheme which provides help for the old and vulnerable to cut fuel bills by using less energy through proper home insulation. The reason it is on target is because there are more gas-powered stations and because Britain has suffered one of the most serious recessions in Europe.

Compare this with the target of *In Trust for Tomorrow* of reducing CO_2 emissions by 20 per cent by 2010. I do not claim that this will be easy to achieve, but we will take action on a number of fronts to try to meet that target – through a nationwide energy-efficiency scheme for homes; by our proposals for a new integrated transport strategy, encouraging the use of swift and environmentally friendly forms of transport; and by a partnership with industry and business to drive down their emissions.

There is also much scope for action at the European level. If we are to tackle pollution which crosses national boundaries and to ensure that our businesses compete on a level playing-field then we need to work constructively in Europe. Much European legislation has been successful. It has improved the quality of drinking-water across the European Union, and it has required action to clean up beaches and bathing-waters, improving the environment for marine life. But there remains much more to be done at a European level.

A huge step forward would be to reform the Common Agricultural Policy. It is clearly failing the consumers, the farmers and the countryside. In the thirty years since its inception, the agricultural industry, food production and land use have been transformed. We know now that the CAP is failing to provide the right incentives in rural areas for land management, for the rural economy and for social protection. It is time that we changed its objectives so that it provides the right economic, social and environmental incentives and support for the next century.

Environment, Economy and Social Justice
The second key approach is to seek new initiatives which promote economic efficiency, social justice and environmental protection together. There will always be hard choices.

At home we need to ensure that we look more closely at the environmental impact of our policies, as many progressive companies do, and ensure that environmental considerations are properly integrated. We cannot take appropriate action without knowing the facts. That is why we proposed a Parliamentary Environment Audit Committee in the House of Commons to scrutinise government action.

We now publish indicators of more and more services – from schools, to the Citizen's Charter, to water leakages. It is right that we now look at new indicators of environmental factors too. That is why Labour will push for new environmental indicators to give a broader measure of our country's health and well-being.

I also want to move away from the argument that, when it comes to protecting the environment, something or someone always loses out. There is a tendency to become overly sacrificial about the environment. It is certainly true that there are hard choices to be made in promoting concern for the environment – about the nature of industrial growth, about the incentives we provide for different types of transport, and about how we regulate to discourage pollution. But for too long the equation has been presented as the environment versus jobs, the environment versus competitiveness, protection of the environment hitting the poorest in our society.

I believe that the arguments presented by the party over the last few years have helped dispel these automatic assumptions of conflict. But the relationship of environmental concerns to those of social justice is not always straightforward. The environment will never be protected unless people are convinced that their livelihoods are protected too. The important point is to see how many ways there are in which the drive for social justice can be enhanced by the drive for environmental protection.

Take the economy and the environment. In many cases environmental sustainability and a thriving economy go together. The key to the relationship between the economy and the environment is the concept of environmental productivity. Most industrialised countries are currently environmentally inefficient. They waste energy and resources and produce far more pollution than is necessary for a given level of economic activity. That is bad for the economy and bad for the environment. Protecting the environment means increasing the economy's environmental productivity. It means using resources more efficiently and producing less pollution per unit of output. This is the key to sustainable development.

Evidence from Germany, Japan, the US and Sweden suggests that domestic regulation provides firms with a 'first-mover advantage' in environmental industries, as firms are stimulated to innovate and create new cleaner processes and attractive greener products. We need to see improving environmental standards as an economic opportunity. The world is adopting higher environmental standards, and it is critical that British industry is ready to lead the way.

We need to see improving environmental standards as an economic opportunity

We should never take this to mean the more regulation the better. One good regulation is better than fifty bad ones. We must always be sure that any new regulations – and, what is more, any existing ones – actually serve the purpose for which they are intended in a cost-efficient way. Our task is to achieve the desired outcome.

There are tremendous opportunities for job creation in new environmental technologies. The environmental sector is now very large. The global market is thought to have been worth some $200 billion in 1990, and to be growing at more than 5 per cent a year to $300 billion in the year 2000. A survey by the German government showed that 50 per cent of this market is shared by three countries – Germany, the US and Japan. Britain should also be leading the way with environmental management techniques, building on schemes such as BS 7750 and Eco-management and Audit Scheme (EMAS) through which companies examine and improve their environmental performance.

It is not only through moving into the newly developing markets that business can benefit from adopting practices and investment strategies which protect the environment. There are many examples of where industry has seen economic benefits as well as environmental ones. For instance Tesco is

231

saving over £12 million a year by recycling cardboard and shrink-wrap in its stores, and is employing 700 more people as a result.

It is also vital to ensure that polices pursued for environmental reasons have a positive social impact too. It is for this reason that we so vigorously opposed the introduction of VAT on domestic fuel. We did not believe it was introduced for environmental reasons, and it caused major social hardship for almost no gain in reducing carbon-dioxide emissions. Instead our policy is to cut fuel bills and emissions by a nationwide programme of energy-efficiency work for householders. It will save millions of tonnes of carbon dioxide. It will immeasurably improve the quality of life for those currently living in fuel poverty by cutting fuel bills for many households. And we estimate it could create up to 50,000 new jobs.

For many years environmentalists have argued that the current rate of growth of roads traffic is unsustainable. The roads lobby now agrees. Businesses are crying out for a more strategic approach to transport planning as their goods are delayed in the snarl-ups on our roads. Commuters already experience crowded, dirty and unpredictable train services, and look for more certainty and better standards. Bus use is dwindling. Car users are fed up with jam after jam. Those who live by roads are suffering the consequences of heavy air and noise pollution.

This country needs a proper integrated transport system. We can't leave our transport system to market forces alone; we must sit down as a country and plan it. These will be the key elements of transport policy:

★ It must be integrated on three levels – national, regional and local – and between different modes of transport: road, rail, air and water. And it must be integrated to take proper account of social, economic and environmental factors.

★ If we are to expect people to use methods of transport other than cars, we must ensure that attractive alternatives are in place. If Britain had the public transport infrastructure it needs, then people would be able to make more environmentally sensitive choices about the way they travel.

★ We must make better use of the planning system to manage transport patterns.

Schemes are already being piloted throughout the country which enable people to make a choice about how they get about. Nottingham's commuter scheme aims to reduce the number of cars with only one occupant. York's scheme aims to reduce reliance on car use and get more people on to their bicycles. We can learn from these local examples how we can promote measures which not only are environmentally sustainable but also create jobs and help unite communities.

Local Community Action
Most people I speak to feel a close attachment to their neighbourhood and local environment. They are proud of their local history and local surroundings. They feel shame when the streets are not clean or local beaches are polluted.

We need to harness the traditional willingness and vigour of British communities to improve their local environment. Over a century ago we saw the rise of the parks movement as local people campaigned for areas of open space and tranquillity for relief from the slums and degradation of their daily lives. Local authorities responded and created parks which became showpieces for the towns. The notice at the opening of the Philips Park in Manchester declared 'This Park was purchased by the People, was made for the People, and is given to the People for their protection.'

Since the Rio Summit, many local authorities have been inspired again to 'think global, act local' under the Local Agenda 21 programme. They have devised local programmes which are designed not only to improve the local quality of life of local residents but to do so sustainably, and they have gained an international reputation for doing so. Labour local authorities are a leading force. The authorities involved have used an open and responsive approach. It is these local Labour authorities which already exemplify the way in which environmental measures not only can provide economic opportunity but also can help some of the most disadvantaged communities in the country:

★ In Kirklees and Lancashire the local councils have pioneered much work under the Local Agenda 21 scheme. They have developed new monitoring systems which are available and usable by local people to find out the conditions of their local environment – from the pollution in the rivers to the quality of air in their streets.

★ In Cardiff and other Labour-controlled areas, recycling schemes have resulted in a massive reduction in the amount of waste going to landfill.

★ In Sheffield the city council has worked with Sheffield Heat and Power to generate energy for the city from its waste. It provides 3,520 homes, 64 city buildings, and both universities with heat, saving 34,000 tonnes of carbon dioxide from being released into the atmosphere.

I don't want just the people in these local authorities to have the benefit of this good practice: I want to see these sort of schemes over the whole country. That is why Labour will place a duty on every local authority to promote the economic, social and environmental well-being of its area and will promote the Local Agenda 21initiative.

Conclusion

If we want a Britain we will be proud to hand on to our children and grandchildren, it must be one in which the environment – in all its manifestations – is protected and enhanced. The Conservatives want a Britain of low wages, low standards and low achievement. Labour's environmental vision is of a high-wage, high-skill economy with high environmental standards.

Our commitment to the environment appears in many areas of policy. It is not just the environmental-protection portfolio that is important. Our health policy commits us to a Minister for Public Health to ensure that we have the highest health standards throughout the country. As part of our policy on open government we want proper environmental information to be available to the public. Our plans to get young people off the dole and back to work include an option to join a green task force.

Our environmental commitment is part of our belief in the need to modernise Britain's economy and society. We will not be able to fulfil this commitment alone. We will need to work with environmental movements, individuals, businesses and local government. But the environment will be at the heart of our decision-making – where it belongs.

From a speech to the Royal Society, London, 27 February 1996

24   *The Rights We Enjoy, the Duties We Owe*

Individuals prosper best within a strong and cohesive society. Especially in a modern world, we are interdependent. Unless we act together to provide common services, prepare our industry and people for industrial and technological challenge, and guarantee a proper system of law and government, we will be worse off as individuals. In particular, those without the best start in life through birth are unlikely to make up for it without access to the means of achievement. Furthermore – though this may be more open to debate – a society which is fragmented and divided, where people feel no sense of shared purpose, is unlikely to produce well-adjusted and responsible citizens.

But a strong society should not be confused with a strong state, or with powerful collectivist institutions. That was the confusion of early Left thinking. It was compounded by a belief that the role of the state was to grant rights, with the language of responsibility spoken far less fluently. In a further strain of thinking, connected with the libertarian Left, there was a kind of social individualism espoused, where you 'did your own thing'. In fact this had very little to do with any forms of left-of-centre philosophy recognisable to the founders of the Labour Party.

The reaction of the Right, after the advent of Mrs Thatcher, was to stress the notion of the individual as against the state. Personal responsibility was extolled. But then a curious thing happened. In a mirror-image of the Left's confusion, the Right started to define personal responsibility as responsibility not just for yourself but to yourself. Outside of a duty not to break the law, responsibility appeared to exclude the broader notion of duty to others. It became narrowly acquisitive and rather destructive. The economic message of enterprise – of the early 1980s – became a philosophy of 'Get what you can'.

All over the Western world, people are searching for a new

236

political settlement which starts with the individual but sets him or her within the wider society. People don't want an overbearing state, but they don't want to live in a social vacuum either. It is in the search for this different, reconstructed, relationship between individual and society that ideas about 'community' are found. 'Community' implies a recognition of interdependence, but not overweening government power. It accepts that we are better equipped to meet the forces of change and insecurity through working together. It provides a basis for the elements of our character that are cooperative as well as competitive, as part of a more enlightened view of self-interest.

People know they face a greater insecurity than ever before: a new global economy; massive and rapid changes in technology; a labour market where half the workers are women; a family life that has been altered drastically; telecommunications and media that visit a common culture upon us and transform our expectations and behaviour.

Duty is the cornerstone of a decent society

This insecurity is not just about jobs or mortgages – though of course these are serious problems. It is about a world that in less than a lifetime has compressed the historical change of epochs. It is bewildering. Even religion – once a given – is now an exception. And of course the world has the nuclear weapons to destroy itself many times over. Look at our children and the world into which they are growing. What parent would not feel insecure?

People need rules which we all stand by, fixed points of agreement which impose order on chaos. That does not mean a return to the old hierarchy of deference. That is at best nostalgia, at worst reactionary. We do not want old class structures back. We do not want women chained to the sink. We do not want birth rather than merit to become once again the basis of personal advancement. Nor does it mean bureaucracy and regulation. Bad and foolish rules are bad and foolish rules, but they do not invalidate the need to have rules.

Duty is the cornerstone of a decent society. It recognises more than self. It defines the context in which rights are given. It is personal; but it is also owed to society. Respect for others

– responsibility to them – is an essential prerequisite of a strong and active community. It is the method through which we can build a society that does not subsume our individuality but allows it to develop healthily. It accords instinct with common sense. It draws on a broader and therefore more accurate notion of human nature than one formulated on insular self-interest. The rights we receive should reflect the duties we owe. With power should come responsibility.

Duty is a Labour Value

The assertion that each of us is our brother's keeper has motivated the Labour movement since the mid nineteenth century. It is time to reassert what it really means.

The Left has always insisted that it is not enough to argue that our only duty is not to infringe on the lives and rights of others – what might be called negative duty. A minimal community creates a society of minimal citizens. It is a broader notion of duty that gives substance to the traditional belief of the Left in solidarity. This was well understood by the early pioneers of socialism. William Morris put it colourfully: 'Fellowship is life, and lack of fellowship is death.'

But solidarity and fellowship are the start of the story, and not the end, because they will be achieved only on the basis of both social equality and personal responsibility.

The historians of *English Ethical Socialism* Norman Dennis and A.H. Halsey argue that William Cobbett, who lived before the word 'socialism' achieved common currency, took it for granted that people stood a better chance of having a happy life if they were not selfish. They write that 'a person matching Cobbett's ideal, therefore, was one who enjoyed the rights and performed the duties of citizenship'.

Early socialists like Robert Owen understood very clearly that a society which did not encourage people voluntarily to carry out their responsibilities to others would always be in danger of slipping either into the anarchy of mutual indifference – and its corollary, the domination of the powerless by the powerful – or the tyranny of collective coercion, where the freedom of all is denied in the name of the good of all.

Ethical socialists have long asserted that there was and is a distinctive socialist view of both human nature and social morality. R.H. Tawney put it clearly in the 1920s: 'Modern society is sick through the absence of a moral ideal,' he wrote. 'What we have been witnessing ... both in international affairs and in industry, is the breakdown of society on the basis of rights divorced from obligations.' And G.D.H. Cole said that 'A socialist society that is to be true to its egalitarian principles of human brotherhood must rest on the widest possible diffusion of power and responsibility, so as to enlist the active participation of as many of its citizens in the tasks of democratic self-government.'

In his book *Liberals and Social Democrats*, the historian Peter Clarke drew a distinction between 'moral reformers' and 'mechanical reformers'. The moral reformers were the ethical socialists like Tawney and Morris. They looked around the communities in which they lived, and called for a new moral impulse to guide them. The mechanical reformers, on the other hand, concentrated on the technicalities of social and economic reform. They were severely practical in their outlook.

Values without practical policies are useless; but policies without a set of values guiding them give no sense of meaning or direction to public life.

Education

Education, as I have said elsewhere, will be the passion of my government. But it cannot be dependent on teachers and government alone. Parents have a duty: to their children, and to others affected by their children. Let me give some examples.

Truancy is a growing problem in many areas, notably the inner cities. Some classes are depleted by 20 or 30 per cent because of truanting. What are truant children doing? They are up to mischief or worse.

What too many people forget is that our education system is founded on two principles: the duty of the local education authority to provide education for the children in its area, and the legal obligation on parents to send their children to school. That latter responsibility is absolute, and LEAs have the authority to take parents to court for continued non-attendance at school by children. For many years this power has fallen into disuse, but the problem is so serious that some local authorities are now using this power to good effect. The number of parents directly affected is small, but the signal to all parents is very strong. Local authorities are saying that they will not tolerate non-attendance at school.

In Lewisham in 1994 the cases of twenty-two children completed the process that ended up in court appearances, though many parents had been forced to mend their ways before their case reached court. Eleven fines of between £20 and £150 were imposed on parents. And the message was clear: attendance at school is non-negotiable.

Of course, parents are every child's first teachers. As a first step towards encouraging a sense of responsibility for children's schooling, schools can also involve parents more closely in their child's learning. I think that home–school contracts, detailing the rights and responsibilities of both schools and parents, can play an important role in ensuring that every child gets the best start. The contracts cover issues like attendance and time-keeping, homework and standards. They are a practical way of building a new partnership between parents, children and teachers.

Of course, parents are every child's first teachers

The contracts are agreed between school and family. They are subject to regular update. And they recognise the essential truth about our education system – that children and parents are not simple customers in a market, but joint producers of education. Teachers teach – and they must teach well – but parents are central to the process too.

Housing
Similar arguments apply to housing. The state has a duty to house the homeless. It should also try to provide affordable rented housing. On that we should be clear. But, equally, those who are housed by the state have a duty to behave responsibly. That is the contract. Families have the right to be housed, but they do not have any right to terrorise those around them – be it with violence, racial abuse or noise. If

tenants do not fulfil their side of the bargain – particularly after repeated warnings – the contract is broken.

Local authorities will soon have the powers to confiscate hi-fi equipment in cases of unacceptable noise. I welcome government attention to this problem.

* More than one fifth of the population say their lives are being spoiled by noisy neighbours.

* There are over 160,000 complaints about noise made every year – a figure that has tripled in the last ten years.

* And any MP will tell you this is a major issue at any surgery.

The problem is not just a matter of noise – though that is the most common complaint. It is also about control of children. Sometimes it concerns rubbish. Sometimes dangerous dogs. But councils up and down the country are tackling these problems. Since the Conservatives do not control many councils, I am pleased to say that many of the initiatives are in Labour authorities.

We should not be afraid to assert that the state's duty is to the whole community – the vast majority of decent tenants – as well as to the individual. What is needed is not a general reduction in tenants' rights, but effective action to deal with those tenants who consistently refuse to behave reasonably but make life a misery for those around them. In failing to take action against individuals who cause trouble, the state fails in its duty to the rest of the community. We will examine how we improve the procedures for taking action where these circumstances apply.

Citizens' Service

Responsibility is not simply taught through lectures but is learned through experience, and that is why I support the creation of a Citizens' Service scheme for young people, to help ally their energy and ideas with community work that needs to be done. This embodies the idea of the 'something for something' society that I want to build in Britain, combining mutual respect and individual fulfilment, mutuality and individuality.

Pilot projects are under way around the country, coordinated by the Prince's Trust and Community Service Volunteers, and already lessons are emerging:

★ the scheme must be voluntary;

★ it must give space for local initiative, and promote development from the bottom up;

★ it must be a partnership of government, the voluntary sector and business; and

★ it should bring young people together to work in teams.

Of course, the notion of duty goes far wider than the individual. Companies have responsibilities too – not only to their shareholders, but also to their employees, to the communities in which they operate, to the environment, and to the nation for which they set an example on issues like pay.

When Conservatives accuse us of the politics of envy over the pay and perks of the heads of privatised utilities, they really do show how out of touch they are. These people are, by and large, in monopoly service industries. They have guaranteed profit levels. It is not true to say, certainly of gas and electricity and water, that they were loss-making before privatisation. They were not. The public, tightening its belt and facing deep insecurity, rightly feels not envy but anger at the behaviour of these people. And it sets an appalling example to industry as a whole.

This applies to politicians too. They should not promise what they cannot deliver. And they should not lie to Parliament or the electorate.

So we can rebuild civil society in different ways, but it remains essential to agree that such a society is desirable, that it must have rules founded on a clear sense of duty, and then to debate openly what those rules should be. Duty and civil society are inseparable. Without the first, the second breaks down; without the second, the first is an idle dream. By uniting the two, we can overcome the central weakness of the individualism of the new Right while avoiding the pitfalls of the old Left.

It will be hard. There are sacrifices in it. But it is not a denial of self-interest: rather, it is its more rational fulfilment. To quote Cobbett again, 'Civil society can never have arisen from any motive other than that of the benefit of the whole.'

There are not new truths in politics, merely new ways of interpreting old truths. Each generation looks for its own philosophy and the politics to accompany it. The mood for change now in Britain is more than about opinion polls or feel-good factors. It is a belief that, as a country, we can be better than we were. It is surely time to try.

From the Spectator *Lecture, London, 22 March 1995*

25 Crime and Family Breakdown

There is nothing more destructive or corrosive in Britain today than the tearing of the social fabric and the rupture of social cohesion. We live in a society increasingly scarred by crime, persistent high unemployment, and family and social disintegration. There are some of our young people – a minority, but still significant – who are growing up in a culture almost entirely alienated from society's mainstream. Drug abuse and the crime associated with drugs have risen dramatically. The cost, financially and otherwise, is huge.

The case made here is that the crude individualism of the Tories' governing philosophy since 1979 should be replaced by a project which has at its heart the rebuilding the foundations of a strong civic society, capable of sustaining and backing the efforts and enterprise of the individuals within it. We should leave behind both the narrow and selfish individualism of the present and old notions of state control. Instead we should fashion a new relationship between society and the individual for the future, where the purpose of social action is to liberate individual potential, and where rights and duties go hand in hand.

The facts now cannot be greatly disputed. The consequences of social breakdown in society lie all around us:

★ Crime has more than doubled since 1979.

★ Violent crime has increased by more than 130 per cent.

★ Robberies have risen by over 300 per cent.

★ British citizens are more likely to be a victim of burglary than citizens of any other country in the European Union.

People are more aware of crime and more frightened of crime. Between 1980 and 1993, the number of people who had no experience of crime fell from two-thirds to a half of the adult population.

244

The cost is enormous. Between 1988 and 1992 household-contents insurance premiums have increased by 50 per cent. Our spending on the criminal justice system has doubled since 1979 and now costs the country £9 billion a year. And a survey has shown that the fear of crime is the single most important factor in reducing people's enjoyment in their local area.

It is crucial to recognise that, while everyone is affected by crime, it is the poor and disadvantaged whose quality of life has suffered most. Residents on the poorest estates face a risk of burglary three times the national average – an unbearable burden for poor families.

The irony is that the policies of the Right have ended up destroying the very thing they were designed to create: individual security and fulfilment. Those that are unemployed and dependent on state benefit suffer directly. The rest suffer as a consequence of the social disintegration around them.

The failure is not just one of policy, but of philosophy. For all its professed radicalism, Thatcherism had at its core a return to nineteenth-century liberalism which sees the individual as the sole social actor – expressed most tellingly by the phrase 'There is no such thing as society.' Traditional Tory paternalism was usurped by a fierce belief that all policy must concentrate solely on the individual, free to make life choices.

Increasingly, the intellectual inadequacy of an analysis based on the theoretical rights of individuals without reference to the specific family and community structures in which they live has been recognised. Former supporters of the new Right,

---

Being tough on crime and tough on the causes of crime is not an empty slogan. It recognises that a sensible and effective strategy to cut crime in this country combines personal responsibility and community action; punishment and prevention; condemnation and understanding; a criminal justice system that works and a society that acts.

From 'Change and National Renewal', Leadership Election Statement
1994

---

such as John Gray, have begun to expound the inadequacy of a strictly individualistic ideology. More importantly for practical politics, in the face of the social breakdown detailed above there has been a recognition that unfettered liberalism will produce an atomised, uncaring, rootless society.

The response of the Right – to break up the welfare state and abandon social provision – will merely make the problem worse. It will deepen the sense of alienation, not lift it.

The task of the Left is not to replace this crude individualism with old notions of an overbearing paternalistic state. The task is to rebuild a strong civic society and base it on a modern notion of citizenship, where rights and duties go hand in hand; where the purpose of social action is to develop individual potential, not subjugate it. In particular, we have to counter the historic belief found on the Right, but sometimes also on the Left, that action by society to improve social conditions is incompatible with notions of personal responsibility. In fact the opposite is true. The purpose of social action should not be to substitute social or state action for personal responsibility but, on the contrary, through social improvement to enhance the prospects of self-improvement. This is not to change the traditional philosophy of the Left but to rediscover it.

Take the much-debated link between crime and social factors. People who become unemployed do not, through some Pavlovian reflex, go out and commit criminal offences. There

---

We should make racially motivated violence a specific criminal offence carrying the most severe penalties under the law. We must set up special police units in order to protect those at risk from racial attacks and, where the BNP or any other party is engaged in the publication of propaganda which incites racial violence, Labour will ensure that those responsible are prosecuted to the full power of the law. No one should play politics with race.

From a speech at the party conference, 30 September 1993

---

are many highly stable families that live in poverty, whose children never stray into delinquency. Nor should we seek to disavow personal responsibility for crime. That is, ultimately, to deny individuality. Those who commit crimes should be brought to justice. Not to do so is unjust to their victims. But it requires not a PhD in philosophy, merely a degree of common sense, to understand that, if children grow up in a culture of low opportunity, poor education, little hope of achievement, and unstable family life, notions of mutual respect and good conduct are less likely to appear. Children are affected by families, families by local communities, and communities in turn by the ethos and policy of society as a whole.

That is the case for social change and renewal. And the family and community are important agents of that change. The very notion of 'bringing up' children implies what is obvious: that children grow up subject to and shaped by their parents.

And both they and their parents in turn react to the world around them. The irrationality in the position of the Right – when they deny the impact of social factors on criminality – lies in their absolute insistence that parental control is a crucial factor in crime, but nothing else. There can be no artificial line drawn around the home. Families live in local communities, which are in turn part of a larger society. Indeed, the stronger the community, the stronger the family – and vice versa.

The breakup of family and community bonds is intimately linked to the breakdown in law and order. Both family and community rely on notions of mutual respect and duty. It is in the family that we first learn to negotiate the boundaries of acceptable conduct and to recognise that we owe responsibilities to others as well as to ourselves. We then build out from that family base to the community, and beyond it to society as a whole. The values of a decent society are in many ways the values of the family unit, which is why helping to re-establish good family and community life should be a central objective of government policy. And that cannot be achieved without policies – especially in respect of employment and education – that improve society as a whole.

This is the philosophical and historical framework within which the Labour Party's policies for jobs, education, housing, public services and poverty are set. And their purpose is not just economic in nature, in the sense of improving our material welfare – important though that is. They are also designed specifically to strengthen local communities and improve our quality of life.

It is time to rebuild. The task is urgent and the choice is clear: to manage our decline or reverse it. And the time to start is now.

From a speech to the Family Breakdown and Criminal Activity Conference,
24 May 1994

I do believe there would be less crime under Labour – I believe that absolutely sincerely.

From 'Blair's Britain', Panorama, *BBC Television, 3 October 1994*

---

26 *Valuing Families*

Children raised by two parents in a stable, loving relationship *do* get a head start. But saying that 'Blair Backs Two-Parent Families' does not mean that 'Blair Blasts Single Parents.' Along with most people, I resent the way the Tories have stigmatised single-parent families.

Most single parents are not single parents by choice. We may wish that all marriages could work, but separation and divorce do happen. The father may have left the mother and children without proper financial support, and many single parents perform heroically in raising their children. But it is common sense to say that a child brought up in a stable and well-balanced family is more likely to develop well than one who is not. And that it can be harder – financially and emotionally – to bring up children alone.

Governments don't raise children – families do. But governments can help. Governments have the power to act to cut long-term unemployment, which destroys families just as it destroys communities. Governments can deal with the crisis in housing, which is another important factor in family breakdown.

It is Labour that understands the concerns of ordinary families, struggling to survive and make sense of a world that is changing at a breathtaking pace. This is what so angers me when middle-class commentators pretend that my speeches on duty and the family are somehow about invading Tory territory. They are about restating *Labour's* values.

At a party meeting I spoke to in Glasgow, a woman describing herself as 'just an ordinary housewife, mother and grandmother' stood up and spoke of the grim reality of her life raising a family in an estate ruined by drugs, crime and poor health. It is people like her that want families strengthened, not weakened. It is people like her who most want our children to learn about right and wrong. And it is in the family that those lessons are learned. It is in the family that we learn that we are part of a community, that we don't just think about ourselves but we think about others too.

Politicians should address these issues not because they want to preach or moralise – politicians are the last people who should do that – but because it should be the policy of government to protect and strengthen families, and to include the impact on families in any assessment of their policies.

And we want a government that recognises that women want to balance family and work, and helps them to do so – whether through retraining, child care, a flexible benefits system, career breaks, nursery education, or through recognising that it is women more than men who are at the sharp end of poor schools and hospitals, crime, low pay and job insecurity. This means that men may have to change their attitudes too.

As far back as 1993, a leaked Cabinet paper said that if a child is raised in a stable family with a decent income and access to high-quality education, raising that child is easier. The paper has been ignored by government ever since.

We want fewer politicians spouting about 'family values' and more politicians who value families – whatever their circumstances. Labour will do just that.

From the Sun, *31 March 1995*

You have this debate about single parents as if most single parents want to be single parents. They don't. The vast majority are because their partners have walked out on them for one reason or another, and what I am really saying is that the family is an important unit and people from my political persuasion on the left-of-centre have got to recognise that . . . I don't think it's my job to inflict moral views on people at all, but I think it is important for the Labour Party to talk about the importance of the family and opportunity within the broader community.

From 'Blair's Britain', Panorama, *BBC Television, 3 October 1994*

---

27 Dear Kathryn . . .

You are growing up in a world with many more opportunities than your grandparents had – but in some ways it is also a more dangerous and less secure world. It is a world where there is no such thing as a job for life. So every new skill you learn, every qualification you get, will make you more adaptable and more able to change jobs and fulfil your potential.

Britain is a great nation. A country where we can watch the most exciting sport – Wimbledon, the FA Cup, Test cricket. Where you can listen to the best pop music – the Beatles, Blur, Oasis and Simply Red. A nation that leads the world in fashion, animation, computer software. A country of stunning beauty – the Lake District, the Yorkshire Dales and Moors, the Highlands of Scotland, Snowdonia, the Cotswolds, seaside towns. A nation blessed with a rich language, fine literature, art and architecture – and a unique sense of humour.

Never let anyone say that there is a better place to live than Britain. But never let others tell you that Britain cannot be better. We are a country of talent, but a country that often does not let that talent flourish. At times we seem to be a nation that has become old, tired, resentful. Relying on our past as a great nation long before you were born, rather than working to make us a great nation in the future. Reluctant to face new ideas. Reluctant to take risks. We are no longer a country that, in the words of the opening to *Star Trek*, wants 'to boldly go'. We are less adventurous, daring, forward-looking. Yet our history is all about being outward-looking, imaginative, clever.

I only have to watch you throwing yourself into new activities – acting, playing the piano, or swimming – to realise that the energy and fearlessness of young people is the energy to make Britain once again a country of enthusiasm and new ideas – a young country.

But if we are to take risks as a country and become envied

for today's achievements rather than only those of yesterday, we must support the doers, the innovators, the young entrepreneurs, the wisdom of older people, the creative talent in each of us. We must put in place the opportunities that allow people to get on, and the pillars of security that enable people to be adventurous. That is the way to greater prosperity.

I want a Britain where the NHS is once again a pillar of security. I want entrepreneurs and innovators to get the backing they need to get their ideas off the ground. I want a Britain where people are not stuck on benefit, unable to go out and work to earn a living. And I dream of a nation where as a parent I am less worried about you going out on your own, where crime does not breed insecurity and fear.

I want a Britain where every child has the chance to go to a good school, where they learn to read, write and add up, but, more than that, where they learn to think and use their imagination.

I have pledged to cut class sizes in all our infant schools. We have set out new ways of improving standards in our classrooms and of taking tough and prompt action against failing schools.

I want a Britain where people have faith once again in politics – where they believe that politicians are not just in it for themselves but are MPs because they wish to serve their constituents and their country. I want the UK to be strong because all parts of it are listened to and have the chance to make decisions that will affect their own lives. That is why we plan to devolve power back to local communities – not least through a Scottish Parliament and a Welsh Assembly.

I want Britain to be leading in Europe, so that we can shape Europe to suit Britain's interests rather than being sidelined and humiliated as the decisions get taken elsewhere.

I want a Britain where people grow up to value friendship, love, kindness, decency as much as material wealth. That means responsibility to others as much as ourselves, compassion as well as ambition, a strong and decent society. Not broken up and pulled apart but one nation.

I want all children to grow up with the idealism that we can change society for the better; that things do not have to be as they always have been but can change; that power, wealth and opportunity need not be held in a few hands but can be shared among all the people.

The great causes still exist – tackling poverty and famine and war in the world's developing nations; working together to ensure that we do not destroy nature, scar the world's beauty, and pass on to the next generation a degraded and polluted environment.

I want you to grow up in a united society, held together by common values of decency, tolerance and respect. A society in which every individual has a stake. A society where you are able to fulfil your potential.

There is no greater responsibility than that which a parent has to a child. My duties as a father come first. But it is to help build that better Britain and that united society that I am in politics.

    Love,
      Dad

From Daily Express, *3 January 1996*

28 The Stanley Matthews Culture

Sir Stanley Matthews is a culture, and it is one that in all too many areas of the game has been eroded. He was never booked, let alone sent off, and was always able to find time for the children crowding around the players' entrance, for he knew that without them and their enthusiasm the game's future is bleak.

People talk of the game's crowd-pullers today, and set them alongside their earnings and transfer fees, but did anyone ever pull them like Sir Stan? When he went back to Stoke from Blackpool in 1961, the average gate went up by 25,000. And he'd cost Stoke just £2,500. Even at the peak of his powers, when he was first transferred to Blackpool, he cost just £11,500. Don't let anyone say Blackpool, and football, did not get their money's worth.

He graced three Cup Finals, including perhaps the most memorable of all – the 1953 win over Bolton. As Frank McGhee has reminded us in the *Observer*, it was one of those very rare occasions when journalists in the press box, barred by both tradition and neutrality from applause, rose to cheer, unable to hide their joy at what they had witnessed.

Clearly television has changed the nature of the game, and, far from lamenting that, I welcome the fact that we get the chance to watch so much quality football from all around the world. But try to imagine that 1953 final without a crowd. Try to imagine any big game played merely for the cameras. It just doesn't work. The game needs atmosphere. It needs crowds. And those people who go to football week in week out cannot and should not be taken for granted.

When multi-million-pound transfers are being paid for players that do not begin to compare with Sir Stan, when even average players are paid wages that most of their fans can only dream about, supporters might be forgiven for wondering if there is a link with the high prices many of them are paying for their seats. Football remains the people's sport. But for many people it is becoming too costly. And for many smaller clubs there is a feeling that they are waging a constant fight for survival while the game's giants grow ever bigger.

I understand the importance of marketing and sponsorship spin-offs to clubs, but there is a fine line between marketing and exploitation. I know the pleasure my own children get in identification with their heroes, and the pride we all get in identification with our club or our national side. That explains in part the phenomenal success of football strips. Times change, and fashions change, but not as quickly, surely, as many clubs would have us believe.

When you take travel, tickets and paraphernalia into account, football has become a pricey pastime. And my message is one which Sir Stan never needed reminding of: You cannot take the fans for granted. There is a market, certainly, but there is a community too, and football clubs are a vital part of it.

I do feel unease about much that is happening in British sport, and I believe that much of what is wrong stems from the overemphasis on the individual, and lack of responsibility to the team. When do we ever hear players express shame or regret at being sent off? Why are referees' decisions so frequently met with snarling and swearing all too clear to the people watching either live or on TV? This is not some Corinthian cry for a return to amateurism, but a belief that basic decent values should not be compromised whatever the commercial pressures, whatever the desire for personal reward, fame or glory.

Hugh McIlvanney recently wrote a very powerful piece lamenting the corrupting effect of commercialism and greed on the idealism that sport represents to so many people. He said:

> What we are witnessing may be quite simply the death of the cherished, though rather flimsily based, assumption that sport can remain permanently superior to the society it serves. If that belief is indeed shown to be a delusion, we are all in trouble. There is no more relevant analogy

in the principle that a society gets the politics it deserves. In politics, as happenings at Westminster are forever reminding us, idealism is a luxury. Without idealism, sport does not exist. Romance and honesty and fair play are not quaint outmoded concepts but the basic apparatus of its survival. If sport ceases to be a slightly fantastic metaphor for life (one that accommodates wild notions of heroes and heroines, triumph and disaster) and becomes just another sleazy part of it, sport is a waste of time.

Romance. Honesty. Those are the values embodied in one man.

I thank Sir Stan for the pleasure he has given, and continues to give. And I applaud him for the credit he continues to bring to a game for which all in this room feel great affection.

From a speech at a Football Writers Association tribute dinner for Sir Stanley Matthews on his eightieth birthday, 15 January 1995

PART V

The United Kingdom and the New World Order

I grew up as part of a postwar generation. I voted for Britain to remain in the EEC in 1975. I fought to persuade my party to become a party of Europe, believing that to be in my country's interests. I support the European ideal of cooperation between nation-states for the mutual benefit of all. I have no doubt that the future of my country lies in being at the heart of Europe.

From a speech to the Friedrich-Ebert Stiftung, Bonn, 30 May 1995

29 New Nation-state

There are now two significant impulses in modern democratic politics around the theory of the state. The first is to bring government closer to the people. Big, centralised government is out. Devolution and decentralisation are in. The second is the realisation of the impotence of isolationism. To be powerful, countries have to develop partnerships with others. They cannot act alone.

New Labour is about exactly these two ideals – devolution within nation-states and cooperation between them. As a new generation has come on, informed by different attitudes and a different outlook, the party has transformed its view of the role of government and of Britain's place in the world. Only fifteen years ago we were the party of big government and the anti-European party. Today we stand for decentralising power and for constructive leadership in Europe, and are enthusiastic proponents of a strong relationship across the Atlantic.

Strangely it is the Conservative Party's right wing – which is growing at an alarming rate – that is increasingly seen as the Little Englander party, content to be on the margins of Europe and often, as over Bosnia, isolationist. And, as Simon Jenkins recently wrote in his book *Accountable to None*, it is the Tories who have 'nationalised the state', becoming the party of centralised government.

The Nation-state
The issue of the nation-state – what it means; where it takes us – will be one of the central political questions of the next few decades. The Left has sometimes feared a debate about nationhood, confusing it with narrower nationalism.

We are all proud of our own countries. But people can be British and Scottish or British and Welsh. They can even be British and feel a close identity with the North-East or with London. And pride in my country is not the same as hostility

259

towards others. So, even at a theoretical level, pride in the nation should not be confused with the status quo, with no change either to central government or towards the rest of the world.

But there are also practical pressures forcing us to change. Power devolved is more accountable. People are better educated and want to take more responsibility for themselves. And nation-states in a new global community of technology, travel, trade and communication have no practical option but to open up to each other.

The real question is whether we have sufficient vision and flexibility to cope with these changes and mould our concept of the nation-state to fit them.

Let me say something about Scotland. Since 1979 the government has been telling us that there is nothing wrong with the way Scotland is governed from Westminster. Since 1979 it has said the Scottish people are wrong to want more control over their own affairs.

Now the government has acknowledged that it is it who is wrong. It admits that the way Scotland is governed from London is inadequate and needs to change. Its argument – that there can be no change because to make any change would be to undermine the Union – is shot. But, while it has finally admitted the problem, it has failed to face up to the solution.

Let me be absolutely clear about one thing. I would never

The Commonwealth is too great an asset to let slide in the way that successive Tory governments have done. It contains one-quarter of the world's population. It includes some of the fastest growing economies, including Asian Tigers such as Singapore and Malaysia. It is the only organisation, outside the United Nations itself, to transcend regional organisations and bring together North and South. It is united by a common language and common cultural roots.

From Tribune, *17 November 1995*

agree to anything which threatened to break up the United Kingdom. I believe in the United Kingdom. Scotland is a vital part of it in every way – economically, socially, politically, historically. To us, devolution is essential if the unity of Britain is to be maintained and strengthened. The real threat to the Union comes from a government that will not face up to the clearly stated desires of the people of Scotland – desires that are well understood by the rest of Britain – to have a greater say over the way Scotland is run.

Scotland already has its own legal system, its own separate education system, its own system of local government. It also has a bureaucracy, based in the Scottish Office. We propose to make that bureaucracy, and those **The era of big, centralised** public services, accountable to the people **government is over** of Scotland. Our proposals for a Scottish Parliament will place power in the hands of the people to have a greater say in the government of Scotland and the running of Scotland's schools, hospitals and key public services.

In the late twentieth century it is preposterous to claim that the only responses to grievances about the lack of democratic accountability are to do nothing or to create a new nation-state. Many of our partners in Europe have successfully devolved power to their regions. The choice is not between separation and changing nothing. The answer is sensible democratic reform.

The era of big, centralised government is over. Ordinary people have lost confidence in the ability of a distant central government to offer solutions to their problems. They have become unprecedentedly cynical about politics and politicians. Many have no interest whatever in Westminster and Whitehall.

If we are to reconnect people to the political system we have to reform it.

We can do this through public/private partnership, and are already doing so in local government – in projects like the Manchester Metrolink, developed by Manchester council and private industry to provide first-class public transport. We should develop partnership with the voluntary sector in providing innovative services, as the Prince's Trust and Community Service Volunteers do for young people. We should make the Employment Service more flexible. For too long it has been about processing large numbers of jobseekers through rigid national programmes. We need a greater focus on the individual, so that training is tailored to their needs.

Most importantly, we need to move decision-making back closer to the people by decentralising government and giving local government more power. I know that it is easy to talk about pluralism when in opposition but much harder to give up power when in government. I am determined that we should do so. That is why, as part of our efforts to restore civic pride, we are exploring the idea of elected mayors.

But it will take more than reinventing government to give people confidence in politics again. Sleaze has become the hallmark of the dying days of this administration. I welcome the adoption of the Nolan recommendations for Parliament. I hope that the work of Nolan can be extended to the funding of political parties, if the Prime Minister drops his objections.

Finally, government needs to be less secretive and more comprehensible. We favour a Freedom of Information Act and reforms in the workings of the Houses of Parliament so that people can have a better idea of how the process of government affects them.

We want a new relationship between the individual and the state. We want to give power back to the people, and in return we expect them to take on greater responsibility for themselves.

Europe and the Atlantic

The second major challenge facing left-of-centre parties over the nation-state is to develop a coherent theory of relations between nations, in the face of the increasing isolationism of the new Right.

In the Cold War it was easy – you were in one sphere of influence or the other, and you could depend on the super-power whose client state you were. But in a multi-polar world it is more complicated.

In the modern world a nation-state of Britain's size can of course act alone, but in the majority of situations it will be far more powerful when acting with others. Turning inwards, as the Little Englanders would have us do, is a recipe for impotence. To be powerful we have to build partnerships with others.

The two main partnerships for Britain are the EU and the transatlantic relationship. We need to use them to maximise our influence so that we can promote and protect our interests around the world, because we cannot do so alone. But to be effective we have to participate fully in each partnership.

The debate over Britain's role in Europe is often a carica-ture: favouring cooperation in Europe is seen as standing up for Europe at the expense of Britain. But the reality is that Britain's interests are best secured by playing a full part in Europe – our influence is enhanced, our **To be powerful we have to build partnerships with others** ability to secure our own commercial interests encouraged, our foreign policy strengthened. The Defence Secretary has said that the notion of Britain needing Europe is 'defeatist'. What is defeatist is the belief that we sacrifice our identity as a nation when acting in concert with others. Tell that to France or Germany. They are hardly indifferent to their own nationhood, but they see no contradiction between being a cohesive nation-state and European cooperation.

This is the patriotic case for Britain in Europe.

Britain's historical role has lain – at least since the eighteenth century – in its unique capacity to be a major global player. Although an island, it has rejected an insular approach. Once we could project our global role through our empire. Now we should exercise it through Europe – not exclusively, of course, but as a powerful part of our destiny.

Our economic power is based on a European internal market of 370 million people, without which our industry and services wither, and on inward investment from the US, Japan and Korea, which would not come here if we were not part of the EU. In trade negotiations, Britain would have far less clout if we were not a member of the EU. It is only through our membership that we can play a significant part in maintaining free trade around the world. And in terms of foreign policy we carry much greater weight in Beijing and

263

Buenos Aires – never mind Washington or Tokyo – if we speak with one voice with our European partners. That is why we attach so much importance to the Common Foreign and Security Policy.

Unless we build our global influence through Europe, we risk being marginalised – without influence on our immediate surroundings or the wider world.

The real question is, What type of Europe?

A Labour government would set out in Europe with its own positive agenda for change – an agenda looking far wider than the IGC.

First, the enlargement of the EU to include the established democracies of central and eastern Europe. NATO membership, while important, may take some time. I agree with Felipe Gonzalez that we should accelerate the timetable for opening negotiations on EU membership. There will obviously be substantial difficulties on the way, and we should not pretend that the negotiations will be speedy or the transitional periods short, but I pledge that a Labour government will open negotiations with the first group of these countries in the first half of 1998, when Britain holds the presidency of the EU. We have the same obligations to these countries as the US had to the war-ravaged countries of western Europe in the 1940s and '50s. We must not allow a vacuum to open up in eastern Europe, and we must help underpin democracy and the growing market economies there.

Second, we need to make a serious effort to reform the Common Agricultural Policy, without which enlargement cannot happen. This government pays lip-service to CAP reform, but seems to have given up in practice. A Labour government with credibility in Europe could use the mounting pressure of enlargement to force reform on to the agenda. Now is the moment to strike. World grain prices are – unusually – at or above EU levels. Dismantling protection would be far less painful if we did it now, when the gap between price levels is so small.

Third, we need to achieve the stronger economic growth in Europe that will bring jobs and increased prosperity. The EU can contribute to achieving that goal through greater efforts to bring open competition in aviation, energy and tele-communications and a tougher approach to unfair state aids. We would make it a priority to remove these barriers.

I do not believe the ultimate goal for Europe should be a federal superstate. Very few people in Europe want that. What we need is deeper cooperation between states. In its early years the EU depended on the pace of integration being forced by the setting of deadlines and the passage of hundreds of pieces of legislation. The driving force was a political élite which paid little attention to what ordinary people thought. Maastricht showed that élites and the people had become far too separated. The EU is now at a more mature stage. Increasingly integration will happen by a process of organic growth, where progress is more and more in the hands of businessmen, consumers and ordinary people, not only the politicians.

The hard issue in Europe is economic and monetary union. Time and again I have set out our position: a single currency could have benefits, but it cannot be forced in defiance of the economic facts and it is a major step of integration, not to be taken lightly. For Britain, EMU would not work economically, let alone politically, unless there were genuine economic convergence.

However, France and Germany are determined to press

The European Union has brought huge benefits to the people of Europe. The EU has helped to bring peace. It has created a vast market for the European economies. It acts as a massive force in world trade, alongside the blocs in South-East Asia and North America. It is a magnet for inward investment. Its citizens enjoy far greater freedom of movement than ever before contemplated across international boundaries. Millions of young people travel and, like I did in the late 1970s, even work and live for short periods of time abroad in other European countries ... Go to any part of the regions of Britain, such as my own constituency in the North-East, and you will see many areas transformed by the EU's regional policy.

From a speech to the Friedrich-Ebert Stiftung, Bonn, 30 May 1995

---

ahead on the Maastricht timetable. There are considerable doubts about the feasibility of such a course, but at present that's their view.

Britain's attitude should not be to set out to obstruct or to glory in difficulties. While keeping our options open, we should be playing our part in trying to ensure that the issue is handled constructively rather than destructively. Such a view is emphatically in British interests.

I see Britain playing a natural part with France and Germany and the other countries of Europe in determining the future direction of the EU. But Europe is not the only partnership we belong to. For me, the relationship with the United States will remain one of crucial importance. It is based on important values that we share as well as the common language that George Bernard Shaw thought divided us. These values remain as strong as they ever were.

I do not believe we have to choose between Europe and America. No other European country would dream of doing so. In fact the two relationships are crucially inter-dependent.

We need to understand that the nature of our relationship with the US has changed. It was always bound to do so after the end of the Cold War. Politico-military issues were at the core, but today economic issues have taken on greater weight. The Europeans no longer have the same incentive to set aside their interests in order to accommodate the Americans. And the Americans no longer have the same incentive to exercise leadership on every issue – nor do they always see as clearly the direction in which they should lead. I do not believe that the US will turn in on itself in a return to the isolationism of the 1930s, and I strongly welcome President Clinton's assurance on this point. But it will be more difficult to get the US interested in overseas activities. Americans will have to be convinced that their interests are engaged.

Let me state this clearly: America is crucial to European security, and it always will be. The UK and the US will always turn to each other in time of crisis. The UK will always be the country the US turns to when it needs military support, as in the Gulf. The relationship between Britain and the US will always be one of special trust. And it must play a crucial role in binding together Europe and America.

But the Atlantic relationship has to be built on more than just military cooperation. Trade with the US is of huge importance to Europe and to the US. We need a framework within which we can deal with the economic disputes that are certain to arise between the two sides of the Atlantic. The EU is a frustrating partner for the US. There is no one centre of power. The Commission cannot be an interlocutor, and the troika system can sometimes throw up collections of countries that do not offer the necessary weight for serious talks. We have proposed the strengthening of the Council secretariat dealing with the Common Foreign and Security Policy, but the relationship will in reality need to pass through London, Paris and Bonn as well as Brussels. Cooperation and consultation on this axis needs to be reinforced.

The way to do so is to take an initiative to build a new relationship of greater economic cooperation across the Atlantic, and I urge EU/US cooperation on the progressive elimination of all non-tariff barriers across the Atlantic to create a new Euro-Atlantic community. As the largest investor in the US and the largest recipient of US investment in Europe, we would be the biggest beneficiaries. It would help us to pursue our agenda for reform in the EU, by speeding up progress in opening up the CAP. If we can make progress in this area we will have taken a major step towards building the foundations of a new, stronger relationship that will survive the peace as well as NATO survived the Cold War.

My argument here is that Britain has to understand that its strength comes from its position at the junction of these two relationships. They should not be looked at separately. The key is the way they interlock and reinforce each other. Europe is not an alternative to the transatlantic relationship. Nor do we have to choose between the Atlantic and Europe. Our influence in each is crucial to our influence in the other. It is only if we are at the heart of decision-making in Europe that we will be taken seriously in Washington. And it is only if we have a new, strong, post-Cold War relationship with the US that we will have the same degree of influence in Europe.

267

This is a patriotism born not of nostalgia but of an under-standing of the changing nature of the world, and a determi-nation to secure our place within it – confident, influential, with a real sense of identity. A new Britain for a new world, finally breaking free of our imperial shadows. Strong in the world because we are cohesive at home, and strong in Europe. A confident nation. A new confidence in the world. Britain as one nation. Britain as a young country again.

From a speech at the Time *magazine 'Distinguished Speakers' Dinner, London, 30 November 1995*

30 *Devolution*

Labour's pledge on devolution is straightforward – we will legislate for a Scottish Parliament and a Welsh Assembly in the first year of a Labour government. Other Labour leaders have made similar pledges; Harold Wilson and Jim Callaghan tried to legislate for it, John Smith said it was his unfinished business but died tragically before he could deliver it. If we win the election, I intend to be the Prime Minister who does it.

The principles we have laid down are clear – to get specific support from the people of Scotland and Wales for what we wish to do, and to be clear about what exactly devolution is and what it is intended to achieve. People want to know this: Are we setting up a Scottish Parliament with taxation powers? Yes. How? By obtaining the mandate of a general election and the specific mandate of the Scottish people. What could be a better symbol of the new politics at the heart of New Labour than that?

Defining Devolution

First let us be clear about what we mean by devolution. It is neither some quasi-nationalist form of government, a watered down form of separatism or a form of federalism. Scotland and Wales do not want separatism. The nationalists might want to tear our country apart and to rip up the United Kingdom. They may wish to tear asunder the common ties of kinship and friendship and the bonds of common history which tie us together in this country but that is because they mistake national pride for separatism. They mistake pride in being Scottish or Welsh and the desire for independence. People do of course feel proud to be Scottish and Welsh but they feel British too. And that sense of being both Scottish and British, or Welsh and British, lies behind the completely legitimate desire to have more control over their own affairs. It also means that people in Scotland and Wales reject the calls of those who would suggest that the only way to gain such control is by breaking up Britain and tearing our country apart.

Some have argued that the response to Scottish and Welsh desires for more control over their own affairs should be a federal system such as exists in Germany or the United States. As a system of government it may have constitutional symmetry but we do not believe it is suitable for the United Kingdom. Here, one of the four constituent parts of our country – England – has four-fifths of the population and the sense of national and regional identity and the desire for autonomy varies greatly. Federalism may appeal to some but it is not what we propose.

What we propose is devolution which requires a decision taken by the UK Parliament – a decision therefore involving representatives from throughout the UK – to establish a subsidiary assembly or parliament to exercise certain functions in one part of the UK. Devolution will not just be good for Scotland and Wales. It will be good for the whole of the UK as it brings power closer to the people and is part of a wider process of decentralisation which allows the centre to concentrate on the strategic needs of the whole country.

A Brief History of Devolution

Demands for devolution or home rule are nothing new in the United Kingdom. For over a hundred years the issue of the dispersal of power within the Union has been at issue, sometimes urgently, sometimes less so, but seldom entirely absent. The first real attempts at home rule were Gladstone's Irish Bills of 1886 and 1893. Gladstone's verdict on the prospects for his proposals was that 'the determining condition will I think be found to be the temper in which men approach the question' – a factor which, then and now, was highly relevant not just to devolution but to British tolerance of the House of Lords and indeed of its entire unwritten constitution. In today's context I believe these proposals will be strengthened if they are seen to have the clear backing of the people.

The Scottish Labour Party was founded in 1888 with home rule as one of its core beliefs. For Keir Hardie and for the Red Clydesiders home rule was a central demand and at Scottish

Labour conferences throughout the early part of the century resolutions supporting this position were adopted. In the early years of this century Ireland dominated the home rule debate with a settlement eventually resulting in partition between north and south, independence for what is now the Republic of Ireland and the establishment of the Stormont Parliament in Northern Ireland.

This remains the only devolved Parliament ever to have been established in the United Kingdom. I make no defence of its political record but its operation over a period of fifty years shows that, constitutionally, it is possible to have a law-making parliament operating within the United Kingdom. Even today, though the politics of Northern Ireland are of course unique in the United Kingdom and will demand a specific settlement, it is part of the government's plans to have a law-making elected body in Northern Ireland. Again this shows that, constitutionally, and where a government supports it, devolution is perfectly possible.

In the middle part of this century interest in Home Rule declined. Only in the late sixties and seventies did devolution return to centre stage. The Labour government appointed a Royal Commission on the Constitution in 1968, chaired first by Lord Crowther, later by Lord Kilbrandon and by the early seventies both major parties were committed to the policy – a fact which should never be forgotten when the Prime Minister continues to denounce devolution as though it marked the end of the world. All of his senior Scottish colleagues – Malcolm Rifkind, Ian Lang and yes, even Michael Forsyth, at one time or another supported devolution and saw the advantages it could bring.

I remember grandad's old Morris Cowley, and he used to take us into the meat market in Glasgow. He'd a bad leg and used to go around with his stick, giving the carcasses a good whack to see what shape they were in. If we were naughty, he'd come after us with that stick and say, 'Ah'll gie ye a richt skelpin'.'

From the Daily Record, *7 March 1996*

The 1974 Labour government eventually succeeded in legislating for both Scotland and Wales but the Acts were scarred by the lengthy and exhausting parliamentary process of the legislation. The attempt was conducted in the most difficult conditions. The government, without a majority, was mercy to the amendments of small groups of backbenchers. And the referendums were eventually held on St David's Day 1979, in the wake of the winter of discontent and in the dog days of the Callaghan government. Wales rejected devolution and the Scots, though they endorsed it, did not do so in the numbers required by the amendment forced on the government during the passage of the legislation. The 1970s marked the most concerted attempt by any government to devolve power to Scotland and Wales and yet it failed.

Our Implementation Plan

We will not fail this time. That is why we have been working on a plan to blow the opposition of the Tories away and speed the legislation through Parliament. Politics is vastly transformed since 1979. Times have changed and the Labour Party has changed. This time we will approach this issue with determination, with vision and with clarity of purpose. Scotland and Wales both have single-tier local government. The Scottish Constitutional Convention process has helped produce cross-party consensus about the case for change – and our implementation plan is firmly based on that consensus.

In England pressure for decentralisation has grown too. Of course it varies but in some regions there is a strong and growing demand for regional coordination of economic development, transport and planning. In Europe, too, more and more countries have gone down the road of devolving power – not just Germany but traditionally centralised countries like France and Italy. In Spain a successful system of devolution has been in operation since the late seventies. Only in Britain does it seem that the government argues change is impossible.

Any government which wants to change Britain for the better has to care about political renewal. It is not an optional extra. It is essential to meeting the challenges of new times.

It is central to my vision of new Britain. And the government I lead will deliver its pledge.

As soon as possible after the election White Papers will be published outlining in detail our proposals for Scotland and Wales. We will then have referendums in both countries on those proposals. We will be campaigning for a massive Yes vote for devolution. There will be no fancy tricks, no special majorities – a simple majority of those voting will be enough. A positive referendum result will scatter the Tory opposition. They will not be left with a leg to stand on if they try to argue against the proposals after they have been endorsed by the people of Scotland and Wales. Not only that, but a Yes vote will be the best long-term security the Scottish Parliament and the Welsh Assembly can have.

Michael Forsyth said recently it was high time that Labour 'committed themselves to seeking endorsement for that programme through a referendum by the Scottish people'. He also said if we did it the Tories 'are not going to abolish it'. We are going to take him at his word – to meet his challenge and to ask him to meet ours. And when the people of Scotland and Wales vote in favour, as I believe they will, let the Tories accept the will of the people and not stand in the way of the legislation. Of course, constitutionally, entrenchment of any legislation in our system is not possible but politically, endorsement by the people will give the new institutions an enormous boost.

Regarding finance we propose that both the Scottish Parliament and Welsh Assembly will be funded through a grant operating on the same basis of expenditure distribution as exists at present. The principle of pooling resources at the centre and then redistributing them on the agreed basis will be main-

---

> The values of the Labour Party are good Scottish values. The need for strong communities, social cohesion, a real meritocracy; the fact that opportunity and responsibility go together – these are our key messages.
>
> *From* Scotland on Sunday, *3 March 1996*

---

tained. That partnership is part of the essence of the United Kingdom. But in addition, for the Scottish Parliament – a body which will have extensive legislative powers – we have made it clear that we want to see revenue powers at the margin: the ability to vary tax up or down with a defined limit amounting to less than five per cent of the annual Scottish Office budget.

The principle that a body with the powers we propose for the Scottish Parliament should have some revenue-varying powers is right. It will be responsible for significant areas of Scottish public life. That it should have some discretion over its budget in those circumstances, and have the responsibility to answer to the Scottish people if that discretion is exercised, is entirely reasonable, is followed in other countries and is constitutionally effective.

On this matter too we believe we should seek the views of the Scottish people. In doing so we will nail for ever the Tory lie that Labour will impose a tartan tax on the people of Scotland. We will ask them, in a second referendum question, if they want a Parliament financed purely from a grant or do they want it to have limited discretionary powers over its budget? And here too we will campaign for a massive Yes vote because we believe that the responsibility which goes with this power is right. And that Yes campaign will be different from 1979. Then we had a Labour plan and a Labour campaign. Now, in the 1990s, we have the consensus the Convention has built and we will have a united, inclusive Yes campaign, working with others to secure the Yes vote on both questions.

We have always said there was a difference between this power and a tax rise or a pledge to raise taxes. If people vote Yes to the second question it does not follow that taxes will be raised. That suggestion is absurd. Political parties will still want to think long and hard before entering an election pledged to raise taxes. The important thing is to establish the principle and we believe the people will back it. By devolving power, Parliament will be deciding that some parts of the UK should be governed in a distinct manner. The sovereignty of the UK Parliament will of course remain undiminished.

We should never forget that John Major's own proposals for a legislative assembly in Northern Ireland proposed no change in their voting powers and no alteration in the representation of Northern Ireland at Westminster. And of course that was subject to a referendum before the Assembly was established. The Conservatives' position is therefore one of abject dishonesty.

I believe Labour's plan – a referendum in both Scotland and Wales before legislation is passed, specific endorsement of the principle of revenue powers for Scotland, a clear statement in the Bill of the sovereignty of Parliament, and a re-examination of the electoral system to be used for the Welsh Assembly – will give us a strengthened package of devolution which can be delivered and established quickly in government.

The changes we have announced will bring devolution closer to a reality. They do not threaten but bring forward the day when Scotland will have its Parliament and Wales its Assembly. They are not a change in policy but a means of implementing policy. They will help ensure the continued unity of the United Kingdom. I am certain that amid all the sound and fury people will believe it is right that they should be given a vote over how they should be governed.

Our country stands on the verge of great change. We can continue with the overcentralised, secretive and discredited system of government we have at present. Or we can change and trust the people to take more control over their own lives. Let no one doubt Labour's determination to make radical changes in the way we run our country and to decentralise power. And let no one doubt that we will do so in a way that can be delivered, is workable, and is in line with our system of government. And let Scotland, Wales and the United Kingdom be stronger as a result.

From a speech in the Playfair Library, Edinburgh University,
28 June 1996

31 The Northern Ireland
Peace Process

For many years the random execution of the innocent was the most familiar image of the politics of Northern Ireland. When the IRA indicated it was time to move from the bullet and the bomb, the present government and all politicians of goodwill sought the chance to put reason back in charge of events. With considerable determination, the British and Irish governments worked together to produce the Downing Street Declaration. Some months later the IRA called a cease-fire. They led us to believe it was permanent.

To provide proof of it, they were asked to start handing in their weapons. They said that was unacceptable. Undeterred, a different route was proposed – a new election, giving a democratic mandate for negotiation.. Although there were reservations from some about this proposal, before it could properly be discussed came the bomb at Canary Wharf.

The vast majority of people in Northern Ireland and in Britain want two things to happen. They want us to stand firm against terrorism, and they want hope kept alive.

Sinn Fein cannot participate in ministerial talks of any kind unless this time it is plain beyond doubt that they have genuinely given up violence for good. All democratic parties in Northern Ireland and in the Irish Republic believe that the future of Northern Ireland must be determined by the consent of the people there. Both Britain and the Irish Republic are saying to Northern Ireland, There will be no change in your constitutional status unless it is supported by a majority of the people in Northern Ireland. The entire historical context of the IRA's position has been overtaken by history, and only they seem not to notice it. Sinn Fein must now play by the rules of democracy or not at all.

We, the politicians, must redouble our efforts to find a way, consistent with the principles we have set out, to let the hand of peace be active once more. The hand of peace is not weak.

276

It is firm. It is patient. It will not surrender to violence or compromise with it. But it will seek any sensible and principled alternative to violence that can provide a way through. Above all, it exists to work for what the people want: not the tiny minority who will indulge in violence, but the overwhelming majority from all traditions who desire peace. To this end all options are open.

So rarely in politics can we see such quick and certain benefits as have come through peace in Northern Ireland. I have seen them myself – businesses reopening; confidence and laughter in the streets where once was fear; Protestants and Catholics at one for peace.

There are many issues of fury and conflict that you will hear across your television screens between ourselves and the Conservative government from now until the general election – great issues of moment to our country, where great differences remain. But on this issue, peace in Northern Ireland, we will work with them, together, united, to put peace above party politics.

The memory that lives in my mind above all others is that of young Catherine Hamill reading her prayer for peace to President Clinton in Belfast in December 1995. It is for her, and countless thousands like her, we bend our mind and will towards building a lasting peace, so that, a generation from now, her children can look forward to a future full of joy, free from fear.

From a statement on the Northern Ireland peace process, 13 February 1996

32 Five Questions for John Major on Europe

I will put five questions to the Prime Minister. What is more, at the conclusion of each question I shall answer it and then ask the Prime Minister to answer it. I cannot put it more fairly than that.

First, does the Prime Minister agree with his Chancellor that a single currency is not a threat to the nation-state? I say that his Chancellor is right; I assume that he says the same.

He cannot say.

Let me put this question to the Prime Minister. Does he agree with his Employment Secretary that having a single currency is a long way to political union, and would mean giving up the government of the United Kingdom? May we have an answer to that? I say that the Employment Secretary is wrong; what does the Prime Minister say?

Thirdly – this is a question that he must surely be able to answer – if he is re-elected, can the Prime Minister say whether a single currency will be a possibility in the next Parliament, assuming that the economic conditions are right? It must logically follow from signing the Maastricht Treaty that the answer to that question is yes. But what is the Prime Minister's answer? Is it a possibility or not?

He cannot say. Anyone would think that I was asking the Prime Minister to do something quite extraordinary. I am merely asking him to agree with his Chancellor. We have a situation, do we not, where I as the Leader of the Opposition can agree with his Chancellor, but he cannot get up and agree with him.

The fourth question is that, if the economic conditions were right, would the Prime Minister be in favour of persuading the country that it was right to join a single currency? He must be able to answer that. I say yes to that. Is the Prime Minister able to answer the question? With all due respect, that is the position of his Chancellor. That is what the Chancellor said in his speech a couple of weeks ago.

Finally, let me ask the Prime Minister whether he can agree with this statement:

> Some observers hope – and others fear – that economic and monetary union as set out in the Maastricht Treaty will be a step in the direction of a federal Europe ... I believe that such hopes or fears are unrealistic.

Can the Prime Minister agree with that? I can; can he?

Shall I tell the House the author of that statement? It was the Prime Minister. That is the position to which he has reduced the government. I find it odd that he cannot agree with his Chancellor, I find it strange that he cannot agree with his Secretary of State for Employment, and I find it unbelievable that he cannot agree with himself.

From Hansard, *1 March 1995*

33 Britain in Europe

Part of the national renewal Labour offers Britain is a more assertive, more confident role in the world. My belief is that the drift towards isolation in Europe must stop and be replaced by a policy of constructive engagement.

In my view, we will not participate fully in Europe until we see how such participation is not a breach with our history but a fulfilment of it. I want to make two points in particular. First, that Britain has always had a powerful historical relationship with Europe – though different from that which we now need. Secondly, and more importantly, I will argue that the true historical role of Britain has lain in its unique capacity, whatever its circumstances, to be a major global player; that, though an island, it has always rejected an insular approach; and that the only way to maintain a global role today is through Europe. Forfeit a central role in Europe and we forfeit our opportunity to play a substantial role in the world. In crude but none the less accurate terms, that is the patriotic case for Britain in Europe.

Europe is not, as the sceptics would have us believe, something that happened to us in 1973. We are Europeans. We are made up of wave after wave of settlers who came to these islands from Europe: Celts, Romans, Anglo-Saxons, Vikings and Normans.

In the seventeenth and eighteenth centuries we began to take on an additional role that distinguished us from most other Europeans. We became a maritime and imperial power. This new role did not replace our European role but was added on to it. The duality was reflected in the existence of separate Foreign and Colonial and Commonwealth offices right through until 1967. Palmerston as Foreign Secretary did not concern himself with the administration of India, but was preoccupied with Europe.

In the nineteenth century we developed down a different track from the Continent. Rather than formalising a system of centralised government based on the Napoleonic code, we were proud of our common law and parliamentary systems.

The empire took more and more of our time and efforts, but 'splendid isolation' was never a serious basis for British policy. A quick look at Palmerston or Grey's papers shows that most of their time was spent worrying about the European balance. Disraeli, with his role in the Congress of Berlin, and Gladstone, with his preoccupation with the Concert of Europe, were acting first and foremost as European statesmen.

When the balance was not maintained at the end of the nineteenth century, disaster descended on Europe. Prussia came to dominate France, and Europe was Balkanised. Having tried to turn our back on the Continent, we were dragged back in and had to pay a heavy price in the First World War.

In the inter-war period, under the influence of appeasers like Neville Chamberlain and Stanley Baldwin, we failed to intervene early enough. In 1937 Baldwin considered Hitler no danger to the West, and even said, 'It would not break my heart if there is any fighting in Europe.'

The Labour Party at the time was more internationalist. It was committed to the notion of collective security (despite the debate over rearmament and the familiar tension between moral sentiment and a pragmatic view of national interest) and was in favour of intervention in the civil war in Spain. But it did not have power. Again, in the Second World War, millions had to pay with their lives.

So we have always been a European power. But we were the only European state to take on truly global responsibilities.

The decade after the Second World War was a special period. The other European powers were flattened. Only we retained our confidence as unconquered victors, and this gave us a peculiar view of ourselves.

Under the leadership of Ernie Bevin, we played an important part in creating with the US the framework of the Western world as we moved into the Cold War: the Bretton Woods institutions, the North Atlantic Alliance and the OEEC to organise Marshall Aid. But we sat on our hands at the Messina Conference, and lost our opportunity to influence the creation of the European Community. We staggered on with our global role, increasingly ragged, on the basis of the special relationship with the United States, which lasted throughout the Cold War.

Churchill believed he could maintain Britain's role with a foreign policy resting on empire, transatlantic relations and Europe. But each pillar can no longer be regarded as of the same strength or significance.

First, the empire dissolved. And to argue that we can sustain a global role solely on the basis of our relations with the Commonwealth – important as the Commonwealth is to us – is simply not serious. We will always have close ties of sentiment with the Commonwealth, but it is not a substitute for our relationship with Europe today.

Secondly, the relationship with the US is, of course, essential. Whatever disagreements there may be from time to time – and under this government there have been quite a few – what binds us together is infinitely more powerful than anything that divides us.

Furthermore, it is possible, at least in theory, to have a relationship with the US that is special even if we were to withdraw from Europe. But that is to miss the point, which is that our transatlantic relationship is multiplied in strength if we are also at the centre of Europe. Indeed, Britain, as a key player in Europe, can use its relationship to huge effect both

---

Some politicians call for the building of a wall of protectionism around Europe. They must be vigorously resisted. Protectionism would be the road to stagnation and decline, not security and prosperity. They are too pessimistic. Our people and industries have the skills, ingenuity and talent to thrive in the global economy.

Our agenda should not be building new barriers in Europe but working to remove them elsewhere in the world, especially in Japan and the Far East, to give our industries fair opportunities to sell. We should explore the idea of talks with both NAFTA and Japan about market access.

From a speech to the Friedrich-Ebert Stiftung, Bonn, 30 May 1995

---

in our own interests and in the interest of Europe. As Dr Kissinger has made clear, the Americans prefer to work through Europe. That is simply a fact of *realpolitik*.

We carry greater weight in Beijing or Buenos Aires – never mind Washington or Tokyo – if we speak with one voice together with our European partners. That is why we attach so much important to the Common Foreign and Security Policy.

And if we want to increase our leverage in trade negotiations and attract foreign investment we have to do so through our participation in Europe. The Euro-sceptics sometimes suggest that the high level of inward investment in the UK demonstrates that we could go it alone. But they miss the point. The Japanese, the Americans and the Koreans invest here because we are part of the European Union. If they see us slipping to a second tier, they will put their investment elsewhere.

Isolationism ignores the strength of the EU, and Britain's role in it, in bolstering free trade and in particular in bringing the Uruguay Round of GATT negotiations to a successful conclusion. Britain outside the EU would simply not have this bargaining clout. Free trade depends on widespread adherence to a set of common rules that are enforceable. In today's world, that adherence is achieved through multilateral institutions, like the new World Trade Organisation, which in turn depend on the support of the world's major economic blocs, the United States and European Union included. It is they who now play the role which once the British navy played in enforcing free trade in Britain's heyday as the 'workshop of the world'.

As for the sceptics' dream of turning back the clock, and reverting to EFTA, what kind of world are they living in? Why did Sweden, Finland and Austria all quit EFTA to join the Union? Because full access to the Single Market requires a full say in setting its rules. They wanted to be in – full members of the club. So does Labour.

The fact is that Europe is today the only route through which Britain can exercise power and influence. If it is to maintain its historic role as a global player, Britain has to be a central part of the politics of Europe.

283

So Labour will be strong in Europe. Strong in defence of the values in which we believe. But not just strong in resisting wrong ideas: strong too in setting the agenda, with the right ideas. That's what our allies are waiting for. That is Britain's traditional role in Europe, and they want us to play it again. For too long they've seen British ministers sent to Brussels to find out what the community is doing and tell it to stop. Or, when it won't, opt out. They want us to help decide what the community should do, and how it can do it better. They want us to be on the inside, arguing constructively for new directions and new reforms.

Naturally, if the rest of Europe wanted to rush headlong

Our first priority should be to create the growth that will bring jobs. We must create the conditions in which business can flourish. We should ensure that every citizen and region of the European Union is able to share in prosperity. That is why we need a well-resourced and effective policy for structural funds for our regions, an active European Investment Bank, and a much more active policy for developing the trans-European infrastructure networks.

The Union needs to remove barriers which hold back the living standards of its citizens. For instance, it should give priority to providing the people of Europe with access to cheaper air travel by introducing greater competition in the market for air travel. The liberalisation of telecom can bring benefits to all our peoples – already the GSM mobile phone system has made communication dramatically easier – an example of European cooperation in practice.

Europe must become more competitive so that our peoples can become more prosperous. We must remove barriers to fair competition within the Union. Distorting government subsidies should be removed and we need to examine the proposal of the establishment of an independent European competition agency, based on the example of the German cartel office.

From a speech to the Friedrich-Ebert Stiftung, Bonn, 30 May 1995

---

into some federalist morass, that would be a mighty argument against Britain participating in Europe, even if it was necessary to maintain influence. But the irony is that the Tory lurch towards disengagement from Europe comes at the very time when the rest of Europe is emphatically not bent on such a course and when, if Britain were only seen to be constructively engaged, it could offer genuine leadership in Europe.

There is a widespread acknowledgement in Europe that the political élites and the people became disconnected from the process of Maastricht. There is a common acceptance that the next steps of integration must happen through consent or not at all. Enlargement to the East inevitably refocuses the EU on how it incorporates new members as much as how it deepens the ties between existing members.

We are not setting out to break up the Franco-German partnership or to engage in a new round of 'balance-of-power' politics. Rather our aim is to join others in the leadership of Europe in the pursuit of our aims. We will be with the French over Bosnia. We will be with the Germans over greater openness to central and eastern Europe. And we will be with the Nordic countries on social and environmental issues. Some of the smaller countries feel left out in decision-making; they would welcome it if we participated actively in the European debate, rather than always being content to be overruled as one against fourteen.

We can lead the case for reform. We are a new generation, not scarred by war. We do not accept that Europe should remain as it is. Our commitment to Europe does not mean that we accept a bureaucratic and wasteful Europe. In fact it suits the Tories to keep it that way so that they have something to attack.

We want a new, revitalised, people's Europe:

★ A Europe more relevant to the real concerns of our people. Instead of being obsessed with the minutiae of institutional reform, the Union should be working to combat unemployment and make European business more competitive in the world economy – in part by removing the barriers to competitiveness within the EU.

★ A more democratic and open Europe. Meetings of the
Council in legislative session should no longer take place
in secret. The Commission should be made more accountable to national parliaments and the European Parliament.
Subsidiarity should be given real effect.

★ A Europe that is less wasteful and inefficient. The scandals
and waste of the CAP are bad for Britain and bad for
Europe. A stronger Britain can work to correct them more
effectively.

A Labour government would not have marginalised the
country by opting out from the Social Chapter – the effort
to ensure that the Single Market has a social dimension.

The system of qualified majority voting needs to be
reformed. Weighted against the large member states, it is bad
for Britain and bad for Europe. It weakens the democratic
legitimacy of decision-taking. We will maintain the veto vigorously in areas such as security and immigration. But, especially with a proper reweighting, we should consider extending
QMV in certain areas such as social, environmental, industrial
and regional policy, and extending a simplified process of
co-decision in the Parliament to those areas where QMV
applies to decisions in the Council. As Sir Leon Brittan has
observed, any sensible Tory government would adopt the same
position instead of threatening to veto any extension of QMV.

The hard issue is EMU. There is no doubt that monetary
union would be a very important step of integration. Labour
has argued that it is vital that the government has a clear policy
upon it: not that it decides whether or not it will join now,
but that it decides the principles upon which such a decision
must be based.

There are some things we will not agree to. We will not agree
to giving up our national veto in crucial areas like security,
taxation, treaty change, and border controls on third-country
nationals.

From a speech to the Friedrich-Ebert Stiftung, Bonn, 30 May 1995

Here again the Tory divisions are shackling sensible government. There is only one immediate question on EMU: is it
inconsistent with the nation-state? If it is, then we must reject
it, even if it would be economically prudent to join. If it is
not – as we believe – then we are free to participate fully in
the formulation of its institutions and structures, while deciding
finally on whether to join on the basis of our national economic interest. We have defined that interest as being satisfied
that there is real economic convergence which is sustainable.

This is surely the sensible line to take. It does not close our
options, but it defines the terms on which they are to be
exercised. Again, provided it is apparent that Britain sees merit
in the objectives of a single currency, in the appropriate economic circumstances, it can exercise far more influence over
the pace and method of its adoption by being fully and constructively involved in the negotiations about it.

Europe will take shape in a constitutional form of its own
making – part shared sovereignty, part inter-governmental
cooperation, permanently resting on the inclinations and policies of its member states, which will always remain the decisive
factor in determining the extent and pace of change.

Labour local government today works closely with the EU.
A younger generation of Labour MPs and activists is broadly
supportive of Europe. The anti-Europeans tend to be older
and less influential. Go to a Labour youth conference and
attack Europe and delegates would look at you in blank incom-
prehension. A Tory youth conference would cheer you to the
rafters. Such differences are much more than symbolic. And
the objections of any Labour MPs to EMU exist less on the
issue of constitutional principle than on economic practicality.

I want a Britain that is true to itself – true to its history,
true to its character and gifts, and above all true to its future.
That is the only way to regain our sense of direction and fulfil
the historic destiny of our country.

From a speech to the Royal Institute of International Affairs,
London, 5 April 1995

PART VI

Stakeholder Britain

New Labour has a vision that strikes a chord with the British people. This vision is quite simple. Everybody should have a stake in the economy . . .

Why is John Major opposed to the people of Britain having a stake in this great country? Why has the man who promised a classless society set his face against plans that will make a reality of that classless society?

From a speech in the Assembly Rooms, Derby, 18 January 1996

34 *The Stakeholder Economy*

I want Britain to be one of the really dynamic economies of the twenty-first century. It is sobering to think that just over a century ago we were top of the league of prosperous nations, we were thirteenth in 1979, and today we are eighteenth. Yet our people, by their intelligence, grit and creativity, are still a people unrivalled anywhere in the world. We must develop their ability and so make ourselves world leaders again.

The key words are 'investment', 'quality' and 'trust'. The reason for investment is to create long-term strength. The better our capacity, the more up-to-date our plant and technology, the higher grade our skills, the stronger the product will be. When very-low-labour-cost countries can outbid us

---

The stakeholder economy is the key to preparing our people and business for vast economic and technological change. It is not about giving power to corporations or unions or interest groups. It is about giving power to *you*, the individual. It is about giving you the chances that help you to get on and so help Britain to get on too: a job, a skill, a home, an opportunity – a stake in the success we all want for Britain. We will fight for that stake, working with you, in partnership. The Tories fight only for the privileged few. We stand for the majority, the many.

Our policies on welfare to work, on education, on welfare reform, on the new technologies, on help for small businesses – they are all designed to create the opportunity on which an efficient stakeholder economy will depend. I want us to win the next election not because the Tories are despised but because the public know our policies and believe they will fulfil that vision.

From a speech in the Assembly Rooms, Derby, 18 January 1996

---

at the lower end of the market we must be moving up continually to higher-value-added products. That comes through quality. We will not sell our goods and services by being the cheapest – important though cost is. We will sell them by being the best.

The easy way to competitiveness has been seen as devaluation. Since 1979 the pound has virtually halved in relation to the Deutschmark. But this is not competitiveness that lasts unless it is backed up by an improvement in quality. In an age of customised design and articulate and careful consumers, it is through making high-value-added products of quality that we will score. The best British companies know this and are doing it. But to build lasting prosperity it is not enough merely for individual companies to be engaged. The creation of an economy where we are inventing and producing goods and services of quality needs the engagement of the whole country. It must become a matter of national purpose and national pride.

We need to build a relationship of trust not just within a firm but within a society. By trust, I mean the recognition of a mutual purpose for which we work together and in which we all benefit. It is a stakeholder economy, in which opportunity is available to all, advancement is through merit, and from which no group or class is set apart or excluded. This is the economic justification for social cohesion, for a fair and strong society – a traditional commitment of left-of-centre politics but one with relevance today, if it is applied anew to the modern world.

We know the pace and effect of new global markets and technological change. Jobs can be rendered obsolete, even whole industries. The world of work has been transformed. There is a revolution happening in media, communications and information. There is a real risk that, in this era of change, some prosper but many are left behind, their ambitions laid waste.

We need a country in which we acknowledge an obligation collectively to ensure each citizen gets a stake in it. One-nation politics is not some expression of sentiment, or even of justifiable concern for the less well off. It is an active politics – the bringing of a country together, a sharing of the possibility of power, wealth and opportunity. The old means of achieving that on the Left was through redistribution in the tax and benefit regime. But in a global economy the old ways won't do. Of course a fair tax system is right. But really a life on benefit – dependent on the state – is not what most people want. They want independence, dignity, self-improvement, a chance to earn and get on. The problems of low pay and unemployment must be tackled at source.

The economics of the centre and centre-left today should be geared to the creation of the stakeholder economy which involves all our people, not a privileged few, or even a better-off 30 or 40 or 50 per cent. If we fail in that, we waste talent, squander potential wealth-creating ability, and deny the basis of trust upon which a cohesive society – one nation – is built. If people feel they have no stake in a society, they feel little responsibility towards it and little inclination to work for its success.

The implications of creating a stakeholder economy are profound. They mean a commitment by government to tackle long-term and structural unemployment. The development of an underclass of people, cut off from society's mainstream, living often in poverty, the black economy, crime and family instability, is a moral and economic evil. Most Western economies suffer from it. It is wrong, and unnecessary, and, incidentally, very costly.

Reform of the welfare state must be one of the fundamental

Business leaders recognise that what New Labour is saying fits exactly with current thinking in industry. Some of our great companies call themselves stakeholder firms – John Lewis, Rover, M&S. Business advisers like John Kay and Charles Handy say that competitiveness and success comes from a stakeholder approach. The great lesson they draw from their research is that companies that treat their workers as partners are the ones that succeed. The same goes for a country.

From a speech in the Assembly Rooms, Derby, 18 January 1996 objectives of an incoming Labour government. Our welfare state, begun by Lloyd George and Churchill (then a Liberal) and carried through by the 1945 Labour government, is one of our proudest creations. But it suffers today from two important weaknesses: it does not alleviate poverty effectively and it does not properly assist the growth of independence, the move from benefit to work. Too many people go on to benefit to stay there. The result is that the welfare state neither meets sufficiently its founding principle, nor is it cost-effective. For Singapore the Central Provident Fund has worked well. But I stress that, though we will examine carefully the CPF system, we cannot transplant one system in one country to another country with a different system born in very different circumstances. But where there are lessons to be learned we will learn them, and it is surely right, for example, to look at a better balance between savings, investment and security in the modern world.

The stakeholder economy has a stakeholder welfare system. By that I mean that the system will flourish in its aims of promoting security and opportunity across the life cycle only if it holds the commitment of the whole population, rich and poor. This requires that everyone has a stake. The alternative is a residual system just for the poor. After the Second World War, the route to this sort of commitment was seen simply as universal cash benefits – most obviously child benefit and pensions. But today's demands and changed lifestyles require a more active conception of welfare, based on services as well as cash, child care as well as child benefit, training as well as unemployment benefit.

Secondly, our education system must be guaranteed to serve all our people, not an élite. Britain has extraordinary talent in science, research and innovation, though occasionally we do not develop it in the way we should. But we need the commitment to excellence at the top to permeate all the way down. This is not just about spending money. Sir Geoffrey Holland, a former Permanent Secretary at the Department of Education, now Vice-chancellor at Exeter University, has argued that there is room for a 30 per cent improvement in the education system within existing budgets – not least by building the system so as to include people rather than exclude them and by developing genuine leadership at all levels of the system.

Thirdly, we must ensure that the new technologies, with their almost limitless potential, are harnessed and dispersed among all our people. Knowledge and technology can combine today as never before to educate, liberate and expand horizons. A class divide in technology in the information age would be a disaster, and it must be avoided.

Fourthly, we must build the right relationship of trust between business and government. For far too long, relations have been dogged by the fear of business that government wants to take it over and government's fear that business left to its own devices will not be socially responsible. In reality, in a modern economy, we need neither old-style *dirigisme* nor rampant *laissez-faire*. There are key objectives which business and government can agree and work together to achieve. This 'enabling' role of government is crucial to long-term stability and growth.

The same relationship of trust and partnership applies within a firm. Successful companies invest, treat their employees fairly, and value them as a resource not just of production but of creative innovation. The debate about corporate governance in Britain is still in its infancy and has largely been focused on headline issues like directors' pay and perks. We cannot by legislation guarantee that a company will behave in a way conducive to trust and long-term commitment, but it is surely time to assess how we shift the emphasis in corporate ethos from the company being a mere vehicle for the capital market – to be traded, bought and sold as a commodity – towards a vision of the company as a community or partnership in which each employee has a stake, and where the company's responsibilities are more clearly delineated.

Finally, stakeholders in a modern economy will today, more frequently than ever before, be self-employed or small businesses. We should encourage this, diversify the range of help and advice for those wanting to start out on their own, and again use the huge potential of the developing technology to allow them to do so successfully. They may work alone or in small units, but they are part of the larger economic picture.

This brings me back to the Asian Tigers. One feature of them, discerned for example by Dr Francis Fukuyama – an economist of the Right who is none the less concerned at the selfish individualism of parts of Western society – is their high level of social cohesion. This may be based on value systems either different or inappropriate for Western economies, but the broad notion of a unified society with a strong sense of purpose and direction can be achieved in different ways for different cultures and nations. And it is really a matter of common sense. Working as a team is an effective way of working, or playing a sport, or running an organisation. My point is that a successful country must be run the same way. That cannot work unless everyone feels part of the team, trusts it, and has a stake in its success and future.

This is where a new economics of the centre and left-of-centre must go: towards an open economy working with the grain of global change; disciplined in macro-economic and fiscal policy, yet distinguished from the *laissez-faire* passive approach of the Right by a willingness to act to prepare the country for this change; and committed to ensuring that its benefits are fairly distributed and all its citizens are part of one nation and get the chance to succeed. That is the real way to combine efficiency and equity in a modern age.

From a speech to the Singapore Business Community, 8 January 1996

It is in the Tories' interests that they cloud the stakeholding debate. They will always say, whatever we do, whatever we propose, that we are going back to the old days. You know, and I know, that we are not: that it is the Tories who are stuck in the past, still arguing about Margaret Thatcher, and that it is New Labour that has a radical and exciting approach to politics, New Labour that can rebuild our nation as a strong cohesive society in which the individual can thrive. That is what the stakeholder economy is about.

From a speech in the Assembly Rooms, Derby, 18 January 1996

35 *The Stakeholder Society*

In 1985 *Faith in the City*, the report of the Archbishop of Canterbury's Special Commission on Urban Priority Areas, sounded a warning note about the direction of economic and social policy in Britain. It argued that economic and social inequality were becoming more pervasive in our society; that this inequality was in part attributable to a governing ideology of unfettered individualism; that the effects of this ideology on those at the bottom were not just material disadvantage but exclusion from national life; and that we all had a moral responsibility – whether we were personally rich or poor, religious or secular, urban residents or country farmers – to contribute towards the creation of a more just society.

Since then, that warning note has become a nagging siren of disaffection, malaise and cynicism. In essence, the reason for this is simple. Britain lacks drive and common purpose. People feel that this country – their country – is at grave risk of losing the values that made it strong. British strengths seem to be melting away. People feel that the fair play for which we are famed is a thing of the past. They believe that values of decency and tolerance are being spurned. They see that a culture of responsibility and mutuality is being eroded. They recognise an outward-looking spirit of adventure and discovery being lost. They sense that national pride is at a low ebb. And they know that, as a result, we are all poorer – left feeling worse off in a country that feels like it is going downhill.

Our society is more divided, it squanders more of our talent in unemployment and low-paid, insecure work; our NHS is creaking at the joints; our children's education is at risk; there is fear on our streets; and our economy is falling behind. No wonder there is a deep-seated 'feel-bad' factor. I believe people want an alternative moral and political compass to take Britain into the twenty-first century, and I want to put on the record my view of what the new direction should be.

297

My vision is of a new Britain that is one Britain – working in the interests of the many and not the few. It has three elements: economic, social and political. Here I want to argue for a *society* in which everyone has a stake.

In the first part of this century we saw the high-water mark of collectivism. The institutions of the welfare state were born. The power and influence of government grew. In the second part there was a reaction. The 1980s saw its peak – the era of the individual fighting against what were perceived as the excesses of the collectivist age.

The question for today is whether we can achieve a new relationship between individual and society, in which the individual acknowledges that, in certain key respects, it is only by working together in a community of people that the individual's interests can be advanced. That means going beyond the traditional boundaries of Left and Right, breaking new ground by escaping from sterile debates that have polarised our politics for too long.

To recover national purpose we need to start thinking and acting as one nation, one community again. But the principles governing it must be different.

'Community' cannot simply be another word for 'state' or 'government'. Both of these have a role to play, but we should aim to decentralise power to people, to allow them to make important decisions that affect them. We must create a society in which people advance through merit and not birth. The blunt truth is that Britain is still, after all these years, a place where class counts, where the best do not always come through, and whose institutions reinforce a sense of us as a country living in our past, not learning from it.

Above all, however, we must create a society based on a notion of mutual rights and responsibilities, on what is actually a modern notion of social justice – 'something for something'. We accept our duty as a society to give each person a stake in its future. And in return each person accepts responsibility to respond, to work to improve themselves.

One Nation: The Reinvention of Community

I believe that the reassertion of one-nation ideals based on Britain's enduring values – social unity, common purpose, fairness and mutual responsibility – represents one of the great tides of thought that govern politics and society in Britain. After the war, the collectivist impulse was supreme. *Laissez-faire* had been seen to fail in the 1930s. Collective action for common ends was seen to work in the war. And after the war, it transformed the lives of millions of working people. Collective provision enhanced freedom and was popular.

But in the 1960s the pendulum swung towards a more individualistic ethos. For a generation or more, the dominant model of human behaviour on Left and Right was highly individualistic. This was true in the liberation of private life and in intellectual debate. The Left was captivated by the elegance and power of Professor John Rawls's *Theory of Justice* (Harvard University Press, 1971). His manifesto for an egalitarian society is a brilliant exposition of the argument that an equal society is in the interests of anyone who does not know which position in that society they would occupy. But it is derived from a highly individualistic view of the world.

Meanwhile, on the Right, the strategy of accommodation to the postwar settlement was replaced with a policy of hostility to it. The lesson of 1945 was taken to be that collective action was necessarily inefficient, bureaucratic, doomed to fail. Today, the Right still say that the only way to move beyond Thatcherism is to have more of it.

But there is also an alternative view gaining currency. It was articulated with courage by religious as well as secular leaders. There was *Faith in the City* in 1985. It has been developed with insight and eloquence by the Chief Rabbi appointed in 1991. People increasingly recognise that to move forward as individuals we need to move forward as a community. And today this alternative view is drawing sustenance from a wide range of sources.

For myself, I start from a simple belief that people are not separate economic actors competing in the market-place of life. They are citizens of a community. We are social beings, nurtured in families and communities and human only because we develop the moral power of personal responsibility for ourselves and each other. Britain is simply stronger as a team than as a collection of selfish players.

Our relationships with and commitments to others are not add-ons to our personalities: they make us who we are. Notions of mutuality and interdependence are not abstract ideals: they are facts of life. People are not just competitive: they are cooperative too. They are not just interested in the welfare of themselves: they are interested in the well-being of others. It was William Morris who wrote, 'Fellowship is life, and lack of fellowship is death.' How right he was.

Those seeking to regain the benefits of strong community need to learn from what is good in the liberal tradition, and preserve and extend it. But we must have confidence in the basic truths: that all people are created equal, that they owe duty to each other as well as themselves, and that the good society is one which works for the good of all and not just the few.

The purpose is simple – to ensure that the country works for the good of everybody, and everybody works for the good of the country. It is necessary because the alternative is decline and decay.

The Collapse of Community Today
The abiding failure of the Tories has been that policies have been pursued which have left us divided and weakened as a society and an economy. At the bottom, what some people call an underclass has been created:

★ One in four men of working age is not in work.

★ One in six of the population relies on a means-tested benefit.

★ One in three children grows up in poverty.

★ Forty per cent of the population have been unemployed at some point in the last ten years – that is, 10 million people.

But even more striking is the contrast with those at the top. While the risks facing the majority have multiplied, those at

300

the top have been served up a one-way bet to a risk-free fortune:

★ Government figures show that, while the income of the bottom 10 per cent of the population has fallen by 17 per cent since 1979, and the bottom 30 per cent have failed to benefit from economic growth, the top 10 per cent are 62 per cent better off.

★ In the privatised water and electricity utilities, salaries of chairmen and chief executives have gone up on average by over 250 per cent since privatisation.

★ The gap between highest and lowest paid is now greater than at any time since the 1880s.

★ A child from an unskilled family is twice as likely to die before the age of fifteen as a child with a professional father.

Between the underclass and the overclass is a new and growing anxious class – people insecure about their jobs, afraid that public services will not be there when they need them, struggling to pay mortgages and new charges, prompted to opt for private pensions and now finding that they get very little in return. These are bank clerks on average income, retail staff on zero-hours contracts, primary-school teachers and police officers now paying top-rate tax, young couples with negative equity, managers facing a lay-off for the first time in their career – all people in work, but dogged by insecurity and struggling to make ends meet.

The Right used to say that to be cruel was to be efficient. In fact it is neither morally justified nor economically sensible. What has in fact happened is that, far from economic success bringing social good fortune, the collateral social damage – unemployment, low pay, crime, ill health – has in turn weakened the economy.

No Way Back, New Way Forward
The policy recommendations of *Faith in the City* covered employment, housing, education, crime and community development. I will address them in turn. Our approach must be, first, to ensure everyone has the means to live a decent

life, and the best way to achieve this is not to boost benefits but instead to help people into work; second, to ensure that everyone has the opportunity to better themselves, and the best way to do this is through education; and, third, to foster among the whole population a sense of community and purpose. The modern welfare state is not founded on a paternalistic government giving out more benefits but on an enabling government that through work and education helps people to help themselves.

A Stake in Employment

The most meaningful stake anyone can have in society is the ability to earn a living and support a family. That is why we have put the attack on unemployment, and especially long-term unemployment, at the top of our economic agenda. We have put forward a comprehensive range of ideas to attack unemployment at source. They include:

★ education, employment and community initiatives for the young unemployed that would slash youth unemployment over a Parliament;

★ welfare reforms to provide hope for the one in five workless households, trapped on benefit by a system designed for a labour market and family structure that no longer exists;

★ a Jobs, Education and Training programme for single parents who need career advice, child care and training;

★ the phased release of the capital receipts held by local authorities, which would not only provide jobs but, equally important, provide homes that so many people are desperate to live in.

A Stake in Housing

Next to employment, secure housing is the foundation of personal security. And together they constitute a double trap: no home means no job, and no job means no home. In the new Britain I want to build, I do not want anyone to have to sleep on the streets, I do not want children growing up in substandard housing on crime-ridden estates, and I do not want communities ravaged by the multiple deprivation which far too many of them face today.

But in Britain for too many people housing is a source of insecurity and fear. There are 160,000 families without a home; 1 million people stuck in negative equity – a figure rising by 50,000 a year – and a housing-benefit bill now greater than the sum we spent on housing investment in 1979.

I welcome the government's decision to extend the Rough Sleepers' Initiative. But it could do much more. Instead of cracking down on rights to housing benefit, as the government is doing, we should be attacking what fraud officers estimate to be the £2 billion a year cost of housing-benefit fraud. There has to be greater cooperation between councils themselves and between councils and the DSS. There is a strong case for a licensing scheme for landlords with multi-occupancy houses. Why not make surplus properties available to housing associations and local authorities? And why not build on the experience of the Camberwell Foyer, where homelessness is tackled at root – by combining it with training so that, as well as housing security, young people are set on the road to financial independence?

A Stake in Education

These two props of a decent society demand an ambitious programme designed to tackle the most obvious sources of social injustice. But they are only a foundation for a more secure and prosperous society.

The core economic challenge facing us as a nation is to use the power of our people – their effort, talent and ingenuity – to reverse a long decline that has taken us from being the world's third economic power in 1950 to eighteenth in the league of income per head today. The key is the education and skills of our people. As leading American economist Lester Thurow said in a speech to the RSA, 'Show me a skilled individual, a skilled company, or a skilled country and I will show you an individual, a company or a country that has a chance to be successful. Show me an unskilled individual, company or country and I will show you a failure in the twenty-first century.'

We have for a long time been very good at educating the élite of our country. The top schools – public and private – have a deservedly high reputation. Some of our universities lead the world. But I am not willing to write off 85 per cent of British young people when in other countries 80 per cent reach university entrance standard. The challenge for British education is to expand opportunity for the majority of people who are not part of the educational élite.

The real lesson of the test results is not about selection in 150 schools but the standards in 25,000 schools. That means overcoming the failures of the Tory years, but it also means making good those things left undone at the time of the ending of the eleven-plus. Comprehensive admission does not of itself make for good schooling.

What is needed is a new move forward, combining inclusiveness with individuality, exploiting a child's individual talent within a context where all talents are developed. It reflects the wider synthesis of community and individual of which I have spoken. It is the essential underpinning of Labour's new approach.

Our education agenda lays the basis of opportunity on which a thriving society rests. But I want to add to it here specifically in the context of improving performance in the inner cities. These are areas in which the National Commission on Education report *Success Against the Odds* says the dice are loaded against educational achievement. There are many good schools in inner cities, succeeding against the odds, but they need help to improve. Schools in LEAs forming the top quarter in terms of advantage are now achieving results over 50 per cent better than those in the bottom quarter.

I want to see us move forward on several fronts.

First, partnership with the community. The Labour Party is placing increasing stress on the need to link school and family in a more concrete and clear way. We have proposed new targets for daily homework from primary- and secondary-school pupils, and we pioneered the idea of home–school contracts detailing the rights and responsibilities of teachers and parents. But many children and parents lack the facilities at home to make good this contract. Therefore I want to look at how we can organise and fund a national network of pre-school and after-school homework centres around the country, to ensure that throughout the population learning is not confined to school hours.

Second, transcending old structures – refusing to go back to the eleven-plus but refusing too to make do with uniformity. In June 1995 I talked about the need to recognise that children do have different abilities and interests that change over time. I talked too about how this could be recognised in primary schools. I want to see this flexibility built into our system, so that accelerated learning is possible in any subject in which a pupil shows talent. This does not mean twelve-year-olds suddenly becoming sixth-formers, but it does mean bright children being stretched instead of being bored in subjects where they have particular aptitude. The initiatives we have announced to bring new technology to the fingertips of pupils, as well as reforms to the 14–19 curriculum, will make this personalised learning possible.

Third, I want to see the best teachers contributing to the revival of our most difficult schools. Labour has already launched the idea of a new grade within the profession to reward the best teachers. In the United States, 'Teach for America' is a corps of outstanding recent graduates funded by charitable foundations to make a two-year commitment to teach in deprived urban schools. There are strengths and weaknesses in its approach, but the basic idea – that we need to make special efforts to raise standards in inner-city schools – is surely right. They could include arrangements for 'twinning' or 'mentoring' with other head-teachers, including those in other countries, and with senior managers in other sectors. We need to match people keen to make a commitment with schools that need them; we need to ensure access to the benefits of the Teachers' Centre that we are setting up on the Internet; and we should explore arrangements to provide sabbatical terms to help people recharge batteries and further develop their skills. All are directed to ensuring that personal resources are of the very highest standard.

Fourth, as a result of local management of schools, LEAs are changing from primarily being deliverers of services to instead supporting schools in their drive for improvement. They are less a chain of command than a spur to improvement. But, just as schools should have targets for year-on-year improvement, so should LEAs. And LEAs should above all be audited, by Ofsted and the Audit Commission, for the pressure they put on schools to set ambitious targets for improvement, and then for the support they give to help meet them.

A Stake in the Community

Successful communities are about what people give as much as what they take, and any attempt to rebuild community for a modern age must assert that personal and social responsibility are not optional extras but core principles of a thriving society today. Without responsibility to each other, we create a nation where community evaporates. If I take without giving, enjoy rights without accepting obligations, then I betray the trust of those who do give, those who do exercise their responsibilities in a responsible way. And then those who were responsible see little point in being so, and we end up without a community at all.

The key is to recognise that we owe duty to more than self. Responsibility applies from top to bottom of society: from the responsibility to pay taxes to fund common services, to the responsibility of fathers to their children after a divorce, to the responsibility of people to respect the lives of their neighbours.

Responsibility is about family and the next generation. My concern in the family policy debate is with the conditions in which children grow up. It is their needs that must be paramount. It is in the family that children learn self-respect and mutual respect, where they are first taught right from wrong, where they learn to value education and learning.

But responsibility is also about service beyond the family, to the community. This is in part about crime and its effects on communities.

It is instructive to see how far the debate has moved over the last fifteen years. The *Faith in the City* report helpfully quotes Lord Whitelaw's view, expressed in 1978. He said, 'Let no one be in any doubt about the danger that has been created

[by the level of unemployment] in terms of crimes of all sorts.'
Today, the government denies any link between crime and
unemployment. It says prison works, so we have more people
in prison than ever before, despite a conviction rate of only
one crime in fifty.

The only strategy with an ounce of honesty or common
sense is to attack with vigour the conditions in which crime
breeds, and at the same time to insist that serious crimes require
serious punishment. That means we should implement the
recommendations of the Morgan Report which advocated
local partnerships of police, business, local authorities and community groups to prevent crime. We need to continue to
crack down on the use of knives and firearms – the recent
knives amnesty shows one way forward. And we need to
ensure proper punishment for crimes like rape and racial violence that are not properly dealt with. Most important of all,
however, we need to increase the likelihood that someone
committing a crime will be caught.

But, in addition to the 'negative' project of reducing crime,
there is a positive one. Across Britain, and perhaps especially
in some of its most deprived neighbourhoods, people give
selflessly of themselves to help each other, because in the
process they are fulfilling themselves as well as helping others.
One of the most striking themes of *Faith in the City* was its
constant insistence that, whoever else moved out of the Urban
Priority Areas, the Church would stay and work for the good
of the community.

Conclusion: Stakeholder Britain

R.H. Tawney wrote in *Social Democracy in Britain* that freedom
means 'the utmost possible development of the capacities of
every human being, and the deliberate organisation of society
for the attainment of that objective'.

That extension of freedom is not possible in the conditions
I described earlier. The divisions in our society identified in
Faith in the City have been exacerbated over the last ten years.
Our social fabric has been tattered and torn. Our economy is
falling behind. Our politics is centralised and aloof.

I see two futures open to this country. In one, Britain's

307

communities follow the process that has occurred in some places in the US, where the affluent have retreated into fort-resses with private security guards, leaving the rest to live in ghettos of low opportunity, crime and insecurity. But the cycle of decay and economic underperformance continues. This is the *Blade Runner* scenario.

That is not the sort of Britain I want to live in in the twenty-first century. And that is not a future in tune with Britain's basic instincts. We are a country that supports the underdog. We are tolerant. We are great adventurers. We are patriotic, but we will always stand up against aggression against someone else.

For the new millennium we need a war on exclusion and a determination to extend opportunity to all. No one should pretend such a war will be easy to win – and I say at the outset it cannot be fought simply by more government money – but it is our duty to fight such a war, and to win it. Everyone has to be involved. This is not just a task for government, but for the private sector too, and most of all for the communities themselves.

Let us talk of rising living-standards, and let's make that mean cash in the pocket. But let's make it mean more than cash too. Let's make it mean rising standards of behaviour, rising standards in schools and hospitals, rising standards of mutual respect. Those are the living standards that make us one nation – a nation bound together by what unites us, not pulled apart by what divides.

In 1941, Archbishop William Temple, perhaps Britain's greatest Christian Socialist, convened the Malvern Conference to discuss the contribution of Christianity to British and world politics. Four hundred clergy listened to diverse speakers. The famous Malvern Declaration includes a fine ideal for anyone involved in politics: it says the Christian doctrine requires that men – the conference was progressive but not wholly enlightened – shall 'have an opportunity to become the best of which they are capable and shall find in the prosecution of their daily tasks fulfilment and not frustration of their human nature'.

To realise the view of human nature I have spelt out here

is a challenge to all of us. On our own, we will never solve it. As one nation, together, we can.

From 'Faith in the City – Ten Years On', a speech in Southwark Cathedral, 29 January 1996

36 *Stakeholder Politics*

John Smith was a passionate believer in constitutional change and in extending democracy. As Elizabeth Smith said recently, his belief in democracy was to him as important as his socialism. The values behind it were embodied in his character – openness, trust, and confidence in the ability of people to take responsibility for their own lives.

The institutions which shaped him – Dunoon Grammar School, Glasgow University, the Scottish legal system, the Labour Party and the Church of Scotland – made him a great example of the 'democratic intellect' which is the hallmark of the Scots. The influence John Smith had on British politics was testament to the powerful contribution his distinctively Scottish brand of socialism makes to our democracy.

John Smith knew that government could be a powerful agent for social justice and individual emancipation. But he was also convinced that if Britain was really to change for the better there had to be change in our institutions of government. He was appalled by the abuse of power during the Conservative years. He felt public service had been tarnished, and the British people demeaned.

In 1993, in a lecture to Charter 88, he said, 'I want to see a fundamental shift in the balance of power between the citizen and the state – a shift away from an overpowering state to a citizens' democracy where people have rights and powers and where they are served by accountable and responsive government.' John died before he could embark on that task. It is his unfinished business which we must now finish.

A New Politics

There are three essential questions in any debate about Britain's constitution:

1. Are we satisfied with the way we are governed?

2. If not, do we agree that the root of the problem is over-

310

centralised government and an undeveloped citizenship?

3. If it is, how do we best devolve power and develop citizenship?

There is, of course, a prior question: Does how we are governed matter? I assume we would answer yes; but, if we are blunt about it, to many this issue seems a long way from the bread-and-butter issues of jobs, health, education and crime.

Yet consider for a moment. Central government will set the economic policy, which affects jobs and industry. Local government has a crucial impact on education. Bodies – quangos – now run our health service. A mixture of councillors and appointees holds our police accountable. The rules on benefits and pensions are determined, in effect, by agencies. A plethora of local councils – large and small – changes for good or ill our quality of life.

These all involve decisions that affect us vitally. Whether the decisions are taken well or badly makes a difference to our lives. Just as companies succeed or fail by the discipline of the market, so governments largely succeed or fail by the discipline of accountability. How government is made transparent, how we know what it is doing and why, how we complain, how we change it, how we influence it – these are the essence of democracy.

This issue of government is not one for the 'chattering classes' – consigned dismissively to the inside pages of the broadsheets. It touches the vitals of the nation.

In part, the reason for the public's disaffection lies in the nature of the modern political battle. As the clash of the all-

---

I hope you will take this as more than just a sort of boring political point, but I genuinely believe that the Conservatives are in such a state now that, in the decisions that they make, first they have to consider the internal questions in the Conservative Party and only then do they move on to the interests of the country.

From Breakfast with Frost, *BBC Television, 14 January 1996*

---

encompassing and absolutist ideologies of the first part of the twentieth century grows muted and distant – the Right having accepted the need for social provision; the Left the necessity of a market economy – politicians feel obliged to generate the same amount of noise over what are really far more limited disagreements. The public sense this and find the battle over-the-top and childish.

That is not to say there are not issues of huge moment or that there do not remain substantial differences between Left and Right, radicals and conservatives, but they fit within a larger body of consensus and sometimes they cross Left/Right lines. In that sense they are more akin to nineteenth- than twentieth-century debate.

In part, however, the disaffection is because people feel no ownership, no stake in much of the political process. The citizen feels remote from power because he or she is remote from power. Britain is *the* most centralised government of any large state in the Western world.

Some large countries are federations, like Germany or the United States. Some substantially devolve power. None has such an extraordinary degree of power held in the hands of central government with such diminished forms of account-ability as Britain. No one knows who to go to, who to com-plain to, where to make the presence of the citizen felt. This is surely because of the way we are governed – power is being kept in the centre.

And it does not make for efficient government. Indeed the opposite is the case. Look at the poll tax or the Child Support Agency or the quangos of each and every description that now run a large part of our public services: they are all imposts of central government. Neither does it release the creative and innovative energy as different centres of power can. A revived local government – with Conservatives as well as others taking it seriously and not giving up on it – could provide ideas and new ways of working, rather than being treated as a punchbag for those who have nothing positive to say.

Of course the detail of specific policy and implementation matters. But the challenge that must first be answered is: Should nothing change?

The Conservative Party Chairman rubbishes the entire agenda of constitutional change. But is this serious politics? Does he really believe no change is needed? The destruction of local government is fine, is it? No need for a proper body for London – alone of all the great cities of the world without one?

Despite huge and genuine pressures for devolution in Scotland and Wales, does he really say there is no case for anything different happening? No requirement for even the most elementary disclosure of information – in this, one of the most secretive democracies in the world?

Are we going to continue, alone of all the democracies, to continue to have laws passed by an Upper Chamber a majority of whose members are there by birth not merit, perhaps because 300 years ago their ancestor was the mistress of a monarch?

Are we, the mother of democracy, unable to take it now any further?

I cannot believe we are so lacking in courage or are so complacent that we cannot rise to the challenge of renewing our democracy. Of course there are crucial points of implementation that can be returned to, in detail, at the appropriate time before the election. But let us first agree the terms of this debate: change or no change. And let those who favour the latter, opposing all change, justify their position as a matter of principle and not avoid it by skirmishing in the thicket of detail.

The Task Ahead

If we are to renew our democracy, we must start with local government – the government closest to the people.

I want to enable local communities to decide more things for themselves through local councils. The future of councils may not be as direct service providers in every area, but councillors have a crucial role in speaking up for the areas they represent and promoting the partnerships necessary to empower the community to realise its ambitions.

Indeed there already exists substantial evidence, even under present arrangements, of what an active, modern local govern-

313

ment can achieve: new transport systems, nursery education, reclaiming derelict land, helping small businesses. If these successes got half as much publicity as some of local government's mistakes, a truer picture of local public service might emerge.

With additional power – removal of crude rate-capping limits, for example – should come greater accountability, with at least some part of the council up for election every year so a verdict can be passed.

We are already committed to a proper strategic authority for London to replace the existing mishmash of boards and quangos. I also favour directly elected mayors, at least for our capital city and other large cities. Thanks in large measure to government destruction of local democracy there has been a dangerous loss of civic pride in many areas, and this is one way that we might address that.

It is hard to defend the way London is presently run. London is a great city and a huge asset to our country. It is a fantastic business and cultural centre, and a great place to live and work. But it is crucially handicapped in dealing with its problems because it has no elected voice of its own. Unemployment, housing, clogged transport and pollution are just some of the challenges that Londoners face. London has been left to drift, and its quality of life has suffered.

A large majority of Londoners want their own city-wide authority. Even Geoffrey Howe has admitted that abolishing the GLC was a mistake. I hope that Lord Howe and others who recognise they were wrong in the past will support our plan to establish an elected authority, able to speak up for London and work together with business and the people to give the city the future it deserves.

Did you notice how the Tories all lined up to say that 'Now we have settled the leadership, we can get on with the real job in hand – attacking the Labour Party'? Excuse me, but isn't the real job of government to govern the country, and to provide clear leadership for the country?

From a speech to the British Society of Magazine Editors, London,
7 July 1995

In the other English regions our aim is clear: we intend to make the tier of regional government which is already in place through the government's regional offices and regional quangos more accountable to the people. I understand that support for elected regional government varies across the country. But, as I travel nationwide, I find more and more enthusiasm for recognising the diversity of England and allowing regions to take greater responsibility in matters like transport and economic development.

Changes like this cannot be imposed. They must enjoy the support of the people living in those regions.

In Scotland and Wales it is now abundantly clear what choice people favour: they want greater control over their national affairs, and that is why we will devolve power to them.

People ask why we offer different packages for Scotland and Wales though both are to be legislated for in our first year of government. The truth is simple: they are different countries, they have different histories, and they are governed in different ways at the moment.

The Welsh Office is a recent creation, and there is very little separate Welsh legislation. But there is real anger at the dominance of public life in Wales by Tory appointees on unelected quangos. And our plans for a Welsh Assembly will address that.

Scotland, on the other hand, had its own Parliament for hundreds of years. The Union in 1707 was forged by two sovereign Parliaments. And the office of Secretary of State has existed since 1885.

Over the past hundred years a huge degree of administrative devolution has been established. The Scottish Office now has an annual budget of over £14 billion a year. It is responsible for more civil servants than the European Commission. And the Secretary of State appoints about 5,000 people to quangos.

Scotland has its own legal and criminal justice system. There is a separate body of Scots law on matters like education, housing and local government, and most Scottish legislation is handled by a specific Scottish procedure at Westminster.

We propose to make this existing devolution and Scottish

law-making properly accountable to the people, so that decisions on specifically Scottish matters can be taken in Scotland.

Even today the Conservatives can't get their line of attack right. Dr Mawhinney says it would wreck the Union by transferring power to Scotland. Lord Mackay says the opposite in *The Times*: 'Westminster would remain the centre of power. The proposed Parliament in Edinburgh would be just a sop.'

I find it odd to say the least that the government proposes devolution for Northern Ireland as part of a package designed to keep the Union together but says that devolution anywhere else is irresponsible and reckless. The truth is that the changes we propose will strengthen the Union by creating a new partnership between government and the people in those areas which demand more power. For let us be clear: devolution is about trust. And our government does not place nearly enough trust in its people.

Trusting people to take their own decisions is a lesson which has been learned by business. In today's economy, successful companies devolve decision-making to their autonomous units, they allow for regional variations, and in doing so they get much more from the people who work for them. Of course the centre still decides on the core functions and sets out the broad company strategy, but the trend is increasingly to give managers on the ground the freedom to decide how to implement its goals.

Yet at the same time as the economy has been changing in this way, and at the same time as virtually every major country in Europe has been engaged in a process of decentralisation, in Britain the state has been pulling in the opposite direction.

So new politics is about a stakeholder democracy as well as a stakeholder economy. And that stake must also extend to the relationship between central government and the people. That is why building the new politics means changing how national government is run as well as devolving power outwards to the people.

The first right of a citizen in any mature democracy should be the right to information. It is time to sweep away the cobwebs of secrecy which hang over far too much government activity.

In 1994 Mr Major published his code and promised further legislation, but the government appears to be trying to keep its commitment a secret. Why, apart from obvious exceptions like national security, should people not know what is available on file about them? It is a great irony that, in a democracy where people have increased information about almost everything else, they often cannot find out the simplest thing from government. If trust in the people means anything, then there can be no argument against a Freedom of Information Act which will give people rights to public information.

But the right to information is only a start. There is also a strong case for a code of citizens' rights which guarantees the rights of individuals to basic freedoms and opportunities.

As a first step we should incorporate the European Convention of Human Rights into British law. We have been signatories since 1951. It is quite separate from the European Union or the European Court of Justice. People in this country have access to the protection and the guarantees of basic human rights that the Convention provides, yet to gain access to those rights British citizens must appeal to the European Commission and the European Court in Strasbourg. It is a long and expensive process, and only the most diligent manage to stay the course.

I believe it makes sense to end the cumbersome practice of forcing people to go to Strasbourg to hold their government to account. By incorporating the Convention into British law, the rights it guarantees would be available in courts in both Britain and Northern Ireland. This would make it clear that the protection afforded by the Convention was not some foreign import but that it had been accepted by successive British governments and that it should apply throughout the United Kingdom.

Some have said that this system takes power away from Parliament and places it in the hands of judges. In reality, since we are already signatories to the Convention, it means allowing British judges rather than European judges to pass judgement.

That brings me to Parliament itself. Parliament has undergone some changes in the past couple of years. The House of Commons now sits more sensible hours, and has acted to curb the unacceptable practices revealed by the 'cash for questions' affair. But do the Conservatives really pretend that this is all that can be done?

We still need to update our legislative procedures to improve the effectiveness of Parliament. There is also a case for effective consultation to produce better-quality legislation. And it does not help produce good government when almost every change in every clause of a Bill is interpreted as a defeat for the government.

Perhaps the oddest and least defensible part of the British constitution is the power wielded by hereditary peers in the House of Lords. The Conservative Party has placed its colours firmly on the territory of no change here either – though I believe some of the more enlightened Conservatives, even those in the Lords, will disagree.

The case for reform is simple and obvious. It is in principle wrong and absurd that people should wield power on the basis of birth not merit or election. What is more, there are over 300 official Tory hereditary peers, but only 12 Labour and 24 Liberal Democrat. Hundreds more rarely appear, but if they did we can be sure very few would side with Labour or the Liberal Democrats. This is plainly and incontrovertibly politically biased.

In addition, these Tory peers do not just use the House of Lords as a drinking and dining club. They vote. Though obviously the Thatcher government must take the blame for the poll tax, but for the hereditary peers the poll tax would never have become law. It was the most expensive fiasco in fiscal history. It cost around £14 billion to implement, modify and then abandon. Lord Lawson revealed that it added more than 4p to the standard rate of income tax. The hereditary peers – Tory backwoodsmen summoned from all corners of the nation to vote – put it through.

In the crucial vote, on 23 May 1988, 317 peers voted in favour of the poll tax, 183 against. Life peers were in fact *opposed* to the poll tax by 125 to 97, but the hereditary peers made all the difference. They voted 220 to 54 in favour of the proposal.

There are no conceivable grounds for maintaining this system. Let me now deal in turn with each argument against its removal.

First, it is said some hereditary peers – albeit a small number – do participate regularly and make a positive contribution. Fine: some of them can be made life peers. But that is not an argument for keeping all of them, the bulk of whom are just Tory voting-fodder.

Secondly, it has been suggested that by changing the House of Lords we would lose the likes of Lord Bramall or the distinguished law lords. But none of these is a hereditary peer. They would remain. We have always favoured an elected second chamber, but some, like my colleague Lord Richard, leader of the Labour peers in the Lords, have suggested that if there was a move to an elected second chamber, provision could also be made for people of a particularly distinguished position or record. We are masters of our own rules and procedure.

Thirdly, it is said that if we don't immediately introduce an elected second chamber then reform of the House of Lords is worthless. More than that, it is said the reformed Lords would be an unelected quango. I find this the most curious and least persuasive argument of all.

At the moment the House of Lords is an unelected body, but it is both unelected and with membership predominantly based on birth, not merit. Whatever the final balance between election and merit, it is impossible to justify doing nothing about a manifest constitutional unfairness, namely membership of the legislature on the basis of birth. Surely we should first make the House of Lords a genuine body of the distinguished and meritorious – with a better, more open and independent means of establishing membership – and then debate how we incorporate democratic accountability.

It is of course elections to the House of Commons which give Parliament its fundamental legitimacy. And it is quite proper for people to ask whether we have the best and fairest available system of election. Some feel strongly about the case for reform and point to the Tory governments elected on a minority of the vote and the fact that smaller parties get squeezed under the current system. I do not dismiss such arguments. But in truth I have never been persuaded that under proportional representation we can avoid a situation where small parties end up wielding disproportionate power.

This is a serious debate, and views on it cross the boundaries of almost all political parties. That is why we are committed to holding a referendum on it.

These reforms would contribute to the health of our democracy. They would tackle the culture of secrecy, enshrine in British law people's legal rights, give us a reformed Parliament which could operate more effectively as a modern legislature, and allow the people to decide how the Commons was elected.

Conclusion

We are only a few years from a new millennium. People in Britain will then look around and see a world transformed since their youth.

We need to respond to the challenge of the new millennium by embarking on a journey of national renewal which creates a new young Britain – a young, self-confident and successful country which uses the talents of all its citizens and gives them a stake in the future. The renewal we need cannot be carried out by government alone but only by government in partnership with the people.

The reforms I have set out will transform our politics. They will redraw the boundaries between what is done in the name of the people and what is done by the people themselves. They will create a new relationship between government and the people based on trust, freedom, choice and responsibility. There is nothing about them that is necessarily party-political, yet they are deeply political reforms because they are concerned with the essence of our democracy and how people can exercise power in our system.

The Tories oppose all measures to give people a real stake in our democracy. They want to keep power for the few, not the many – for the centre, for the unelected and for hereditary peers.

New Labour wants to give power to the people – to be a government working in partnership with the people, which gives them freedom, choice and responsibility, and where the country is more united, more open and more confident about the future than it has been in decades.

That is the choice and this is the future we want to build in the name of John Smith.

I conclude with some words of Thomas Jefferson:

Men, by their constitutions, are naturally divided into two parties. (1) Those who fear and distrust the people, and wish to draw all powers from them into the hands of the higher classes. (2) Those who identify themselves with the people, have confidence in them, cherish and consider them as the most honest and safe depositary of the public interests. In every country these two parties exist, and in every one where they are free to think, speak and write, they will declare themselves.

I know which was the party of John Smith, and I am proud to follow in his footsteps.

From the John Smith Memorial Lecture, London, 7 February 1996

Index

Page references for pictures are shown in *italic*.

Accountable to None (Jenkins) 259
Act of Union (1707) 315, 316
Advisory Committee on Business and
  the Environment 228
Africa 203
age of consent 186–9
Agriculture and Fisheries, Ministry of
  179
Appeal Court 136
apprenticeships 92
Archbishop of Canterbury's Special
  Commission on Urban Priority
  Areas 297
Asia 98, 110, 203, 212
Asia Pacific region 119, 203, 204, 212
Asia/Europe Leaders' Meeting
  (1996) 212
Asian Tigers 110, 260, 296
Asquith, Herbert Henry, lst Earl of
  Oxford and Asquith 15
assisted places scheme 24, 67
Associate Teachers 169, 176
Attlee, Clement, lst Earl 4, 7, 10, 11,
  16
Audit Commission 306
Australian Labour Government 100
Austria 210, 283

balance of payments 79
Baldwin, Stanley 281
Balfour administration 15
Bank of England 81, 87, 88
banks 35, 37, 87–8, 94, 95, 119, 122
Barings group 129
Barnett, Corelli 10
BBC *see* British Broadcasting
  Corporation
bed-and-breakfast accommodation
  30, 69, 194, 199

benefit fraud 43
Benefit Transfer Programme 117
Bevan, Aneurin 4, 7, 9
Beveridge, William, lst Baron 7, 11,
  142
Beveridge Report 8, 9, 10, 19, 141
Bevin, Ernest 4, 10, 161, 281
Bill of Rights 20, 47
Birmingham 166
block vote 18, 32
Blunkett, David 53, 67, 170, *322*
BMA *see* British Medical Association
BNP (British National Party) 246
boom and bust 52, 63, 113, 122, 193,
  200
border controls 286
Bosnia 259, 285
Bradford and Bingley Building
  Society 194
Brammall, Lord 319
Bretton Woods agreement 281
Britain
  democratic 70
  divided xi
  in Europe 210, 211–12, 252,
  263–7, 280–87
  in the information economy
  104–5
  Japanese investment 120, 122–3,
  204, 263, 283
  Knowledge Britain 66–7, 114,
  125
  looking outwards 209–12
  relationship with the United States
  210, 266–7, 281–2, 283
  stakeholder 68–9, 307–9
  strong 70–72
British Broadcasting Corporation
  (BBC) 104, 106

British empire 10, 65, 210
'British Experiment' 75, 77, 79–84, 96
British Medical Association (BMA) 181, 187
British National Party (BNP) 246
British Telecom (BT) 67, 101, 104, 115, 127, 204
Brittan, Sir Leon 286
broadcasting 66, 103
Brown, Gordon 112, *290*
Brundtland Commission 227
BS 7750 231
BT *see* British Telecom
budgetary policy 76, 80, 81, 89–90
Bundesbank 87, 88
burglary 19, 35
business
    and the environment 228–9
    and government 295

cable technology 41, 67, 101–2, 127, 204
Callaghan, James 79–80, 269, 272
Camberwell Foyer 200, 303
Cambridge University 209
Camelot 69
Campaign for Freedom of Information 219
Canary Wharf, London 276
CAP *see* Common Agricultural Policy
capital assets, sale of the nation's 36
capital flows 86
capital markets 84, 86, 119–20
capital projects 40
capital receipts 30, 117, 196, 302
capital spending 89
capital stock 84
capitalism x
carbon dioxide emissions 228–9, 232
Cardiff 234
care-in-the-community provision 198
Castle, Barbara 8, 152
CBI *see* Confederation of British Industry

Central Provident Fund (Singapore) 294
centralisation xi–xii, 32
Chamberlain, Neville 281
Chambers of Commerce 107
Channel Tunnel 40, 114
Charter 88 310
child benefit 131, 142, 143, 146, 152, 294
child care 68, 93, 131, 143, 155, 157, 250, 294
Child Support Agency 312
children 50
    abuse of 64
    and computers 67
    disadvantaged 155
    and drugs 30
    and poverty 36, 300
    teaching values 37–8
    and welfare system 9
China 111, 119, 212
Christianity 57–61, 308
Churchill, Sir Winston Spencer 282, 294
Circle 33 Housing Trust 194
CIS (Commonwealth of Independent States) 224
citizens advice bureaux 103, 204
Citizen's Charter 230
Citizens' Service (proposed) 148, 241–2
citizenship 11, 218, 238, 246, 311
city centres viii
    see also inner cities
Clarke, Peter 14
class x, 9, 12, 45, 65, 121, 161–2, 221, 298
Clause IV (of the Labour Party constitution) 6, 15–16, 51, 52, 54, 55, 159, 226
climate change 225
Clinton, Bill 100, *202*, 266, 277
Cobbett, William 238, 243
Cold War 262, 266, 267, 281, 282
Cole, G.D.H. 239
collective action 14
collectivism 215, 298

Index

command economy 32
Commission on Social Justice 44,
    132, 141, 145–50
Common Agricultural Policy (CAP)
    70, 108, 116, 128, 211, 229, 264,
    267, 286
Common Foreign and Security
    Policy 264, 267, 283
Commonwealth 65, 210, 212, 260,
    282
Commonwealth of Independent
    States (CIS) 224
communications 67, 203, 292
communism 16, 77, 224
community xi, 29, 51, 237, 247, 298
    collapse of 300–301
    and duty 59
    and the environment 233–4
    fractured x, 121
    the individual within a 22, 39
    power of 156
    rebuilding 35–9
    reinvention of 299–300
    responsible 148
    a stake in the 147, 306–7
    strong 23, 178–9, 238, 273
    working together ix, 36, 37, 53,
    56
Community Service Volunteers 242,
    261–2
companies
    and competition 40
    failing 94
    investment funds 40
    taxation 113–14
    and the workforce 36, 42, 53, 92,
    295
competition
    and communications 67
    companies and 40
    global ix, 205
    in the information revolution
    100–101, 102, 104–5
competitiveness 111, 114–15, 118,
    124, 230, 285, 293
Concert of Europe 281
Confederation of British Industry
    (CBI) 95, 107, 113, 228

Congress of Berlin 281
Conservative Party
    and competitiveness 100–101
    forced to adapt and change 14
    and the NHS 10, 33
    and self-interest 37, 58
constitutional reform 219, 222
construction industry 196
Council of Mortgage Lenders 192,
    195
Council for the Preservation of Rural
    England 225
crime 63, 68, 116, 143, 151, 218,
    250, 308
    being tough on crime and its causes
    24, 25, 30–31, 43, 245
    burglary 19, 244, 245
    cutting 64
    and drugs 24, 244
    and the elderly 64
    fear of 244, 252
    increase in 121
    and the information superhighway
    104
    mugging 19
    punishment of 31, 307
    and responsibility 42
    robberies 244
    and taxation 37
    victims 136
    violent 43
    young offenders 24, 44
crime-prevention programme 43
Criminal Injuries Compensation
    Scheme 136
criminal justice 24
Crosland, Anthony 7
Crowther, Lord 271
currency 83, 116, 204
current-account deficits 83

decentralisation xi, 259, 262, 270,
    272, 275, 298, 316
defence 12, 20
demand management 75–6, 77, 80
demobilisation 4
democratic socialism 4, 6, 7, 12, 54,
    143

Dennis, Norman 238
dentistry 42, 180
Department of Social Security (DSS) 199, 303
deregulation 76, 85, 92, 93, 97, 124, 131
deskilling 92
Deutschmark 211, 292
devaluation 211
devolution 213–14, 259, 269–75
  see also under Scotland; Wales
digital technology 119–20, 203
discrimination 54, 69, 186
Disraeli, Benjamin 281
divorce 142, 249, 306
Docklands, London 114
doctors 19, 30
  see also general practitioners
Downing Street Declaration 276
drugs 68
  anti-drugs initiative 43
  children and 30
  and crime 24, 244
  young people and 44
DSS see Department of Social Security

Eco-management and Audit Scheme (EMAS) 231
economic and monetary union (EMU) 211, 265, 279, 286, 287
economic change 18, 38, 55, 207–8, 291
economic cycle 86
economic growth 10, 19, 36, 38, 76, 77, 78, 83, 84, 87, 90, 112, 120, 193, 212, 264, 284, 301
economic policy 9, 75, 124, 297
economic reform 14
economic regeneration 40
economic renewal 20
economy
  dynamic 48, 52, 226
  global xi
  government-industry partnership 32
  mixed 14
  stakeholder 39, 191, 200, 291–6

supply side 84, 89, 96
education 5, 24, 50, 52, 63, 91, 117, 142, 143, 148–50, 215
  A-levels 53, 93, 114, 148, 160–61, 168
  baseline assessment 166
  broad-based 127
  choice in 32
  comprehensive 24, 159, 173–6
  curriculum 165, 167, 168, 305
  eleven-plus 163, 173, 176, 304, 305
  further 159, 168, 176
  GCSEs 114, 160, 164, 166
  health 187
  higher 12, 125, 148, 149, 159, 160
  home-school contracts 240, 304
  investment in 40, 149, 207
  league tables 168
  as a life-long process 126, 207
  mass 33, 162
  nursery 53, 148, 157, 165, 250
  on-line 103
  parents and 19, 148, 239–40, 304
  political 62
  pressure and support 162–4
  primary 24, 159, 160, 164–7, 174, 252, 304, 305
  remedial 155
  secondary 159, 160, 304
  setting 166, 175–6
  specialist teaching 98
  spending 12, 110, 203
  a stake in 303–6
  standards in xii, 19, 24, 32, 41, 53, 78–9, 97, 126, 127, 148, 159–61, 171–2, 174, 178, 240, 252, 304, 308
  streaming 175
  target grouping 166
  and taxation 37
  and technology 66, 113, 126, 127, 167, 176
  truancy 168, 239
  vocational 53, 93, 114, 127, 167, 168
  see also schools; teaching; universities

Education Act (1944) 8
EFTA (European Free Trade
  Association) 210, 283
elderly people 141
  care of 19, 44, 56, 143
  fears of viii, 30, 35, 64
  and VAT on fuel 31
EMAS *see* Eco-management and
  Audit Scheme
employer/employee partnership 40
employment 77, 143, 200, 215
  changing jobs 120
  fairness at work 24, 123, 295
  full 4, 5, 18, 39, 46, 53, 76, 77,
    146
  health and safety in 123
  high 19, 39, 53, 87
  increased 10
  insecurity in 35, 130, 177–8, 192,
    297, 301
  job creation 192
  low-skill 131
  minimum standards at work 53, 92
  part-time 131, 132, 133, 154, 156,
    157
  replacing unemployment benefits
    30, 32, 131, 146–7
  short-term 63
  a stake in 302
  temporary contracts 131, 132
  women in 64, 131, 133, 142, 147,
    155, 156, 157, 237
  working conditions 15
  young people 24–5
Employment Service 262
EMU *see* economic and monetary
  union
energy 52, 128, 230, 234, 265
English Churches Housing group 194
English ethical socialism (Dennis and
  Halsey) 238
entertainment markets 103
environment ix, x, 20, 54, 116,
  223–35, 253
environmental projects 44
Equal Opportunities Commission
  155
Equal Pay Act (1970) 152

equality 51, 55
  racial 65, 189, 206
  sexual 152, 154, 158, 189, 206
  sexuality 186–9
ERM *see* exchange-rate mechanism
Essex 12
EU *see* European Union
Euro-sceptics 210, 211
Europe
  British role in 24, 210, 211–12,
    252, 263–7, 280–87
  competitiveness 111
  devolving power 272
  federal 279
  food policy 32
  government attitude towards
    (1945–51) 10
  international cooperation 20
  minimum wage 45
  reform 32, 70, 211
  troika system 267
  and the United States 267, 283
European Commission 100, 211,
  267, 286, 315, 317
European Community 33
European Convention of Human
  Rights 317
European Council 267, 286
European Court of Justice 317
European Free Trade Association
  (EFTA) 210, 283
European Investment Bank 284
European Parliament 286
European Union (EU) 24, 108, 120,
  123, 128, 129, 136, 210, 211, 224,
  263–7, 283, 284, 285, 287
exchange controls 124
exchange rate 80, 83, 211
exchange-rate mechanism (ERM) 80,
  116, 128

Faith in the City report (Archbishop
  of Canterbury's Special
  Commission on Urban Priority
  Areas) 297, 299, 301, 306, 307
family
  changes in 143, 147, 302
  Conservatives and 37

family – *contd.*
  and crime 247
  nuclear 142
  responsibility 148, 306
  stable 250
  standard.of living xi
  strengthening 68–9
  unstable 43, 64, 141, 205, 247, 249, 293
  and welfare system 9
  women at work 19
  working together 37
Family Allowance Act 152
family credit 133, 147
'family values' 250
federalism 270
fibre optics 119, 203
financial sector, long-termism in 93–5
financial services 123
Financial Services Act 195
Finland 210, 283
firearms 43, 307
First World War 65, 281
fiscal policy 81, 86, 88–91, 112
fixed-interest bonds 120
Food Standards Agency (proposed) 179
football 254–6
foreign policy 70, 263–4
Forsyth, Michael 271, 273
'Forum for the Future' 227
France 263
  devolution of power 272
  education 160–61
  and Maastricht 265–6
  nuclear testing 224
free market 32, 38, 148
free trade 210, 283
Freedom of Information Act 20, 47, 54, 70, 219, 262, 317
Friends of the Earth 227
Fujitsu 122
Fukuyama, Dr Francis 296

G10 countries 110
GATT (General Agreement on Tariffs and Trade) 283

GCHQ, Cheltenham 45
GDP (gross domestic product) 76, 77, 80, 81, 88, 91, 105, 110, 113, 203
General Agreement on Tariffs and Trade (GATT) 283
general practitioners (GPs) 19, 182–4
  fundholding 69, 183
GP commissioning 69, 183
General Teaching Council (proposed) 126, 169
Germany 263
  cartel office 284
  economic record 87–8, 94–5
  education 160–61
  and the environment 231
  as a federation 270, 272, 312
  and Maastricht 265–6
  and the minimum wage 108
gilt market 84
Gladstone, William Ewart 270, 281
GLC (Greater London Council) 314
global economy xi, 118–29, 160, 237
global markets 23, 56, 86, 91, 100, 111, 112, 121, 292
globalisation 78, 118, 120, 121, 124, 128, 204, 227
GMB (General, Municipal, Boilermakers) 135, 136
GNVQs 168
'golden rule' of public finance 113, 122
Gonzalez, Felipe 264
Gore, Al 100
government
  and the Bank of England 81
  borrowing 25, 88, 113
  and business 295
  coalition 5, 8
  collectivist 216
  and commerce 91
  de-centralisation xi
  and industry 19, 32, 40, 91, 109
  open 234
  outdated system 50
  in partnership x, 321
  role in a modern economy 110
  spending 36, 37, 76, 89, 90–91, 93, 110, 116

GPs *see* general practitioners
Gray, John 246
Greater London Council (GLC) 314
greenhouse effect 225
Grey, Charles, 2nd Earl 281
GSM mobile phone system 284

Hackney 12
Halifax Building Society 191
Halsey, A.H. 238
Hamill, Catherine 277
Handy, Charles 293
Hardie, Keir 226, 270
head teachers 170–71, 305
Healey, Denis 10, 80
health authorities 19, 179
health centres 204
health insurance 180, 185
health and safety at work 123
Heathrow Airport 114
Hennessy, Peter 10
hereditary peers *see under* House of
    Lords
Heseltine, Michael 108
Higginson Committee 161
High Performance Asian Economies
    110
High Scope programme 155
Hitachi 204
Hitler, Adolf 281
Hobhouse, Leonard 14, 15
Hobson, J.A. 15
Holland, Sir Geoffrey 294–5
home rule 270–71
homelessness 37, 69, 194, 196,
    199–200, 240, 303
homosexuality (age of consent)
    186–9
Honda 119
Hong Kong 110
hospitals 38, 48, 250
    and cable technology 98, 103, 115,
    204
    operational freedom 20
    standards 308
    state/private 23
House of Commons, reform of 47,
    319–20

House of Commons Social Security
    Select Committee 199
House of Commons Trade and
    Industry Select Committee 102,
    115
House of Lords 270
    hereditary voting peers 20, 30, 47,
    70, 209, 318–19, 320
    reform of 15
housing 5, 178, 190–200, 215, 314
    bed-and-breakfast accommodation
    30, 69, 194, 199
    building 30, 37, 69, 190, 194,
    196, 199, 302
    capital receipts 30, 117
    flexible tenure schemes 194
    government spending on 198–9
    and interest rates 80
    leaseholders 196
    mass 33
    mortgages 191, 193, 194, 237,
    301
    negative equity 191, 192, 194, 195,
    303
    private 190
    privatisation of council 197
    public and private partnership 40,
    196–7
    rented 190, 193, 196–9, 240
    repossessions x, 191, 194
    shared-ownership 194–5
    social 190, 196, 197, 198
    a stake in 302–3
Housing Act (1924) 190
housing associations 194, 197–8
housing benefit 37, 199, 303
Howe, Lord 80, 314
human rights 317
Hume, John 46

ICI (Imperial Chemical Industries)
    204
identity cards 68
IGC 264
In Trust for Tomorrow (Labour Party
    environment policy statement)
    227, 229
income controls 124

income support 36, 141, 147, 155, 192
India 10, 203, 212
individualism 4, 206, 208, 209, 215, 217, 236, 242, 244, 246, 297, 299
Indonesia 111, 203
industrial action 78
industrial policy 114–15
industrial relations 82, 132, 135
industrial revolution 100, 119, 162
industrial revolution, new 98, 99–101
industrialisation 110
industry 31, 40
  government and 19, 32, 40, 91, 109
  investment in 52, 217
  long-termism in 94–5
inflation 25, 38, 63, 76, 77, 79–87, 93, 96, 97, 110, 112, 113, 122, 193
information revolution 40, 98, 99, 292
Information Society 100
information superhighways 40, 41, 100, 101, 103, 104, 105, 115, 127
infrastructure, investment in see under investment
inner cities 52, 124, 225, 304
  see also city centres
insurance 44, 64, 245
interest rates 76, 80–81, 83, 88, 96
Intergovernmental Panel on Climate Change 225
International Monetary Fund (IMF) 80
Internet 103, 104, 127
Invest in Britain Bureau 122
investment 90, 291, 294
  capital 37
  causes of low 94
  in economic regeneration 40
  in education 82, 149, 207
  in human capital xi, 78, 97, 124–5
  in industry 52, 217
  in infrastructure xi, 40, 52, 78, 82, 91, 110, 114, 124, 207

inward 122, 210
  long-term 40, 79, 110, 124
  low 111
  and low inflation 122
  in manufacturing 40
  and public borrowing 88
  reduction in 84
  in research and development xi
  in skills 207
  spending on 24
  in training 82
investment funds 40
investment trusts 198
Ionica 101, 104, 115
IRA see Irish Republican Army
Irish Bills (1886, 1893) 270
Irish Republic 271, 276
Irish Republican Army (IRA) 276
isolationism 259, 262, 266
Italy 79, 272

Jaguar 119
Japan
  competitiveness 111
  education 127
  and the environment 231
  investment in Britain 120, 122–3, 204, 263, 283
  market access 282
  relations between government, banks and industry 94
  and the superhighway 100
Jefferson, Thomas 321
Jenkins, Simon 259
job centres, electronic 106
Jobs, Education and Training Programme (proposed) 302
jobseeker's allowance 147
John Lewis 293
Jung, Carl Gustav 59
justice ix, 55, 208
juvenile delinquency 155

Kant, Immanuel 59, 60
Kay, John 293
Keynes, John Maynard, 1st Baron 7, 11
Kierkegaard, Sren 59

Kilbrandon, Lord 271
Kinnock, Neil 3, 5, 10–11, 29
Kirklees 234
Kissinger, Dr Henry 283
knives amnesty 307
Komatsu 122
Korea 77, 119, 203, 263, 283

Labour government (1945–51)
    achievements of 4, 9–10, 12, 77,
    178, 226, 294
    and electoral map (1945) 12
    leads national mood for change and
    renewal 5
    mistakes of 10, 77
    objectives 5
    reasons for success in 1945 election
    4–5, 8
Labour government (1964–70) 12
Labour government (1974–79)
    12–13
labour market 147, 157, 302
    change in 53, 56, 237
    flexibility 92–3
    insecurity in 130
    reform of 18, 93
Labour Party
    constitution x, 5, 15, 25, 49, 54,
    62, 226
    and Europe 210
    and fairness 44–6
    founded 17
    governing for more than one term
    8, 63
    ideology 16–17
    law and order 42, 60
    and leadership 47–50
    lessons of 1945 13
    as the majority party 35
    membership x, 12, 13, 16, 17–18,
    23, 25, 32, 60, 221
    National Executive Committee
    (NEC) 49, 153
    and opportunity 39–42
    organisation 16, 17–18, 55, 62
    as the party of the people 22
    as the patriotic party 9
    pledges 24–5

programme 16, 18–20, 25
    reason recent elections lost 6, 13,
    48, 55, 221
    and responsibility 42–4
    revolution inside 22
    and the trade unions x, 6, 16,
    62
    and trust 46–7, 49
    values 18
Labour Party conferences 17
Labour Representation Committee
    14, 17
laissez-faire 14, 15, 109, 207, 295,
    296, 299
Lancashire 226, 234
Lang, Ian 271
Latin America 203, 212
Lawson, Lord (Nigel) 75, 76, 80, 82,
    318
'Lawsonomics' 80
leadership 46, 47–50, 159, 228–9
Learning Bank (proposed) 149
left-of-centre 7, 8, 31, 51, 55, 59,
    143, 207, 209, 211, 215, 223, 236,
    262, 293
Lewisham 240
Lewisham East 12
Liberal government (1906–14) 15
Liberal Party 14
'liberal socialism' 15
liberalism 14, 207, 245, 246
Liberals and Social Democrats (Clarke)
    239
liberty 11, 14
libraries 103, 115, 204
living standards 87, 114, 203, 216,
    308
Lloyd-George of Dwyfor, David
    Lloyd George, lst Earl 7, 15, 294
Local Agenda 21 programme 233,
    234
local authorities
    and capital investment 37
    and the environment 233, 234, 235
    and housing 30, 69, 117, 196–200,
    302
    and noise pollution 241
local development 115

local education authorities 19,
239–40, 304, 305–6
local government 70, 220, 313–14
London 70, 119, 314
low pay 133, 143, 147, 234, 250, 293,
297, 301
Low Pay Commission 108

M3 see monetarism
Maastricht Treaty 265, 266, 278, 279,
285
Macara, Sandy 179
McGhee, Frank 254
McIlvanney, Hugh 255–6
Mackay of Clashfern, Lord 316
Macmurray, John 59–60
macro-economic policy 75–6, 79,
80, 82–6, 89, 91, 96, 97, 113,
121–2, 123
Mais Lectures 75, 80, 92
Major, John 191, 275, 278–9, 317
Malaysia 212, 260
Malvern Declaration 308
management, trade unions and 78
Manchester Metrolink 261
manufacturing
dividends 40
and foreign firms 120, 204
investment 40
profits 40
market capitalisation 203
market economy 40, 109, 217
markets, opening up foreign 24
see also global markets
Marks and Spencer 119, 293
Marquand, David 13
marriage 142, 249
Marshall, T.H. 11
Marshall Plan 10, 281
Marx, Karl 38
Marxism 30, 58–9
maternity leave 157
Matthews, Sir Stanley 254–6
Mawhinney, Dr Brian 316
means-testing 9, 144, 145, 147, 300
media 203, 204, 205, 237, 292
Medium Term Financial Strategy
(MTFS) 82–3

members of parliament see MPs
Mercury 67, 102, 104, 115
meritocracy 173, 209, 273, 298
Messina Conference 281
micro-economic policy 76, 83–4,
85, 89, 91, 92, 96
Midland Bank 157
Millennium Archive 106
minimum wage 45, 53, 107, 108,
109, 131, 133, 147
Minister for Public Health 179,
234
MIRAS (mortgage interest relief at
source) 192
monetarism 80, 82
monetary policy 80–81, 86–8, 96,
112
monetary union 116
money-supply targets 80
monopolies 102, 242
Morgan, Kenneth 10, 307
Morgan Report 307
Morris, William 238, 239, 300
Morrison, Herbert, Baron Morrison
of Lambeth 4, 12, 83
mortgages see under housing
MPs, women as 47, 153
MTFS see Medium Term Financial
Strategy
mugging 19

NAFTA (New Zealand and Australia
Free Trade Agreement) 282
NAHAT (National Association of
Health Authorities and Trusts)
184
nation-states 204, 259–68, 278, 287
National Association of Health
Authorities and Trusts (NAHAT)
184
National Children's Bureau 187
National Commission on Education
170, 304
National Health Service Bill 10
National Health Service (NHS) 5, 63,
177–85, 252, 297
co-operation 181–2
and the Conservative Party 10, 33

and investment 40
as a Labour achievement 4, 9, 69,
178, 226
management 19, 24, 30, 43, 69,
179, 181
modernisation 183–5
opting out 42
as a public service 41
reform 19, 177, 180–81
renationalisation of 53
standards in xii
structure of 9
using money from cuts to make
improvements 42
waiting lists 24, 25, 42
see also general practitioners;
hospitals
national insurance 9
National Insurance Act 152
national lottery 69–70
National Parks and Access to the
Countryside Act (1949) 226
national renewal 3, 8, 16, 20, 29, 31,
105, 107, 280, 320
National Savings Pension Plan
(proposed) 145
nationalisation 62
nationalism 122, 209, 269
NATO (North Atlantic Treaty
Organisation) 10, 264, 267
New Britain 22, 25, 50, 72
'New Labour, New Britain' phrase
16
New Labour, New Life for Britain
document 22
New Liberalism 14, 15
new venture capital 115
new world order 10
NHS *see* National Health Service
Nissan 122
noise nuisance 232, 240, 241
Nolan committee 181, 262
Norfolk 12
North Atlantic Alliance 281
North Atlantic Treaty Organisation
see NATO
North Sea oil 12, 36, 81
Northamptonshire 12

Northern Ireland 46, 70, 271, 275,
276–7, 317
Nottingham 166, 233
NSK 122
nuclear weapons 237
nursing 19, 30, 42

OECD (Organization for Economic
Cooperation and Development)
203
OEEC (Organisation for European
Economic Cooperation) 281
OFCOM 102
Ofsted (Office for Standards in
Education) 306
old-age pensioners *see* elderly people
old-age pensions 9
One Member One Vote x, 17, 32,
134
one nation ix, 16, 22, 29, 48, 56, 117,
178, 191, 196, 199, 200, 268,
292–3, 298, 308, 309
Open University 12, 41, 106, 159
Open University of the World 106
Organisation for European
Economic Cooperation (OEEC)
281
Organization for Economic
Cooperation and Development
(OECD) 203
Orwell, George 17
Owen, Robert 238
Oxford University 209

Pacific Basin 98
Pakistan 212
Palmerston, Henry Temple, 3rd
Viscount 280, 281
Panel on Sustainable Development
228
parents
and education 19
and home responsibilities 156
responsibility for their children 42
Parliament, reform of 54, 262,
318–20
see also House of Commons; House
of Lords

Parliamentary Environment Audit
  Committee (proposed) 230
partnership 51, 71, 313
  between the government and
  industry 19, 32, 40
  between the government and the
  people 321
  between public and private sector
  40, 143, 207, 220, 261
  and education 159–60
  in society 53
  in the workplace 36, 40, 53, 66,
  92, 121, 295
paternity leave 156
patriotism 71, 268
patronage xi-xii, 30, 170
Patten, John 53
Pearson 104
peers, hereditary see under House of
  Lords
pensions x, 12, 43, 95, 136, 142–5,
  294, 301
PEPs (personal equity plans) 113
Philips Park, Manchester 233
police 24, 37, 213
  providing more police officers on
  the beat 68
  as a public service 41
  reducing paperwork 42
  using money from cuts to make
  improvements 42
Policy Forum 18
political parties, financing of 262
political renewal 20
politics
  a new 310–13
  stakeholder 310–21
poll tax 312, 318–19
pollution 225, 228–34, 253, 314
population growth 225
Post Office 41, 52, 134, 135
postwar Keynesian economics 77, 79,
  81, 82, 84
poverty 63, 143, 204, 293
  attack on 16, 18, 55, 253
  children and 36, 300
  costs of ix
  decreased 10

and education 53, 149
empowering the poor 54
and national income 37
power
  abuse of 54, 310
  of community 156
  devolution of 260, 272, 311
  of the state 62
prejudice 16, 54, 71
Prescott, John 49, 133, 290
price controls 124
Prince's Trust 242, 261
Private Finance Initiative 113
private sector xi, 19, 40, 52, 55, 66,
  67, 76, 83, 85, 101, 124, 149, 197,
  198, 207, 220, 308
privatisation 76, 134, 242, 301
privilege 31, 32, 36, 54
'progressive dilemma' 13, 14
property rights 15
proportional representation 320
protection 79, 101, 102, 121, 282
Public Interest Disclosure Bill 219
public sector x, 19, 40, 55, 63, 83,
  85, 110, 124, 135, 145, 149, 207,
  216, 220
public services x, 18, 41, 50, 51, 53,
  69–70, 85, 90, 106, 152, 217–18,
  312

qualified majority voting (QMV) 286
quangos 32, 42, 47, 54, 70, 151, 311,
  312, 314

Race Relations Act 13
racial discrimination 13
racial violence 43, 65, 240, 246
rail transport 24, 232
railways 41–2, 52
Rank Xerox 157
Rawls, Professor John 299
Reagan, Ronald 206
recession 83, 229
recycling 223
regions 41, 52, 70, 110, 115, 315
religion 121, 237
  see also Christianity
repossessions see under housing

rescue spending 90–91
research centres 66
research and development xi, 78, 124, 125, 294
restrictive practices 209
retirement
    and national insurance 9
    and pensions 144, 145
Reuters 104
Richard, Lord 319
Rifkind, Malcolm 271
Rio Summit 233
road transport 24, 232
Rough Sleepers' Initiative 303
Rover 293
Rowntree report (February 1995) 154–5
Royal Commission on the Constitution (1968) 271
Royal Commission on Transport and the Environment 228
Royal Society for the Protection of Birds 223

Sanyo 122
satellite technology 40, 41
Save the Children Fund 187
savings 90, 110, 124, 294
schools 38, 48
    allowed to run their own affairs 19
    buildings 30, 35
    and cable technology 103, 115, 127, 204
    class sizes viii, 24, 25, 67, 252
    comprehensive *see under* education
    failing 160, 250, 252
    grammar 173
    homework 240, 304–5
    improvement 306
    inner city 305
    paperwork 42
    primary *see under* education
    private 23, 304
    public 209, 304
    secondary *see under* education
    standards *see under* education
    successful 162
    two classes of state 65

science 24, 52, 55, 64, 115, 124, 125, 294
    as a school subject 166, 175, 176
Scotland, devolution of 54, 252, 260–61, 269–70, 313, 315–16
Scottish Constitutional Convention 272, 274
Scottish Labour Party 270–71
Scottish Office 261, 274, 315
Scottish Parliament 47, 70, 252, 261, 269, 273, 275, 315
Sea Empress 225
Second World War 5, 8, 9, 65, 281, 294
second-generation welfare 142–3
secrecy xi–xii, 219, 275, 317
security 18, 31, 39, 45, 143, 157, 178, 191, 203–14, 245, 252, 266, 286, 294, 302
self-employment 52, 124, 131
separatism 269
SERPs (State Earnings-Related Pension Scheme) 12, 144, 145, 152
Sex Discrimination Act (1975) 12–13, 152
sexual equality 152, 154, 158
sexual revolution 64
Shaw, George Bernard 161, 266
Sheffield 234
Shephard, Gillian 53
Shore, Peter 13
Singapore 110, 212, 260, 294
single currency 128, 211, 265, 278, 287
Single Market 115, 123, 128, 211, 283, 286
single parents 68, 93, 155, 249, 250
Sinn Fein 276
skills 52, 66, 303
    access to 41
    improved 92, 93, 123, 126, 130
    investment in 207
    lack of 111, 217
    language 165
    multi- 113
    new 131, 148
    reform 53
    standards 78–9, 97
    undervalued 31

small businesses 24, 35, 52, 91, 115, 124, 207, 291
Smith, Elizabeth 310
Smith, John 3, 5, 34, 58, 269, 310, 321
social breakdown/decay 19, 207, 208, 244
'social capital' 116–17
social change 208–9
Social Chapter 45, 53, 108, 109, 129, 131, 135, 136, 286
social democracy 7
Social Democracy in Britain (Tawney) 307
social justice ix, 7, 9, 10, 23, 30, 50, 51, 107, 136–50, 154, 155, 158, 229, 230
Social Justice Commission *see* Commission on Social Justice
social legislation 12
social policy 297
social reform 14, 15
social renewal 20
social security 8, 11, 150
socialism 30
  Attlee on 11
  Christian 59
  ethical 16, 59, 239–40
  Morrison defines 83
  nature of 9, 11, 18, 31, 38–9, 62
  values 31, 33, 39, 62
Socialisms (Wright) 18
society
  belief in 38
  divided ix, 31, 36, 50, 64, 68, 155, 297
  egalitarian 299
  idealism and 252
  the individual within 218
  power of 30
  a stake in ix, 53, 148, 297–309
  thriving 304
  united 253
Somerset 12
Sony 119, 204
Soros, George *202*
South Africa 33
South Korea 110

Soviet Union 64
Spain 272
Spanish Civil War 281
stakeholder economy 39, 191, 200, 291–6
stakeholder politics 310–21
stakeholder society ix, 53, 148, 297–309
state control 38, 40
state ownership 5–6, 16
  of public services 41, 52
state, power of 215–16
Stormont Parliament 271
strike ballots 46, 132
Student Loan Scheme 63
Success Against the Odds report (National Commission on Education) 304
Sweden 210, 231, 283

T&G *see* Transport and General Workers' Union
Tawney, R.H. 239, 307
tax rebates 93, 117
tax relief 44, 113
taxation 63, 76, 178
  capital-gains 95
  corporate 112–13
  cuts 24, 64, 81, 85–6, 89, 90
  evasion of 43
  a fair system 44–5, 112, 123, 293
  and health 37, 180
  lower marginal tax rates 76
  and pensioners 144, 145
  poll tax 312, 318–19
  progressive 15
  rises in x, 35, 37, 64, 90, 192, 274
  top rate of 44, 124, 146
  VAT *see* VAT
  and the world economy 89–90
'Teach for America' 305
Teachers' Centre 305
teaching 24, 30, 42, 166, 169–71, 240
  Advanced Skills Teacher grade 126, 169–70
  associate teachers 169, 176
  head-teachers 170–71, 305

Index

mixed-ability 175
  specialist 98
  standards 32, 41, 163
  training 67
  see also education; schools
technological change ix, 18, 38, 204, 237, 291, 292
technology
  education and 66, 113, 126, 127
  harnessing new 24, 52, 91, 207, 295
  telecommunications 40, 66, 105, 115, 128, 204, 212, 237, 265, 284
Temple, Archbishop William 159, 308
Tesco 231–2
Tessas (Tax-Exempt Special Savings Accounts) 113
Thatcher, Margaret, (later Baroness) 14, 35, 60, 80, 141, 156, 165, 190, 206, 236, 296
Thatcherism 43–4, 216, 217, 245, 299
Theory of Justice (Rawls) 299
Thurow, Lester 303
Times, The 135–6, 316
Toshiba 204
Toyota 119
trade barriers 115
trade unions 33, 130–37, 215
  and the block vote 18
  and financing of political parties 47
  growing assertiveness of 14
  legislation 46, 82, 123, 132
  links with the Labour Party x, 6, 16, 62
  and management 78
  the right to join 45, 54, 132–3
  strike ballots 46, 132
training 36, 38, 41, 53, 68, 82, 91, 92, 93, 97, 114, 131, 133, 143, 157, 200, 262, 294
transport 128, 212, 314
  and the environment 230, 232–3
  infrastructure 114
  public 40, 114
  and public/private sectors 124
  transport policy 48, 52
  see also rail transport; road transport

Transport and General Workers' Union (T&G) 136
Treasury 78, 87

UCW (Union of Communication Workers) 134–5
UN see United Nations
'underclass' 116, 142, 218, 293, 300, 301
unemployment 12, 52, 63, 68, 110, 293, 297, 301, 314
  and crime 19
  cutting 37, 64, 141
  fighting 16
  high 43, 96
  long-term 68, 84, 85, 91–4, 117, 131, 132, 141, 142, 146, 147, 249, 293
  mass ix, 131
  and national insurance 9
  statistics 36, 81, 192, 300
  talents of the unemployed 155
  and taxation 37
  work instead of benefits 30, 32, 131
  and young people viii, 117, 302
unemployment benefit 131, 294
Union of Communication Workers (UCW) 134–5
United Biscuits 135
United Kingdom 269, 271, 278
United Nations (UN) 10, 33
United States of America
  British investment in 212
  competitiveness 111
  and education 169, 170, 305
  and the environment 231
  and Europe 267, 283
  as a federation 270, 312
  and health 180
  investment in Britain 263, 283
  minimum wage 45, 108
  relationship with Britain 210, 266–7, 281–2
  Savings and Loans crisis 129
universities 24, 35, 42, 63, 66, 125, 149, 304

337

University for Industry 41, 66, 93, 105, 126, 149
Urban Priority Areas 307
Uruguay Round talks 120, 283
utilities 25, 31, 43, 54, 68, 69, 112, 242, 301

VAT (value-added tax) 31, 44, 64, 89, 232
Vietnam 111
violence 43, 68, 240, 244, 276, 277
vocational education *see under* education
voluntary national task force 44
voluntary sector x, 117, 208–9, 220, 261

wage control 76
wages (a living wage) 30
Wales
  destruction of environment in South Wales 224
  devolution 54, 269–70, 272, 313, 315
Wandsworth, London 194
war, ending 55, 253
Water Act (1945) 226
Watson, Sam 10
wealth, socially created 14–15
Webb, Sidney 15–16
welfare state 50, 217, 298, 302
  an embryonic welfare system (1910) 15
  and the Conservative Party 14
  as the envy of the world 9
  getting off benefits into work 30, 32, 45, 46, 93, 146–7, 291
  as a Labour achievement 4, 77, 226, 294
  new dividing lines on welfare 143–50
  reform of 18, 19, 124, 142, 291, 293–4
  second-generation welfare 142–3

Social Justice Commission report 141
spending on 24, 64
Welsh Assembly 47, 70, 252, 269, 273, 275, 315
Welsh Office 315
Wheatley, John 190
White Paper on employment (1944) 39
White Paper on transport 114
White Papers on devolution (proposed) 273
Whitelaw, Lord 306–7
Wilson, Sir Harold, Baron 13, 175, 269
women 30, 151–8
  in employment 64, 131, 133, 142, 147, 155, 156, 157, 237
  first woman Cabinet minister 152
  increase in women MPs 47, 153
  role of ix
  suffrage 152
women's rights 12–13
working class 14
working hours 154
world financial crisis (1973) 12
world foreign exchange market 119
world prosperity league 109–10, 193
World Trade Organisation 283
World Wide Fund for Nature 227
Wright, Tony 18

York 233
York City Council 197
young offenders 24, 43, 44
young people 63, 68
  Citizens' Service 148, 241–2
  and crime 44
  and drugs 44
  and employment 24–5
  and the environment 234–5
  and Labour Party membership 33
  unemployed viii, 117, 302
  and a voluntary national task force 44